THE
APOCALYPSE
CONSPIRACY

THE APOCALYPSE CONSPIRACY

Why the world may <u>not</u> end as soon as you think and what you should be doing in the meantime.

JOHN NOĒ

Wolgemuth & Hyatt, Publishers, Inc.
Brentwood, Tennessee

The mission of Wolgemuth & Hyatt, Publishers, Inc. is to publish and distribute books that lead individuals toward:

- A personal faith in the one true God: Father, Son, and Holy Spirit;

- A lifestyle of practical discipleship; and

- A worldview that is consistent with the historic, Christian faith.

Moreover, the Company endeavors to accomplish this mission at a reasonable profit and in a manner which glorifies God and serves His Kingdom.

Wolgemuth & Hyatt, Publishers, Inc.
1749 Mallory Lane, Suite 110
Brentwood, Tennessee 37027

Library of Congress Cataloging-in-Publication Data

Noē, John R., 1945–
    The apocalypse conspiracy : why the world may not end as soon as
you think and what you should be doing in the meantime / John Noē. —
1st ed.
       p. cm.
    Includes index.
    ISBN 1-56121-040-4
    1. Bible. N.T. Revelation—Criticism, interpretation, etc.
I. Title.
BS2825.2.N64 1991
228'.06—dc20
                                       91-20563
                                        CIP

Glory be to the Father,
And to the Son,
And to the Holy Ghost.
As it was in the beginning,
Is now and ever shall be.
World without end,
Amen.

Gloria Patri

WARNING

The ideas contained in this book might be radically different from everything you've heard and been taught about biblical prophecy. They cannot be lumped together with any of the prophetic doctrines, movements, or labels that are being espoused today. Further, reading this book may be hazardous to your spiritual complacency.

CONTENTS

vii

PUBLISHER'S PREFACE

O ver the course of the last century, evangelical Christians have become increasingly preoccupied with trying to predict when the Second Coming of Christ will occur. Initially, this quest was relegated to the status of a fringe movement. In fact, in the ancient church, this type of endeavor was considered to be a flat-out heresy. Even in the 1920s, when the liberal-fundamentalist debate was raging, the doctrine of Christ's imminent return was not considered to be foundational to the faith—even by fundamentalists. However, within fifty short years it has become a central tenet of American Protestanism.

Certainly one of the milestones in this advance from fringe theology to status quo was the publication of *The Late Great Planet Earth* by Hal Lindsey. In this volume (and a raft of sequels), Lindsey made the bold assertion that we are living in "the terminal generation." Although Lindsey attempted to identify the period of history in which our Savior's second coming would take place, he was not so bold as to try and predict the year or day. Subsequent writers have not been so careful.

In recent years, we have seen a barrage of Bible teachers, armed with a vast array of detailed prophecy charts, brashly assert that Christ will soon return "to rapture the Church" and bring an end to the world. Each new war or global disturbance has given birth to a new wave of books and tapes. Missed dates have come and gone. And in their wake, all these writers and teachers have been left with one thing in common: they have all been wrong. Unfortunately, however, this has not seemed to deter the next wave of time-liners and date-setters.

All of this has, of course, had a profound effect upon the evangelical churches that espouse it. In addition, it has greatly damaged Christian credibility in the eyes of the world. In placing so much emphasis upon a future coming, many Christians have forgotten the fact that Christ promises to come to us in a variety of ways—right now! Christians don't have to wait for some distant, future event in order to experience the fullness of His presence. They can exchange their let's-just-hold-on-until-the-rapture defeatism for a biblically-based optimism that is rooted in Christ's promise to come to them now and meet their every need.

So what credentials qualify the author to counter conventional wisdom and set forth a view of biblical prophecy that is so different from nearly everything that is being taught today? Well, it is true that Mr. Noē is not a trained theologian. He's not a seminary professor, nor is he a pastor or professional minister. But, even though these may appear to be deficiencies in his resumé, they are, in fact, the very things that qualify him to write such a book. How so? Because, as we say in Tennessee, "he doesn't have a dog in the hunt." In other words, he doesn't have a denominational or academic position to protect. He's a dedicated Bible student who got frustrated with the failed predictions and outlandish claims of the so-called experts. He began with the simple assumption that the book of Revelation was, as the Greek derivation of its name suggests, an "unveiling." As such, it was meant to be understood and applied by ordinary Christians of *every* generation.

You won't need a prophecy chart to understand this book, but you will need an open mind. In the final analysis you may not agree with every detail of the author's interpretation, but if you can grasp the author's central thesis—that we can't afford to limit Christ's coming to a single future event—it will revolutionize your Christian life.

THE PUBLISHERS

INTRODUCTION

T ed Turner, the famous business tycoon and owner of Cable News Network, recently told a group of news media executives that he was thinking about offering a reward of a half million dollars to anybody who could show him *a way the world could end happily*. Later he changed his offer to include only works of *fiction* "ensuring the survival and prosperity of all life on our planet."

Well, Mr. Turner, it's not fiction, but the Revelation offers just such a scenario, although one would never know it by the way we have been twisting and distorting it during the last few decades.

In fact, it's not hard to see how any person growing up during the last half-century could become as pessimistic and fearful about the world's future as Ted Turner says he is.

When I was born again some years ago and started attending a church, one of the most frequent messages I heard was "Welcome to the final generation!" It seemed that almost everything I read from my church and from a wide range of religious teachers proclaimed a message of impending global—even universal—disaster.

Of course, I was no theologian, but these messages of gloom and doom didn't seem to fit at all with the Scriptures I knew and understood. What's more, the imminent destruction doctrine I was being taught seemed to poke holes in all the other doctrines I was expected to accept. I wondered, for example, why I should be a good steward over my possessions and invest my resources in future generations when everything I owned and invested in was going to be wiped out anyway. Why should I be concerned about spreading the gospel around a world that was soon going to be blown apart? And how could

I live in joy, peace, and hope when people I dearly loved were about to be annihilated?

When I actually asked such questions, I got all the trite answers most Christians have come to accept without challenge. "Just do it because God's Word commands it," "You just can't worry about all those things," and so on, and so on.

Journey into the Apocalypse

The most perplexing question of all was this: Why is there so much controversy, conflict, and confusion among the churches over biblical prophecy—especially over the book of Revelation? Why, for instance, can't a typical, ordinary layperson like me study the Revelation and trust the Holy Spirit to guide me into its truths?

"Oh," my teachers and pastors cautioned, "it's all very complex. . . . First, you'd need years of education in such subjects as hermeneutics, theology, ontology, biblical and contemporary history, millenarianism, literary and form criticism, apocalyptic imagery, and so on. Plus, you'd have to have an in-depth knowledge of at least the ancient Hebrew, Chaldee, Greek, Aramaic, and Latin languages."

Wait a minute, I thought, the guy who wrote the book of Revelation was a commercial fisherman—unschooled[1] according to the religious leaders of his day. What he had going for him was a personal intimacy with Jesus Christ, a sincere heart, and the anointing of the Holy Spirit.

What's more, the Apostle Paul (a trained theologian) didn't tell the Ephesians he was praying that God would open the door for them to go to the best theological seminary in the world. Instead, he told them that God had "made known to us the mystery of his will."[2] He thanked God for their faith and said, "I keep asking that the God of our Lord Jesus Christ, the glorious Father, may give you the Spirit of wisdom and revelation, so that you may know him better."[3]

Besides, the very person the Apocalypse reveals, Jesus Christ, promised that "the Holy Spirit . . . will teach you all things and will remind you of everything I have said to you."[4]

So, with an open and hungry heart, I began an in-depth, exhaustive study into the Revelation and related Scriptures. And, to my great delight, the Holy Spirit began to open up their mysteries to me. I began to discover that the Revelation message was not so much a pre-

---

"It seemed that almost everything I read from my church and from a wide range of religious teachers proclaimed a message of impending global—even universal—disaster."

---

diction of distant, future events, but a vital and vibrant description of the ongoing, timeless kingdom of God as a present reality. I began to see that it not only paints a most hopeful picture for the future; it is extremely pertinent to each of us in our daily lives—right now!

Why Don't Most Christians Know All This?

"Why don't most Christians know the pertinent truths and realities the Revelation teaches?" I began to ask.

After all, if the stated purpose of the book is to unveil Jesus Christ and what He says is taking place, and if it promises blessings to those who hear it, heed it, and obey it, and if there are severe warnings to those who don't,[5] why are most Christians either ignorant, confused, or deceived about its contents? It's as if someone had taken the veil that had been removed by God and laid it right back over the mysteries.

Gradually, I began to see that this is exactly what has happened. There has been (and still is) a deliberate conspiracy to cover up the very truths and realities the Apocalypse was given to uncover—a conspiracy against the Apocalypse itself.

In this book, you'll discover who the conspirators are, why they have plotted against the Apocalypse, and how they are executing their evil plot. You'll also discover that there are many sincere, well-meaning people and organizations that have unwittingly aided the conspirators in their efforts to blind masses of people to the crucial, present-day realities God has so carefully revealed to us.

Like the people of John's day, I think you'll be "astonished"[6] at who the conspirators are, how they work, and what they are doing in God's world in our generation.

Why Did I Write This Book?

The book you are about to read is a synopsis of the most relevant truths and realities I have discovered in my search into prophetic Scriptures. I do not intend to provide an exhaustive explanation of the Revelation, nor do I intend it to be the last word on this subject. Certainly, under guidance of the Holy Spirit, others, even I, can and will improve upon my findings. My primary goal is to encourage believers to take a new look at what they believe about prophecy and see how it squares with the Scriptures.

Many people tend to get caught up in doctrines, movements, and labels rather than confronting the reality of what the Scriptures actually say. It is not my objective to present *new* doctrines (they aren't), but to cause people to re-examine the whole doctrinal and labeling approach to prophecy. My desire in this work is to open the beauty of Jesus in the Revelation and in His present-day ministry through His body, the church. The last thing I want to do is create another movement or propagate another doctrine. There are far too many of both now.

I also hope this book will provide some common ground upon which Christians can come together to worship and serve God in greater harmony. In recent decades, Christendom has experienced far too much controversy, confusion, and conflict over prophecy. This has made a mockery of the church in the eyes of the world. This book is offered in the same spirit Moses exhibited when he threw a tree into the bitter waters of Marah and made them sweet.[7]

Oh, I know that one book won't suddenly wipe away all the doctrinal squabbles and conflicts over prophecy that have plagued the body of Christ for decades, even centuries. But, if it enables the sweetness of Christ to take out even a little of the bitterness, it will have been more than worth all my years of labor, prayer, and study.

A Plea for Openness

I've had to face the fact that this book may have the opposite effect from what I desire. It may be controversial. No doubt, many will brand me a heretic simply because the contents of this book are so

---

"Like the people of John's day, I think you'll be 'astonished' at who the conspirators are, how they work, and what they are doing in God's world in our generation."

---

radically different from what they've always been taught. Let me remind you that the dictionary defines heresy as "any belief that is against a belief of a church or most people." By that definition, Jesus was a heretic, and so was the writer of the Revelation. But history reveals that the majority is often wrong.

Also, some people—especially those who insist on a literal/physical interpretation of all symbols—may feel that I have greatly over-spiritualized the Revelation symbols. They will argue with me (as one Bible scholar did) that, if you start spiritualizing a few things, pretty soon you'll have nothing to take literally.

I did not start the process of interpreting material and physical symbols spiritually. God did! Read the first five books of the Bible, and notice how often God used physical objects—a rainbow, the blood of a lamb, a pillar of fire—as spiritual symbols. And look how often Jesus used physical/material objects—a coin, weeds, yeast—in His parables and teachings to convey realities of the spiritual world.

Nearly everything in the Bible can be spiritualized, but the opposite is not true. You can attach a spiritual meaning to nearly every physical/material object or event in the Scripture, and the writers of the Bible very often did. Yet, you cannot always reverse the process. For example, Jesus spoke of being born again as a spiritual reality.[8]

But try to interpret that analogy literally and physically (as Nicodemus did), or reverse it (as some have), and you come up with reincarnation.

Let me urge you to be open as you read this book. Even if you disagree with some of my specific interpretations of prophetic symbols, don't throw out the whole reality the symbols represent. Ask the Holy Spirit to reveal to you His interpretation of those symbols.

In the final analysis, I am beholden to God and will be measured by His plumbline. I have constantly prayed that God would give me His Spirit of wisdom and revelation, and that I would neither add my personal theories to the Revelation message nor subtract from it the truths and realities of the Apocalypse.

What You'll Find in This Book

Much of the confusion over the Revelation stems from the widespread practice of interpreting its visual images as literal, physical, and historical realities to support theories about God's timetables and specific plans. Over the centuries, many Christians have built layers and layers of such faulty theories upon flawed theological foundations. Speculating about the future is neither the task nor the prerogative of individuals or of the New Testament church. We can, and must, leave the future in God's hands and get on with being the people of God in our present generation.

In the first four chapters of this book, I will provide an overview of the muddled mess of confusion over biblical prophecy, explain how it got that way, and chart a course for a fresh direction in understanding and applying prophetic writings.

In the remaining chapters, I examine in detail the most controversial and troublesome passages of the Revelation and Daniel, and the doctrines that have grown up around them.

I have made a great effort to avoid getting caught up in the complex jargon and confusing rhetoric usually associated with writings about biblical prophecy. I've tried to offer, instead, insights here-and-now on how individuals can tap into the tremendous spiritual power and reality explained in prophetic writings and can overcome evil in both the spiritual and the physical/material world.

The book ends on this triumphant, inspiring note: the bottom line of the Revelation is that God has removed the veil from the full reality of Jesus Christ, enabling believers to overcome the world, to live in perfect fellowship with Him, and to reign and rule in the kingdom of God.

And since the Revelation is not a prediction of a disastrous end but a proclamation of a glorious beginning, let us begin to search out its infinite riches.

1

CLEARLY, SOMETHING IS WRONG

S cared? I really got scared when I started reading *The Late Great Planet Earth*," a deeply troubled young man recently told a Christian counselor.

"I couldn't put it down! All that stuff about Israel becoming a nation in 1948 . . . and Russia . . . and the European Common Market . . . and the end times made me stop and think. . . . I'd never read anything about prophecy. . . . It really got to me," he continued.

"I started going to End Times conferences, reading books on prophecy, and listening to tapes. The more I heard, the more uptight I got. . . . I dropped out of college, all but abandoned my family, and just bummed around the country, listening to any teacher who seemed to know what he was talking about. . . . I even went to Israel to try to sort it all out.

"Then, I began to notice something strange," he observed. "No two teachers seemed to agree. I mean, they'd argue over which came first—the rapture or the millennium. Some would say that every word of Revelation should be taken literally; others would say that some of it was symbolic. They'd argue over the interpretations of various images. . . . And, they were all one hundred percent sure they were right and that the others were wrong."

"So, what came of all that?" asked the counselor.

"I just got more and more confused," he lamented. "Eventually, I just had to push the whole thing out of my mind and get on with my life."

"Are you still frightened about the future?" the counselor asked.

"I don't know what to think any more," came the quick response. "I just try not to think about it."

Countdown to 2000

Questions about what's going to happen in the future are reaching an almost feverish pitch as we inch closer to the year A.D. 2000. Predictions of dire events are growing in frequency, in drama, and in scope with each passing day. Seers, prognosticators, and prophets of all kinds are rushing to prey on the rampant fears and uncertainties of the masses.

"Fears of Apocalypse Spark Plans for Rescue by Blimp," screamed a recent *Wall Street Journal* headline.[1] The article cited a number of indicators of just how far the frenzy is going:

- "Richard Kienenger is racing to assemble a fleet of blimps to rescue hundreds from the major earthquakes he believes will rumble across the globe on May 5, 2000. . . . So far, he says, 250 have reserved seats on the blimps, which will take off from sites in Texas, Illinois, and an island in the South Seas."

- "Publishers are beginning to cash in on the burgeoning fears of an apocalypse. They're bringing out a spate of new books on Nostradamus, a prophet of the 16th century, who predicted an apocalyptic ending for the world around 2000."

- "Video stores in New York and California report waiting lists of up to three months to rent a film on the prophet [Nostradamus] narrated by Orson Welles."[2]

The various media are adding fuel to the fire by running quotes almost daily from any so-called authority who can demonstrate a modest following—and from some who simply offer outlandish claims that make good copy.

There Are Legitimate Concerns

All the furor might be brushed aside were it not for an overabundance of legitimate political, economic, and scientific concerns which seem to grow in intensity every day.

- Middle East wars and political upheavals come and go but keep the world on edge.

- The 1991 war with Iraq once again brought forth a fevered pitch of cries from various church leaders, teachers, and writers about the imminency of fulfillment of biblical prophecies regarding "Armageddon," "Apocalypse," and "the end of the world."

- With the war over, these same voices urgently predict "it's not over," "there's more to come," "the Antichrist," "the false peace," and other apocalyptic events of the "last days." "All the pieces are falling into place," they continue to warn us.

- Worldwide terrorism is a ticking bomb that now inflicts fear on millions of travelers and has the potential to create major problems for the world's transportation, food and drug supplies, and water systems.

- Illegal drug trafficking threatens to destroy whole nations, including the United States.

- The overwhelming debt burden in Third World countries, and even in America, poses the threat of worldwide economic collapse and widespread depression.

- The AIDS problem appears totally out of control, and many reputable medical experts predict that it could be killing millions worldwide by the year 2000.

- Scientists generally agree that our environment is reaching a pollution saturation point.

- Medical advances continue to raise moral issues like genocide, genetic manipulation, and mind control.

- The moral fabric of society, the values of family, and the relevancy of the church continue to deteriorate at an accelerating pace.

With all these concerns parading across our television screens night after night, along with an abundance of natural and man-made disasters, it's easy to see why so many people have the feeling that something cataclysmic is about to happen.

Besides, as one historian pointed out, people have a way of attaching significance to years that end in zero; the more zeros a year has, the more significance we tend to give it.

There seems to be a widespread feeling that something's going to happen soon.

People Once Turned to the Church for Answers

Traditionally, people have looked to the Christian church for answers in confusing and troubled times. After all, if anybody should understand where the future is going and how we should prepare for it, it should be the institution which claims to have an inside track with the Creator and Controller of our universe.

It makes sense, doesn't it, that people would turn to the one source which should be able to interpret the confusing imagery of prophetic writings to give them some clues about what to expect in the future and how to prepare for it?

Unfortunately, when people turn to the church today for answers about the future, they simply find more confusion.

First, they don't find one church speaking with a unified voice. Rather, they find literally thousands of denominations and countless independent churches, each interpreting the Scriptures in its own way.

Second, even within denominations (and often within the same local church) they find more controversy than agreement over what the Bible says about the future and how to prepare for it in the present.

Third, they may have a hard time finding out what a church really believes about prophecy. Most churches seem to have a chronic case of prophetic laryngitis, especially regarding the book of Revelation, which they themselves often don't understand.

Fourth, they may turn to the media. Unfortunately, in the absence of a clear and cohesive message from the church, anybody who can put together enough words to write a book or raise enough money to get on radio or television to talk about prophecy can quickly become identified as the authentic voice of the church. And most of the prophetic lone rangers of the last two decades have been so far afield that they've made a laughing stock of the church.

Fifth, since bad news sells and good news doesn't, they find only the more dire predictions and dramatic timetables in the media versions. Thus, they rarely hear the more responsible prophetic voices.

All this disunity leaves the majority of people to fend for themselves at a time when they desperately need guidance and hope. So people cope (or fail to cope) in a variety of ways.

"Unfortunately, when people turn to the church today for answers about the future, they simply find more confusion."

---

1. Most People Simply Ignore Biblical Prophecy

Most people are so confused by the so-called apocalyptic imagery of many prophetic Scriptures that they ignore their teaching and busy themselves with the daily concerns of their lives.

I recently heard about a new convert who began immediately plowing through the Bible, starting with the New Testament. Several weeks later, a fellow Bible student noticed a bunch of staples in the new convert's Bible, thought it odd, and asked, "Why have you put staples in your expensive new Bible?"

"Oh, that," replied the novice Christian. "That's Revelation."

"But why the staples?" his friend pursued.

"Look," he said flatly, "My pastor can't understand anything in that book, my Bible teacher can't understand it, and I certainly can't figure it out. So I just stapled it shut."

Imagine! Here was a Christian at the turn of the twenty-first century stapling shut a book that was more dear than life itself to Christians at the turn of the second century! Surely, a book that once brought so much comfort and life, a book that God saw fit to preserve as a part of the Canon, cannot have lost all its meaning in this generation!

2. Most Churches Neglect Biblical Prophecy

Perhaps one big reason most people no longer look to the church for answers to questions about the future is that the typical church avoids biblical prophecy like the plague.

Many Bible scholars push prophecy either so far into the past or so far into the future that it has little relevance to the here and now. Many ministers I've questioned about the book of Revelation quite frankly admit they just don't know what to do with it.

"There are sixty-five other books in the Bible," one minister noted, "so why do we even need to talk about Revelation?"

"I recently took an informal poll in my church and asked what book of the Bible people would like most to study," an announcer from a radio station in my area told me a few days ago.

"And what did you find?" I asked.

"To a person, they all said they'd like to study Revelation," he answered.

"That's interesting," I replied. "Then what did you do?"

"I went to my pastor and told him what I'd found. I asked if he would teach some classes on Revelation."

"What was his answer?" I queried.

"He told me he'd rather not get into Revelation."

"But why?" I wanted to know.

"He said studying Revelation is too divisive . . . that he knows a number of churches which have split wide open over such a study."

Can you believe that? Churches splitting over a book that was given by the Holy Spirit to bring unity of heart and spirit to the Body of Christ? Yet, it's happening.

3. Some People Get Carried Away with Dramatic Predictions

It's not surprising that most people, at the mere mention of the book of Revelation, start conjuring up mental images of grotesque beasts, global devastation, and vanishing loved ones. Virtually all of the popular books on biblical prophecy focus mainly on such themes, and many have gained credibility by basing their predictions on historical (or what they think are historical) events and people.

Humans are naturally curious about the future, and many are also quite fearful about coming events. It's not hard to convince many people that the world is quickly coming to an end.

The countdown-to-doomsday approach causes people to react in several destructive ways:

> ## "Perhaps one big reason most people no longer look to the church for answers to questions about the future is that the typical church avoids biblical prophecy like the plague."

Some are immobilized by anxiety and depression. "Look, man," a blurry-eyed street person told a volunteer in a shelter for the homeless, "we're all gonna be blown away one of these days. . . . What's the use in trying?"

Many psychiatrists now routinely ask depressed patients about their views on biblical prophecy. They've found that fears about the end of the world frequently appear as symptoms of a mental breakdown.

Some lapse into escapist lifestyles. Some people are convinced that the end of the world is just around the corner but that they're going to be removed from planet Earth in time to escape all the holocaust. They develop what we called in the military service a FIGMO (**F**orget **I**t **I**'ve **G**ot **M**y **O**rders) attitude and become "short" sighted.

"The Rapture could occur at any moment," a woman in a troubled marriage told her pastor, "so I find it hard to even think about my work or raising my children or paying bills or getting along with my unbelieving husband. . . . Praise Jesus, it won't be long until I leave all this pain and sorrow behind me."

Others are simply looking for an easy way to push aside what they fear will inevitably be their own destruction. "Why not live it up?" they ask. "Living it up" may involve substance abuse, sexual promiscuity, extreme materialism, or a host of other modern-day magic carpets that whisk people away to exotic states. "Don't Worry, Be Happy," proclaimed the title of a Grammy-winning song of the late eighties. And that's exactly the philosophy many have adopted.

Some retreat into cynicism. "When I was a little boy, I used to go to church and hear preachers telling hair-raising tales about how the Second Coming could happen that very night," said a cynical humanist to a friend of mine. "They'd show all these charts about the Millennium and frightening pictures of beasts and swarms of locusts.

"I'd go down to the altar and cry my eyes out and confess every sin I'd ever thought of committing, but it never seemed to help," he continued. "I'd still get up and go home scared half to death and lie awake until I saw the morning sun peeping through the windows.

"All night long, I'd keep tiptoeing into my mother's room to see if she was still there. . . . I figured that if anybody was going to get raptured it would be her.

"Gradually," he continued, "it began to dawn on me that as soon as Adolph Hitler was disqualified by death as a candidate for the Antichrist, the preachers would replace him with a Joseph Stalin or a Henry Kissinger or whoever seemed to be the biggest threat to them at the moment. The absolutely certain dates for the Rapture kept slipping further and further into the future.

"Eventually," he chuckled, "I just dismissed the whole business as superstition born of ignorance."

"Has that eliminated your anxieties about the future?" my friend questioned.

"No . . . not really," the skeptic replied thoughtfully. "I don't think you can be certain about anything. But, at least I don't go to bed with goose bumps all over me anymore."

Perhaps most people are simply indifferent to biblical prophecy. Part of it stems from the fact that most of us have about all we can deal with each day. With all of our family needs, job demands, and other concerns, we never seem to have time to sort through all the confusion about prophecy.

Besides, there seems to be no place a person can turn in order to get straight answers about all the conflicting views of various prophetic

> ## "Such misuses of prophecy— predicting historical events and dates, fighting over the Millennium, and neglecting the prophetic message —produce the bad fruit of divisiveness, fear, confusion, and escapism."

Scriptures. Even churches, teachers, and theologians seem to be at odds over what prophecies all mean.

So most people take the attitude, "Okay, you guys figure it all out, and when you agree, let me know."

4. Some Use Scare Tactics to Get People Converted

Many churches and teachers use apocalyptic imagery to frighten people into what they call "making decisions for Christ." Very often, their hearers do not convert to true discipleship of Christ; they merely make a profession of faith to escape damnation. As soon as the fear factor is discredited (as with specific predictions that don't come true) or wears off, the so-called decisions often lose their meaning.

Clearly, Something Is Wrong

If, as Jesus said, the measure of a message's validity is the fruit it produces,[3] it's pretty clear that something is drastically wrong with the way many Christians are handling biblical prophecy.

Perhaps this is why much of the church is such a muddled mess of confusion and mediocrity. Such misuses of prophecy—predicting historical events and dates, fighting over the Millennium, and neglecting the prophetic message—produce the bad fruit of divisiveness, fear, confusion, and escapism. This kind of misuse discredits the entire gospel message and emasculates the effectiveness of the church and its people. And this is not unique to this generation. Misuse of prophecy has been a pastime of many for centuries.

Not What God Had in Mind

Ironically, as we'll explore throughout this book, the Revelation was given to produce precisely the opposite effect in the church. It was given to produce good fruits like unity, comfort, faith, understanding, and personal and corporate power.

The church of the late first and early second centuries, to which the Revelation was originally addressed, was under severe persecution from the Jews and from the Roman government. Historical accounts show that, in many parts of Europe and Asia, Christians were brutalized and killed by the thousands because of their faith in Christ. And, despite all their prayers and trusting in Christ, the persecution, or tribulation,[4] seemed to grow worse every day.

"Where is God while all this is happening?" any Christian might have had good reason to ask.

John's prophetic message, the Revelation, provided God's resounding and timeless answer to that question. It explained that the horrors they were experiencing in the material/physical realm directly resulted from spirit-realm activities.[*] Thus, it used visual parables to show spiritual/physical realities. Revelation made it clear that, no matter what the situation might look like at any moment in the visible world, God is in charge. Jesus Christ is the King of kings and Lord of lords,[5] and His kingdom belongs to those who have experienced the new birth and follow Him.[6] Further, it shows that those who obey and remain faithful in the midst of great troubles will receive the power to overcome the worst that Satan can do to them.[7]

What a glorious reality! It's the kind of message that produces good fruit.

The Prophetic Message Is for Here and Now

Does this mean that the Revelation message was meant only for Christians at the turn of the second century? Indeed not! The whole book echoes the theme that it is for all who live and die for Christ from the

---

[*] Throughout the book we will be using "spiritual" and "spirit-realm" terminology interchangeably. Too often in today's usage, "spiritual" is restricted to mean only a moral or ethical condition of the heart. This, of course, is true but much more is involved—specifically, the interaction of spirit beings in our physical universe.

time of the writing forward.[8] This exciting message proclaims the on-going involvement of Jesus Christ in the struggles of both the spirit realm and the physical/material realm, for all ages.

So why all the confusion? Many people who heard Jesus' parables during His earthly life failed to see the spiritual/physical reality behind them[9] and misunderstood their meanings. Even today, the pertinent reality of the Revelation remains hidden except to those who receive it through spiritual eyes and ears.[10]

"The whole book echoes the theme that it is for all who live and die for Christ from the time of the writing forward. This exciting message proclaims the ongoing involvement of Jesus Christ . . . for all ages."

Many teachers have interpreted the visual images of the Revelation as distant, one-time events to support their theories about God's timetables and specific plans. They're like the Samaritan woman at the well who totally missed the point of Jesus' teachings. When Jesus promised to give her water that would forever quench her thirst, she quickly pointed out that He had no bucket to draw with and that the well was deep.[11] He was speaking to her on a spiritual level, but she was trying to understand His words on a physical/material level.

Many of the popular ideas about the End Times have grown out of such misinterpretations of the Revelation and other prophetic Scriptures. Over the centuries, many Christians have built layers and layers of faulty theories over these flawed theological foundations. We humans have often been so busy looking for what was not in Revelation that we've overlooked what God actually put there. In short, we've complicated the simple by over-simplifying what appeared to us to be complicated!

What the Book Says About Its Prophetic Message

I don't claim to have any direct new revelation from God, or even inspiration beyond what's available to any Christian. It's just that I have examined carefully the Revelation and discovered that this vital book has always been God's present-day message to His church. What's more, the book of Revelation explains itself.

Let's take a brief look at some of the glaring examples of how the simple truths of Revelation have become distorted by human interpretation.

The Apocalypse. What image comes to mind when you see the word *Apocalypse?* Total devastation? A nuclear holocaust? An exploding universe? That's the kind of imagery most people in our day have come to associate with it. Hence, we have books and movies like *Apocalypse Now* and *The Four Horsemen of the Apocalypse.*

But what did the word mean to John, who wrote it, and to the Greek-speaking people for whom he wrote it nineteen centuries ago? The Greek word is *apokalypsis*, which simply means an unveiling or an uncovering.

And, what is revealed? In the first verse of the Revelation, John calls his writing "the Revelation [unveiling] of *Jesus Christ*" (emphasis added). This statement makes it clear that the book's basic purpose is to reveal Jesus Christ, not to satisfy our intellectual curiosity about distant, future events. The Apocalypse was given to people in the first century (and all people since) to enable them (and us) to live out the will of God and to experience the fullness of Christ and His kingdom in their (and our) daily lives.

Yet, from most of the current mass literature and movies on the Revelation, one could easily conclude that the book is primarily about Satan and his cohorts and what they are going to be doing to our world at some future date. Think, for example, about the emphasis of blockbuster movies like *Rosemary's Baby* and *The Omen.* Such images are gross distortions of God's purpose for the book, yet many people, some within the church, believe the theology of such works to be accurate.

No wonder people are frightened! Clearly, something is wrong.

At Hand. "Seal not the sayings of the prophecy of this book: for the time is *at hand*."[12]

This instruction to the writer of the Revelation stands in stark contrast to God's command to the prophet Daniel to "shut up and seal" the message because, in Daniel's time, the fulfillment was not at hand.[13] But the Revelation was at hand.

There is no good English equivalent for the ancient Greek expression *engys*, which the King James Version translates as "at hand" and most later versions translate as "near." It includes meanings such as graspable, squeezable, within reach, and close enough to take hold of.

Engys is the same expression used in Matthew 26:46 to describe Judas Iscariot's proximity to Jesus. The King James Version says, "behold, he is *at hand* that doth betray me" (emphasis added). The New International Version translates the expression simply, "*Here comes* my betrayer!" (emphasis added).

The same expression is also used in John 2:13 to describe an approaching event at the outset of Jesus' ministry: "And the Jews' passover was *at hand*" (KJV, emphasis added), or "When it was *almost time* for the Jewish passover" (NIV, emphasis added).

Most likely the Christians in the seven churches of Asia who received this prophecy interpreted it as available, pertinent, and fulfillable for them—not a message about something that would happen more than nineteen centuries later.

Just in case these first-century readers (and we today) should have failed to understand the pertinence and practical application of the prophecy in its entirety, the very same expression, "at hand," is used both at the beginning and the end of Revelation.

"The Revelation of Jesus Christ, which God gave unto him, to shew unto his servants things which must shortly come to pass . . . for the time is at hand."[14]

Perhaps a reader could misconstrue that "the time is at hand" means thousands of years away. But together with the phrase "which must shortly come to pass," each so interprets and clarifies the other that to make these words futuristic is utterly ridiculous.

Christians throughout the centuries have always drawn strength, faith, and courage from the Revelation as a message that was within reach for their times—as with all other New Testament writings. To limit its symbolic imagery to speculation about single historical events that have either already occurred, or future events that might someday occur, is to rob this vital book of its pertinent reality and practical guidance for our daily lives in this present age.

The widespread emphasis today on interpreting the Revelation as a message only about the future or the past is a far cry from what God intended. Clearly, something is wrong.

Keepable, Heedable, Obeyable. "Blessed is he that readeth, and they that hear the words of this prophecy, and keep those things which are written therein."[15]

"Blessed is he that keepeth the sayings of the prophecy of this book."[16]

This expression is used at both the beginning and the end of Revelation. Why? Obviously, to once again emphasize the wholeness of the prophecy. To *keep* means to heed, to hold fast, to obey. It should not be too difficult for the reader to understand, therefore, that in order to keep, heed, and obey *all* of this book, it must *all* be keepable, heedable, and obeyable. If, as the end-timers tell us, the prophecies refer only to future, historic events, what could people of any generation keep, heed, or obey? Oh yes, it may satisfy an intellectual itch for some to know what will be happening out in the distant (nineteen hundred plus years) future; but what relevance would it really have in how first-century believers lived their lives or received comfort from their persecutions?

The Revelation is not a futuristic *foretelling* of events that will occur, although the prophecy indeed contains dynamic future fulfillments. It is a *forthtelling* of the gospel of the kingdom of God. It is the good news of who Christ is, what He is doing throughout history, and what He expects of His disciples of every generation. More than half a century before the Revelation was written, Jesus had said, "the kingdom of God is within you."[17]

Everything in the Revelation is graspable and fulfillable as a present-day reality. It is all keepable, heedable, and obeyable—right now. It always has been, and it always will be. To focus most of our attention on speculating about past or future events is to draw people's minds away from what God wants to fulfill in their lives here and now.

> **"Most likely the Christians in the seven churches of Asia who received this prophecy interpreted it as available, pertinent, and fulfillable for them —not a message about something that would happen more than nineteen centuries later."**

Does It Really Matter, Anyway?

So what's the big deal? What does it really matter if some people use the Revelation to speculate about the future? More than you might realize!

Our view of the future determines our philosophy of life. Whether we have a positive view or a negative view or simply don't know what to think about the future, our expectations shape the way we live and the way we define and carry out our mission today. It matters to the church, and it matters to us as individuals.

It Matters to the Church. Nothing divides Christians and discredits the Christian message so effectively as does all this distortion of the Revelation. While we fight among ourselves over how history is going to come out in the end, much of the church is abdicating its present role of guiding people into the reality of Christ and His kingdom.

As a result, the media, special interest groups, and opinion polls have taken over the role of deciding moral issues like abortion, gay rights, prolonging life, and the boundaries of medical research and practice. Secular humanists now choose the curriculum for our schools, governments increasingly take over the responsibilities of families, and scientists shape our values.

As the late Reinhold Niebuhr once said in a sermon, "The church has become trivial."

It Matters to the Individual. People who get caught up in speculation about the End Times usually struggle with needless anxieties, doubts, and confusion. They often lead anemic Christian lives because they are waiting for God to do something more. The good news of the kingdom is that He has already done everything that needs to be done.

The kingdom of God is not some abstract, ethereal place where we will live some day. It is at hand now. It is within our reach at this very moment.

We don't have to wait for the end of the world before Christ comes to us in power and glory. He is coming in all His fullness, right now. We can be overcomers in the daily experiences of our lives. We can live victoriously and abundantly, no matter what is happening in our lives today or what may happen tomorrow or twenty years from now.

Yet, most Christians aren't aware that the Revelation has any meaning for them today; and millions of people have lost the power of the faith because they've missed the vital truths of this thrilling book.

What Can We Do About It?

As a businessman, I've learned that it is never as important to fix blame as it is to try to fix a problem. Therefore, my purpose in this book is not to throw stones at any person or group but to suggest that we take a diagnostic, therapeutic approach to fixing the problem which has arisen in the church over prophecy.

Most of us would like to wave a magic wand and make the problem go away. After all, this is the age of instant everything. The solution is simple, but it is not easy—just like running a marathon is simple but not easy. Running a marathon is as simple as putting one foot down and picking up the other—for 26.2 miles. But, as one who has run a marathon, I can tell you it is not easy.

The first step in the diagnostic, therapeutic process is to ask, "What is wrong?" In this chapter, we've at least begun to search for answers to that question by looking at some of the good fruits biblical prophecy should produce and by examining some of the bad fruits that human interpretations are producing.

Yet, I suspect you've already experienced some anxieties, just in taking a look at the symptoms. I confess that re-examining a lifetime of religious conditioning has certainly created anxieties for me. But it has also been a liberating, exhilarating experience.

I think most of us allow our psychology to shape our theology, rather than allowing our theology to shape our psychology. We decide what we want to believe about the present and future, then we look for Scriptures to support our beliefs. But, when the Scriptures begin to rattle our theology, most of us become psychologically uncomfortable.

The next step in a diagnosis is to ask, "How did things get this way?" That's the question we'll explore in the next chapter. However, I can tell you that things didn't get this way by accident. There is a deliberate conspiracy to distort the truth about Christ, as He is unveiled in the Revelation. This cosmic conspiracy wants to seal up the

---

"I think most of us allow our psychology to shape our theology, rather than allowing our theology to shape our psychology."

---

glorious truths about Christ and the kingdom of God which are unveiled in the Revelation. The conspirators want to blind the very people God wishes most to receive its message, to live in its fullness, and to proclaim its reality in a desperate world.

Only when we understand what's wrong and how it got this way can we comprehend what we can do to begin correcting it.

2

THERE IS A CONSPIRACY AGAINST THE APOCALYPSE

T he very trap the Revelation warns us about—the trap of focusing attention on the world and away from Jesus Christ—has ensnared millions of people and thousands of churches.

Make no mistake about it; this trap was set deliberately and is constantly being reset. There is a conspiracy against the Apocalypse itself—a diabolical plot to continuously distort and discredit the revelation of Jesus Christ and the present reality of His kingdom.

The ongoing goal of the conspirators is to strip the Apocalypse of all its present, pertinent reality and lifegiving power. One of their most productive strategies, as we near the turn of the century, is to try to focus people's attention—especially Christians'—on dramatic predictions about the future.

The Nature of the Conspiracy

To get a clear picture of how the conspiracy operates, we must understand where it originates, why it exists, and what the conspirators hope to achieve.

Jesus constantly spoke about a universe in which everything is divided into two simultaneous, adversarial kingdoms: the kingdom of

God and the kingdom of this world. These two kingdoms exist simultaneously and have certain distinct characteristics:

- Both are spiritual kingdoms with physical/material manifestations in the visible world. The world is the battleground on which their conflict is being fought.

- The end goal of each kingdom is total control of the whole universe.

- Their methods of obtaining control are precisely opposite, and the tactics of each kingdom reflect the nature of its respective ruler.

Jesus Christ, by His death, resurrection, and ascension, has established His permanent lordship over the kingdom of God and has triumphed over the kingdom of this world and its ruler Satan.

Satan's Dilemma

Of course, Satan is smart enough to know that he cannot hold back the emergence of the kingdom of God by force. Like all clever revolutionaries who seek to overthrow their more powerful rulers, he tries to lure enough people to his side to shift the balance of power.

In this case, it's a flawed plan, because the power of Christ's kingdom does not come from human numbers but from the unconquerable God Himself. Satan and his spiritual cohorts[1] have, however, deluded themselves into believing they can win; and they continue to try to deceive human beings into aiding and abetting their efforts.[2]

Meanwhile, we humans live in the physical/material battle zone, where the spiritual struggle between the two kingdoms rages. Yet, moment by moment, we have the freedom to decide to which kingdom we will yield control of our lives. Given that choice, and given the ability to understand clearly what is of God and what is not, most sincere Christians would always opt to go with the winning team.

So the enemies of Christ's kingdom have a real problem on their hands. They cannot win the war against the kingdom of God. Jesus Christ has already delivered the decisive blow and holds in His hands the keys of death and hell.[3] All they can do is carry on a form of guerrilla warfare aimed at keeping individuals from receiving Christ's kingdom in all its fullness and from leading others into it.

As if that were not enough of a problem for the rulers of the kingdom of this world, everything Christians need to enter and live in the fullness of the kingdom of God has been provided by Jesus Christ and

---

"The ongoing goal of the conspirators is to strip the Apocalypse of all its present, pertinent reality and lifegiving power. One of their most productive strategies, as we near the turn of the century, is to try to focus people's attention—especially Christians'—on dramatic predictions about the future."

---

is clearly revealed in the Word of God.[4] Since they have been unable to destroy the Bible, the only recourse these spirit-realm conspirators have is to try to keep human beings ignorant, confused, and distracted from what it says. To accomplish this end, they constantly plot ways to distort and discredit the Word of God.

The conspirators, knowing that human beings are quite curious and anxious about the future, have seized on prophecy as one of the most fertile fields for sowing their seeds of confusion and deception.* The End Times speculation, which has become so popular in recent years, is one of their primary strategies.

The Apocalypse: A Safeguard Against Confusion and Deception

Since the two kingdoms operate in both the visible (material) and invisible (spirit) realms, Christians must be able to discern whether actions, events, and influences come from Christ or from the conspirators. Therefore, the book of Revelation gives us visual parables of the

---

* There are other fertile grounds where the seeds of confusion and deception are being sown, but for the sake of clarity, we will only address this one.

spiritual reality of the two kingdoms in conflict. It is one of our primary safeguards against being deceived.

So why does the book use bizarre images such as beasts, plagues, and cosmic conflict? If God knew that understanding the Revelation would be so critical to our following Him and resisting evil, why didn't He just explain everything in simple, direct language? Why not make the Revelation a simple how-to book?

I don't propose to explain God's motives, but one valid answer to those questions is that the human mind cannot grasp spiritual reality in the same way as scientific or historical knowledge. Spiritual reality can only be grasped by faith, through spiritual ears.[5] When the people asked Jesus why He spoke in parables, He said of the Pharisees, "Though seeing, they do not see; though hearing, they do not hear or understand." [6]

We need to interpret the stories and images of the Revelation just as we interpret the parables and symbols Jesus used in the Gospel narratives—figuratively, as metaphors and similes that express both spiritual and physical realities. The parables and symbols of the Apocalypse become complicated and frightening only when we take the book's language literally, purely physically, or connect it with future events and people—something that, according to the Scriptures, God never intended for us to do.

If we take the Revelation precisely for what it is, visual parables of spiritual/physical reality, any sincere and seeking believer can understand it. God has not complicated the Revelation; it is the conspirators who insist on reducing everything to distant persons, places, and events.

Who Are the Conspirators?

The conspiracy against the Apocalypse originates and is guided by the spiritual forces behind the kingdom of this world, but it is carried out by human beings in every generation—and this generation is no exception.

I know that conspiracy against the kingdom of God is a serious charge, and it's not one I make lightly. Again, I don't intend to cast stones at any individual or organization, or to encourage anybody to break fellowship with any church. Rather, I want to show how we human beings and our institutions carry out the conspiracy in the real world, whether knowingly or unknowingly.

So who are the conspirators? Many of them are Satan's human agents who conspire knowingly and willingly to twist the truth and deceive the unsuspecting. They may be avowed enemies of God or people who simply claim He does not exist. We have seen, for example, a marked increase in recent years in both the number and boldness of satanic and occult groups who twist parts of the Bible. Many secular humanists and new age metaphysical practitioners regularly distort the Scriptures (especially prophecy) to support everything from transcendental meditation to reincarnation.*

Tacit Conspirators

However, millions of people and many organizations, unknowingly and without malicious intent, also aid and abet the willful conspirators in misleading the masses. These individuals and groups are, to use a term from the legal profession, tacit conspirators. The word *tacit* comes from the Latin term *tacitus,* which is literally translated *silent.* One of its key meanings is arising without express contract or agreement.

In other words, a tacit conspirator unintentionally acts in a way that furthers the goals of the willful conspirators. They are not like Goëthe's aging philosopher Faust who, knowing full well what he was doing, sold his soul to the devil for a moment of complete pleasure. Rather, they are like the many good German people who were duped by Adolph Hitler into supporting the Third Reich, only to find out later that they had enabled a tyrannical madman to seize their motherland and mount a real threat of taking over the whole world.

Tacit conspirators, then, are those who unsuspectingly aid the cause of the willful conspirators. They may be sincere people who are doing what they believe is right. Many of them operate under the name of religion. They may be theologians, church leaders, ministers, teachers, authors, laypeople, or religious institutions.

---

* e.g., Jesus' statement to Nicodemus that "You must be born again" (John 3:7) is often used literally to support the doctrine of reincarnation.

May I Confess?

Please hear what I'm *not* saying. I'm not trying to single out any person or group and call them tacit conspirators. Nor am I saying that I have all the answers about the Apocalypse and that anybody who disagrees with me is a false prophet.

I confess that I have been a part of the conspiracy. We may all have aided the conspiracy, whether knowingly or unknowingly. What's more, I can easily fall back into it. Religion, not true Christianity, makes conspirators of us all. Any doctrine that becomes more important than the reality of God behind it aligns us with the conspirators.

"Woe to you, teachers of the law and Pharisees, you hypocrites!" Jesus charged the religious leaders of His day. "You shut the kingdom of heaven in men's faces." And how did He say they did that? "You yourselves do not enter, nor will you let those enter who are trying to."[7]

That's the key—whether or not we enter and live constantly in the kingdom of God. Unless we do that, we fall victim to the conspiracy and become blind guides or kingdom killers who lead others astray.

The reason so many people are vulnerable to the conspiracy is that, when it comes to the kingdom of God, they simply won't take *now* for an answer.

How the Conspiracy Works

Let me be more specific as to how you can recognize when and where the conspiracy is at work.

A handful of willful conspirators can mobilize millions of innocent people, who then become tacit conspirators. Consider, for example, how in 1959 a bearded young revolutionary named Fidel Castro overthrew the government of Fulgencio Batista with a few thousand men and gained complete control of Cuba. Millions of Americans applauded the efforts of this man, whom they thought to be an idealist wanting to restore democratic rule to one of our closest neighbors. Even the United States government came to his aid. Only after Castro had firmly established his power base did we learn of his hidden agenda: to set up a communist dictatorship, in league with Russia, on the island nation ninety miles from our coast!

**"I confess that I have been a part of
the conspiracy. We may all have aided
the conspiracy, whether knowingly or
unknowingly. What's more, I can
easily fall back into it. Religion,
not true Christianity, makes
conspirators of us all."**

Willful conspirators usually cloak their real motives and objectives
in secrecy to gain the support they need to achieve their goals.

The End Times Frenzy

I'm sure you've seen magicians use this simple ploy. They draw your
attention to one hand so you won't see what the other one is doing.

One of the best examples of how the willful conspirators use the
sleight-of-hand trick to cloak their hidden agenda is the frenzy they
are creating over the so-called End Times prophecies.° Their hidden
agenda is to draw attention away from what God is doing today and
what He wants Christians to be doing in the here and now. To achieve
that objective, the conspirators try to get people so caught up in what
might happen in the future that they miss what is actually happening
now.

- Some of them insist on interpreting the Apocalypse as ancient history. They say it was completely fulfilled within a few decades after
  it was written, and that it is important only because it contains
  useful principles.

° This is certainly not the only ruse the conspirators utilize. Others will be dealt
with in later chapters, and still others lie beyond the scope of this book. My purpose
for highlighting this one is that the conspirators are having so much success with it as
we approach the year A.D. 2000.

- Others push its fulfillment out into the future (although they may caution that it can happen any day) and use its imagery to predict coming events.

- Others claim that apocalyptic language and imagery are literal descriptions and use them as false evidence to convince people with a scientific mindset that nothing in the Bible can be taken seriously.

- Still others seize on frightening images (which they take literally and embellish) to create terror in people who don't know any better.

In other words, they will do whatever it takes to focus attention away from the spiritual and practical realization that the kingdom of God is in our lives here and now. To put it bluntly, the conspirators are those people and organizations who add their own interpretations to, or take away from, the reality of the Revelation of Jesus Christ—practices the Bible expressly condemns.[8]

Deception: The Great Cloaking Device

The truth, as revealed in the Scriptures, is the greatest obstacle the conspirators face in their efforts to thwart the continuous emergence of God's kingdom. Since they cannot disprove it, they will do anything to try to discredit it, distract people from it, and make it irrelevant to the present world. One need only look at the wide range of controversies over prophetic interpretation in the church today to see that somebody (maybe many somebodies) is being deceived.

The conspirators use a variety of clever tactics in their efforts to deceive. Here are only a few of the most common ones, with illustrations of how they show up in our day.

(1) Counterfeit: To be deceptive, a counterfeit has to look very much like the original. By literalizing the language of the Revelation and connecting it with distant, historical events, the conspirators turn the truth—that Christ's kingdom is unfolding daily—into the ruse of millennialism. By fixing dates and places, they can hide the present reality of the unveiled Christ.

(2) Trickery: By getting Christians to fight with each other over the timing and nature of the Second Coming, the conspirators call attention away from the biblical truth that Christ can come to us in all His reality right now.

(3) *Distortion of truth:* Conspirators often twist Scriptures to explain how prophetic verses could have a scientific basis. For instance, they put forth a nuclear holocaust as a plausible explanation of how the old earth will be destroyed to make way for a new earth. Pretty soon, masses of people believe that's what the Bible says.

(4) *Half-truths:* Many half-truths parade as whole truths to the point that they become lies. We've all heard a great deal, for instance, about the Antichrist. Prophetic literalists try to name one specific person who will deceive the nations. Yet, if we spend our time speculating on one person who will fit the exact description, we overlook the many antichrists who are deceiving millions in our own day.

(5) *Fear:* One of the oldest sleight-of-hand tricks is to get people so busy looking at all the drastic things that could happen to them that they miss the reality of the kingdom of God. Some people, for example, spend much more time looking in their newspapers for evidence of the mark of the beast than they spend searching their Bibles for the reality of Christ.

The good news is that deception doesn't work against Christians who know the Bible and yield to the Holy Spirit. But the bad news is that many Christians today do not meet those two conditions.

Why the Church Today Is Such Fertile Ground for the Conspiracy

"Be on your guard against the yeast of the Pharisees and Sadducees," Jesus cautioned His disciples.[9] What was the yeast of the Pharisees and Sadducees? It can be summed up in one phrase: doctrines of men.[10]

So many layers of human doctrine have built up around the Revelation, and so many Christians are so ignorant about biblical prophecy, that masses of people have no idea what the Scriptures actually say about the unveiled Christ. Yet, early Christians were constantly on guard against deceptive teachers and doctrines.

The dividing line between the kingdom of God and the kingdom of this world has eroded over the centuries to a point that today's typical Christian cannot distinguish between them.

Jesus compared our efforts to impose worldly values on God's kingdom to trying to preserve new wine in old wineskins. If we try to do that, He said, "the skins will burst, the wine will run out and the wineskins will be ruined."[11]

Yet, that's precisely what religion does. It joins in with the conspirators to substitute the physical/material perceptions of man for the spiritual realities of God. Thus, many churches and Christians today provide fertile ground for the conspiracy against the Apocalypse.

Let's briefly examine some key reasons why so many Christians today find the End Times deception so attractive. In later chapters, we'll look much more closely at these factors and see how they work together to produce anemic Christians and lifeless, irrelevant, mediocre churches.

The End Times conspiracy appeals to a strong, anti-supernatural bias which is widespread in the church today. Many people love God but just can't tolerate His supernatural ways. They may accept the idea of God doing something in the future, way up in the heavens. They may even believe that God works on earth, using human methods and devices to accomplish His purposes. But they find totally offensive the very notion that God could or would work miraculously in the lives of individual believers here and now. Most churches accept science, knowledge, and doctrinal orthodoxy more readily than the present reality of the Spirit of God.

Yet Jesus clearly taught that His kingdom and the kingdom of this world were both spiritual and material. Indeed, according to the entire Bible, spiritual forces exert a major influence on people and events in the physical world. We will never be able to understand the visible world until we recognize the invisible realm of the spirit.

De-spiritualizing the spiritual message Jesus delivered and modeled makes the message intellectually acceptable. (In fact, Thomas Jefferson attempted to do just that by publishing a version of the New Testament in which he had deleted all references to miracles.) And pushing the kingdom of God back into the past or out into the future conveniently avoids having to deal with an *active* Christ who does not *act* in our "orthodox" ways.

It should be noted that denying or minimizing the relevance of the supernatural (both good and evil) to our present existence eliminates neither its reality nor the need people feel for it. The new age movement is growing by leaps and bounds, even infiltrating the church,

"Pushing the kingdom of God back into the past or out into the future conveniently avoids having to deal with an active Christ who does not act in our 'orthodox' ways."

because it offers such an authentic-looking alternative for the spiritual/physical reality the Bible proclaims—a reality for which many people hunger but know little about.

The End Times frenzy appeals to a widespread aversion to evangelism. The church, and even many end-timers, talk a lot about evangelism. Yet studies show that 95 percent of all Christians have never led a single person to Christ.

In fact, most Christians would secretly rather see the world destroyed than pay the price of witnessing openly to the reality of Christ and His kingdom in our present world. You can get yourself subjected to all sorts of persecution by actively sharing the good news of the gospel in a hostile world, they reason. Let's just let God destroy it and prove to those sinners that we're right.

The End Times frenzy appeals to an escapist psychological desire. Many Christians would rather be jerked out of the difficulties and pains of their lives than pay the price for intimate, moment-by-moment fellowship and co-laboring with Jesus. It's the same sort of escapist psychological desire that causes people to long for a knight on a white horse to come and take them away from it all.

Too many people are like the Jews of New Testament times; they are so busy looking for a particular type of coming, future Messiah that they completely overlook the Messiah who has already come and who continues to come.

The End Times doctrine is fiercely defended by denominational protectionism. End Times doctrine is deeply embedded in many church denominations, and they strongly resist any challenge to it as heresy.

For example, church denominations own some of the largest publishing houses in the world, and they carefully censor any material that does not support their particular doctrine about the Revelation. Even many privately-owned publishers hesitate to publish a work which may offend certain religious leaders.

This kind of denominational protectionism also exerts pressure on ministers to comply with their denomination's stance on the Revelation. Theological seminaries often screen students about their views of the End Times before they admit them. And, of course, no theological degree means no church. Many ministers who stand up to proclaim that the kingdom of God is here and accessible now find themselves removed from the approved pastor or evangelist list.

The End Times doctrine is reinforced by decades of religious conditioning. One reason the End Times doctrines meet with so little questioning in the church is that most Christians have been conditioned all their lives to believe them. It's as though we have a set of End Times filters on our hearts, and we systematically filter out whatever does not fit.

Most people tend to settle into churches with doctrines and practices that are comfortable for them. They find a theology to support their psychology, and any message that threatens their comfort zone—even if the message is clearly stated in the Bible—is vigorously resisted.

Shoving the kingdom of God into the future relieves us of having to take greater responsibility now. Most of us have our hands full just meeting the demands of our daily lives; so the idea of rearranging our religious prejudices is something we can easily put off until later. A futuristic view of the kingdom of God gives us a convenient way to do that.

Given the pace and complexities of our citizenship in the world, not many of us want to tackle the challenge of finding out what it means to be a citizen of God's kingdom now. We can handle church membership and attendance, and we've been led to believe that's all being overcomers involves.

Yet, the Revelation clearly states that everything in God's Word is at hand—graspable and keepable—right now. God may choose to do all kinds of things in the future; after all, God can do as He wills. But

He doesn't have to do anything else to fulfill all the prophecies of the Bible. They have been and are continually being fulfilled. To bury our heads in the sand like the proverbial ostrich does not change the present reality that God intends for us to reign with Him in the heavenlies and to express our spiritual dominion through our actions in the physical realm—*now*.

Admittedly, we've only scratched the surface of why so many Christians today find the End Times deception so attractive. Throughout the book, we will look at other reasons.

What Can We Do About the Conspiracy?

Hopefully, I've awakened you to the reality that there is a diabolical conspiracy to discredit the revelation of Christ and His kingdom by making it solely futuristic or historical—not relevant to our day. And, by now, it should be clear that it takes more than cleverness on our part to avoid the conspirators' deceptiveness.

So, what can we do about it? If all I had to offer were more of the confusion and fear that surround the Apocalypse, I would never have undertaken the writing of this book. But the Scriptures which warn us about the conspiracy also show us how to deal with it. That's the subject of the next chapter.

3

HOW TO AVOID BEING TAKEN IN BY THE CONSPIRACY

Neither individuals nor the church have the task nor prerogative to speculate about the future. We can and must leave the future in God's hands and get on with our task of being God's people in our present generation.[1]

I believe that far too many Christians have been duped by the conspiracy into accepting a literalistic, futuristic theology—hook, line, and sinker. Yet, that theology fits neither the teaching, pattern, nor terminology of Jesus' earthly ministry or of any other Scripture.

Does that mean that God has done all He is ever going to do? Does it mean there will be no future Rapture or global holocaust? No! God is sovereign, and He can do whatever He chooses at any time.

It simply means that biblical prophecy does not give us enough information to enable us to predict when God might wrap up human history. If we get caught up in trying to figure it all out intellectually, we are likely to be as wrong about God's future plans as the Jews of Jesus' day were about the coming of the Messiah.

But how can we avoid being duped into chasing after End Times doctrines or other deceptions?

When the Best Defense Is a Strong Offense

We can live in the fullness of God's Word, made alive to us by the Holy Spirit. That is the best defense against any kind of deception.

The Revelation clearly reveals what God expects us to be doing in our daily lives, and it also promises great blessings and benefits to those who heed it. It gives three basic instructions which can help us avoid being taken in by the conspiracy. If we follow them, we can, instead, live according to God's expectations for us.

First, we are to read it (both publicly and privately), to hear (understand) what it says, and to keep or obey its commands. "Blessed is he that readeth, and they that hear the words of this prophecy, and keep those things which are written therein: for the time is at hand."[2] Please note that we must do all three to qualify for the promised blessing.

Second, we are to live out our daily lives as *rulers and priests in Christ's kingdom.*[3]

Third, we are to overcome—to *be faithful to God* and to *overcome the evil one.*[4]

In short, we are not to look for a quick and easy way out of this troubled world but to get on with being Christ's kingdom, temple, bride, and servants in the world—no matter what happens.[5]

So how do we do all that? I have exciting news! Jesus has provided everything we need, and the Bible explains very clearly how we can live in the full victory of Jesus Christ. Let's begin in this chapter to examine how we can tap into God's infinite power and live, moment by moment, in the kingdom of God—here and now.

Read, Hear, Obey

Let me ask you an unsettling question: How much of your belief about the Revelation is based on your personal search of the Scriptures, and how much is based on what others have said?

When I began to seriously study the Revelation and other biblical prophecy some years ago, I quickly discovered that I had picked up most of my beliefs from other people, not from direct reading and study of God's own Word. And, quite frankly, much of what I had been taught did not square with the Bible.

Again, please hear what I am saying, and don't infer what I'm not saying. I don't at all mean to imply that we shouldn't listen to teachers and read other books on the subject. But listening to others and reading books about the Bible cannot take the place of our personal reading and study on any subject, including prophecy. We each have the responsibility to measure everything we hear and read (including this book) against God's Word.

"In short, we are not to look for a quick and easy way out of this troubled world but to get on with being Christ's kingdom, temple, bride, and servants in the world—no matter what happens."

"Blessed is he that *readeth . . . the words of this prophecy . . .* " the author of the Revelation says.[6] He also warns, "If anyone adds anything to them, God will add to him the plagues described in this book. And if anyone takes words away from this book of prophecy, God will take away from him his share in the tree of life and in the holy city, which are described in this book."[7] John gives us an exciting promise and two dire warnings. Let me urge you to constantly re-examine the Scriptures to make sure that no message you believe adds to or takes away from the content and spirit of the Apocalypse.

Consider these points:

All Scripture is prophetic. What book is John talking about? Obviously, the words *this book of prophecy* in chapter 22:18–19 refer directly to the book of Revelation. They imply that John regarded the Apocalypse as Scripture—a direct revelation from God. Earlier, he had expressly stated that its message was delivered personally to him by an angel of the Lord.[8]

There is, however, a sense in which all Scripture is prophecy. Most of us have been taught that prophecy has only to do with *foretelling* the future. Yet, throughout the Bible, the term *prophecy* also refers to *forthtelling* the Word of God. A prophet is one whose message is of divine origin—one who, like John the Baptist, proclaims a message from God.[9] As the forerunner of Christ, John did predict (*foretelling*) the coming of Jesus in His incarnate form; but he also had a great deal to say about what was going on at that moment in history (*forthtelling*).

Likewise, the Revelation is the Word of God for the here and now—not merely a set of clues about what will happen. It was at hand in the first century, and it is at hand now. Don't get so carried away with any biblical message about the future (as the conspirators would like for you to do) that you overlook the Revelation's spiritual and practical message about the here and now.

Also, remember that the Revelation does not stand in isolation from the remainder of the Bible. Everything it contains is consistent with and supported by all other Scriptures.[10] In fact, one of our God-given safeguards against deception is to constantly check our understanding of any one Scripture against all other Scriptures.

Rely only on what the Bible says, not on human interpretations of what it says. There is often a big difference in what man says and what the Bible says. Nowhere is this more evident than in the book of Revelation.

Here are only a few examples of how human doctrines about prophecy often stand in conflict with the Word of God.

The Bible Says	Doctrines of Men Say
It is done	No, it is not yet done!
At hand	Out in the future, somewhere
Heed / keep / obey	Know about
For first century, on	We may be *the* generation to which all this applies
Within and among you	Up in the sky, by and by
World without end	The end of the world is near
Jesus: "Lo, I'll be *with* you always, even to the end of the age."	Jesus is *off* somewhere waiting to come back at the end of the age

The Bible Says	Doctrines of Men Say
Not for you to know times and dates	But we can speculate
The kingdom is here	Kingdom not here (in its fullness)
Reign and rule	Just hold on
Kings and priests	Unworthy worms
Do the works of Jesus	Wait until Jesus comes back and does them
Disciples lived in the last days	No, the last days only apply to this (or some future) generation
We have been living in the Day of the Lord	The Day of the Lord is coming soon
My words are spirit and life	His words are predictions of future events

The list could go on for pages, but I think you get the idea. When we base our faith and actions on what some people say, we will be acceptable by human standards but not necessarily by God's standards. Thus, we must read and know what God says to us in His Word.

Examine the fruits of any interpretation. If we are living with a firm conviction that the kingdom of God dwells within and among us now, as Jesus said, we will produce the fruits of His kingdom. Conversely, if we are living with the belief that the kingdom of God will come someday, we will produce the fruits of this present world. Jesus spoke of being in the world but not of the world.[11] There is an enormous difference.

Let me illustrate.° One of the most popular themes in Christianity today is that serving God will make us blissfully happy and materially wealthy. Some religious groups even hold seminars designed to teach people how to amass wealth and get more pleasure out of life. But

---

° We will cite many specific examples throughout the remainder of the book.

that often produces fruit like: excessive materialism, anxiety about possessions, and compromise with the world system.

Now, take a look at Revelation's picture of how God's saints experience the world. They are awed only by the majesty of Christ; and their primary focus is serving God, not enjoying life or amassing wealth. Although they live under great tribulation, even to the point of losing their lives, they are called upon to "wait a little longer."[12] That message produces good fruit like patience, faith, endurance, and the advancement of Christ's kingdom.

It may be intellectually convenient to push the persecutions back into the first and second centuries or to think of the tribulation as a one-time event, limited to seven years, that will occur at some future time. However, to remove tribulation from the present produces the negative fruit of spiritual blindness; it is to ignore Jesus' warnings about the coming persecution[13] and His prediction, "In the world ye shall have tribulation."[14]

Scripture emphasizes that we are to rule and reign over the world, not to get caught up in its ways.

I'm not saying that Christians should be morbid about life. After all, Jesus was the most joyful person who ever lived, even the night before His crucifixion.[15] My point is simply that we need to read, hear, keep, and obey the Revelation message. We must check our doctrines and credos against God's Word, not simply accept what others say.

Do the Works of Jesus

According to the Bible, the kingdom of God is full of action. We are expected to be doers of the Word, not merely hearers of it.[16] Yet, the work God calls us to do is not busywork or the empty religious works that took up so much time for the Scribes and Pharisees.

God's Word specifically instructs us to do the works of Jesus.[17] And it promises that all who do the work of Jesus will be given authority and will rule with Christ over the nations.[18] Christ has already made us His kingdom and His priests.[19]

That's not pie in the sky by and by—that's real world, here and now. Jesus spoke of the kingdom of God as a glorious, present-day reality (there and then, here and now), not in part, but in all its full-

"Scripture emphasizes that we are to rule and reign over the world, not to get caught up in its ways."

ness.[20] He had much to say about His present kingdom, but of a future millennial kingdom, absolutely nothing! Not even a small number of poetic and figurative Old Testament passages used by the conspirators can be identified with a future millennial kingdom. No, we don't have to wait for any prophecy to be fulfilled before we can enter Christ's kingdom to reign and be priests with Him.[21]

What, then, are the works of Jesus? The Bible suggests that they involve a lot more than church work. Attending worship and Sunday school, singing in the choir, and giving to missions might be outward trappings of the works of Jesus; but pagans do those things. Even a cursory reading of the Revelation shows that the works of Jesus involve intense activities such as discerning and resisting evil spirit-realm beings and forces and spreading the good news of the kingdom.*

Now maybe all that sounds ethereal and hard to grasp. Admittedly, it's a lot different from merely raising budgets and increasing attendance. But it is not as other-worldly as you might think. If we accept the basic theme of the Revelation—that many events in this world originate in the spirit realm—we can begin to grasp the importance of what Paul described as spiritual warfare.[22] As we read Christ's unveiling of the events that "must soon take place,"[23] we see one visual parable after another demonstrating how Jesus has overcome the world and how He enables us to overcome it—moment by moment.

Doing the works of Jesus, then, includes conquering the spiritual forces that are constantly struggling to gain control of our personal lives and of the world around us. It means winning against evil in the spirit realm and expressing that victory by the way we live our daily lives.

Let's take a closer look at what doing the works of Jesus implies.

---

* For examples, see the letters to the seven churches in Revelation 2–4.

We must enter the kingdom and live there continually. To do the works of Jesus, we must first belong to His kingdom.[24] Entering is as simple as Jesus' command to Nicodemus: "You must be born again."[25] But the ongoing nature of statements like "those who wash their robes"[26] suggests that living in the kingdom is a continual process of receiving the Spirit and life of God. If we do that, we gain access to the "tree of life and go through the gates into the [Holy] city."[27]

Again, don't let the conspirators convince you that all this is out in the future. Jesus said, "It is done."[28]

The kingdom is spiritual, but we express it in physical actions. We are to be Christ's kingdom—to be spiritually in Him and have Him in us.[29] Only then can we live victoriously in an evil world and do the works of Jesus.

It is still possible to know the King without knowing the kingdom.

Many people buy into the notion that the age of miracles has passed, if it ever existed. Some can accept the ideas that Jesus performed miracles and fought with spiritual beings during His earthly ministry and that the Second Coming will be miraculous; but they somehow believe that all supernatural activity has been put on hold for the present. That's why it's so comfortable to interpret the events of the Revelation literally and push them out into the future or back into the past.

For example, it's more intellectually appealing to speak of a literal, physical Battle of Armageddon over in Israel someday than to accept the reality that citizens of the kingdom are constantly fighting a spirit-realm/physical-realm Armageddon—right now. We'll have a whole chapter about this later. For now, it is vital to see that we must first do the works of Jesus in the spirit realm before we can do the works of Jesus in the physical/material realm from day to day.

Doing the works of Jesus, then, means doing what Jesus did in the same power in which He did them. And, what power was that? When the Jews challenged Him for "making himself equal with God," Jesus replied, "I tell you the truth, the Son can do nothing by Himself; he can do only what he sees His Father doing, because whatever the Father does the Son also does."[30]

Any way you slice it, doing the works of Jesus means being energized by the supernatural power of God.

God is actively involved in our world—now! One question that continues to trouble the church today is "Where was God during the Nazi holocaust?" Millions of Jews were slaughtered by a world system that seemed totally out of control. Millions of Christians who are being persecuted around the world today may still be asking, "Where is God?"

The answer is "He is where He has always been." He is here— with and among us. Our struggle is His struggle; our pain is His pain. The Lamb of God knows what it's like to go through what we may be enduring, because He paid the ultimate price—His own life. He is worthy to rule and reign, not only in our hearts, but throughout all creation.[31]

Doing the works of Jesus means demonstrating the good news of the kingdom by the power of the Spirit. And what is that good news of the kingdom? "Now the dwelling of God is with men, and he will live with them."[32]

So God calls us to "come out of Babylon" (the confusion of the world and religious systems),[33] to reign and rule with Him as His kings and priests, and to do the works of Jesus by the power of His Spirit— right here, right now!

Finally, let's look at the third way we can get on with being Christ's kingdom, temple, bride, and servants in the world—no matter what happens.

We Can Overcome

Don't think for one minute that God doesn't know how hard it is to live victoriously in a world besieged by evil spiritual powers. Anytime we feel like no one understands what we're up against, all we have to do is to compare our scars with those of Jesus. If anyone knows what it means to overcome evil, He does. Now He asks us to do the same and promises great benefits to all who do.[34] And no matter what our world may look like to us now, God *is* in charge.

Why doesn't He just wipe away all the evil? Surely, as the omnipotent, all-powerful God, He could! Why doesn't He just wave His great hand and get rid of all the evil forces?

Well, He doesn't tell us why. But He does warn us to expect tribulation (literally, *trouble*). And the Revelation warns that, for some reason, these things must take place—as a present reality, not in some
distant, seven-year time period. Yet we are not helpless pawns caught
up in the spirit-realm struggle of good against evil. God gives us the
power, moment by moment, to overcome all the evil that besets us.

What does it mean to overcome in the midst of tribulation? Certainly more than waiting for God to jerk us out of the world! Let's look
at what overcoming means to those who seek to rule and reign with
Jesus in His kingdom.

***Overcoming requires us to recognize the presence and activi-
ties of real spirit-realm powers.*** It is one thing to think of good as
ethics and morals and to characterize evil as a sinful condition of the
heart or as wrongful deeds. But, if you stop there (as most churches
do now), then you reduce overcoming to a process of merely deciding
what is right and wrong and then living accordingly. Thus for many
Christians overcoming means little more than living by the golden
rule, going to church, and being a good person.

As noble as that approach may seem, however, it reduces Christianity to a religion of works—another one of the many religions of the
world. It's the "yeast of the Pharisees and Sadducees" of which Jesus
warned His disciples to beware: religion.[35]

What distinguishes biblical Christianity from all other religions and
moral codes, however, is that Jesus Christ is the only person in history
who solved humanity's two biggest problems: sin and death. He overcame sin by His sinless life and death on the cross, and He overcame
death by His resurrection. Thus, He can empower believers to overcome sin and death.

To the Christ of the Gospels and the Revelation, sin meant much
more than our propensity to do evil, and death much more than the
cessation of life. Christ spoke of sin as the activity of spiritual forces
(epitomized by Satan and his demons) which led men to resist the
emergence of God's kingdom.[36] And He spoke of death as a direct
result of the actions of "the prince of this world" (Satan).[37]

The underlying theme of the Revelation, then, is that much of the
visible evil in the world results directly from invisible spiritual forces
and activities. Therefore, we can overcome evil only when we recog-

nize that these forces exist and when we can discern their influence, both in our world and in our personal lives.

I'm not suggesting that we have to see a demon behind every tree, but we simply cannot ignore or deny the supernatural realm if we are to be victorious kings and priests in the kingdom of God.

> ### "The underlying theme of the Revelation, then, is that much of the visible evil in the world results directly from invisible spiritual forces and activities."

Overcoming requires supernatural empowerment. Recognizing the involvement of spirit-realm beings is vital, but it is not enough. We must have within us the supernatural power to overcome them.

Acts 19 tells a tragic story about what happened when the seven powerless sons of a Jewish chief priest named Sceva tried to drive the evil spirits out of a man by invoking the names of Jesus and Paul. "The evil spirit answered them, 'Jesus I know, and I know about Paul, but who are you?' Then the man who had the evil spirit jumped on them and overpowered them all. He gave them such a beating that they ran out of the house naked and bleeding."[38]

Of course, most encounters with evil spirits are not that dramatic or explosive. But don't think for one moment that the cosmic powers will roll over and play dead as the kingdom of God emerges. "From the days of John the Baptist until now, the kingdom of Heaven has been forcefully advancing, and forceful men lay hold of it,"[39] Jesus said. The New English Bible uses the language, "subjected to violence and violent men are seizing it."

Make no mistake about it. We are involved in a cosmic war energized by spiritual beings. The platitudes and clichés which most people in the church count on for power prove no match for the "spiritual forces of evil in the heavenly realms."[40] We are foolish if we think we can overcome cosmic forces with human intellect or positive thinking. To rule and reign with Christ, we have to seize the kingdom by force; and to do that, we simply must operate within the supernatural power of God.

"I hold the keys of death and Hades,"[41] said Jesus. He is the "King of Kings and Lord of Lords,"[42] and He has promised to give us His full authority and power. But we have to tap into that infinite power source spiritually before we can overcome in the material realm.

Overcoming gets very nitty-gritty. Revelation emphasizes the interplay between the spirit realm and the material realm. So, while overcoming begins in the spirit realm, it is executed primarily in the nitty-gritty of our daily lives in this world.

The Revelation message given to John stands in complete harmony with John's gospel account of Jesus' discussions with His disciples and of His prayer for them the night before His crucifixion.[43] "My prayer is not that you take them out of the world but that you protect them from the evil one,"[44] He prayed. A few verses later, He made it clear that He was not praying only for the disciples but "also for those who will believe in me through their message."[45] That includes us. Both messages focus not on getting people out of the world (as with the end-timers) but on enabling believers of every generation to overcome in the world.

Then, He made it clear that we are in the world on a definite mission: "As you sent me into the world, I have sent them into the world."[46] What is that mission? Jesus said, "that the world may believe that you have sent me."[47] A few weeks later, He instructed them, "Go and make disciples of all nations, baptizing them in [literally, *into*] the name of [literally, *the reality of*] the Father and of the Son and of the Holy Spirit, and teaching them to obey everything I have commanded you."[48]

So overcoming means more than simply escaping the enemy of God. We are to engage God's enemy and win—all day, every day. But how are we to do that? Revelation says, "[The overcomers] overcame him [Satan] by the blood of the Lamb and by the word of their testimony; they did not love their lives so much as to shrink from death."[49]

Spiritually, Jesus has cleansed us and given us power through His blood. That is done *for us*, and all we need to do is receive it.

Our part, however, is to exhibit that supernatural redemption and empowerment in the material world through "the word of [our] testimony," even to the point of risking our lives. That implies much more than witnessing for Christ, although it may include that.

"The kingdom of God is truly a glorious, present-day reality—there and then, here and now—in all its fullness. We don't have to wait until some future day to enter and participate in Christ's kingdom."

The Greek word used for *testimony* in that passage is the same word from which we get our term *martyr*. And, if you glance through the book of Acts, you will discover that the first-century Christians who were persecuted or killed for the sake of the gospel were not merely witnessing in the modern sense of the word. They were demonstrating the power of God's kingdom by doing the works of Jesus, in the power of God.[50]

Certainly, if you do the works of Jesus, you can expect to meet with opposition. But the good news of the kingdom is, "Take heart! I have overcome the world."[51]

The bottom line of the Revelation is that God has done and will continue to do everything He can to overcome evil with good—and He asks us to do the same. We have to live *in* this evil world, and that means tribulation. But the good news of the kingdom is that we don't have to be *of* the world. We can overcome evil with good. And we can share as priests in God's ongoing ministry of reconciliation.

Looking Ahead

So you see, the kingdom of God *is* truly a glorious, present-day reality—there and then, here and now—in all its fullness. We don't have to wait until some future day to enter and participate in Christ's kingdom. We can rule and reign with God in this universe, today.

We may not have enough information to predict when or how God might wrap up human history. But we can and must leave the future in God's hands. We must trust Him completely and get on with being God's people in our present generation.

I know that many of the ideas in this chapter beg for further explanation. In later chapters, we'll speak in detail about many of the exciting things God has made available for us—here and now. In the next chapter, we'll explore how you can make sense of all the confusing imagery of the Revelation.

Hopefully, I've inspired you to re-examine the truths of biblical prophecy. If so, before you move on, let me urge you to take a moment and ask the Lord for the "spirit of wisdom and revelation."[52]

4

HOW YOU CAN UNRAVEL THE MYSTERIES OF THE REVELATION

I f you've had trouble unraveling the mysteries of the Revelation, you're not alone. Bible scholars over the centuries have been puzzled by the book's strange symbolism and what theologians call its apocalyptic imagery.

Martin Luther, for instance, felt that the book should be dropped from the Canon because it was too different from other New Testament Scriptures and neither taught nor acknowledged Jesus Christ. Ulrich Zwingli, the sixteenth-century Swiss reformer and Bible translator, called it insignificant and refused to concern himself with it.

Why does the Revelation use such bizarre creatures, descriptions, and symbols to tell its message? If God had something important to tell us, why didn't He just come right out and say it in simple, everyday language?

In fact, God does have something very important to tell us, and He did say it clearly and simply. The problem is that the conspirators keep garbling His message by trying to attach their own meanings to it.

In this chapter, we'll examine four simple keys you can use to unlock the mysteries of this vital book.

Key #1:
The Revelation Uses Figurative Language And
Symbols to Reveal Spiritual/Physical Realities

The strange imagery of the Revelation and other prophetic Scriptures is not God's way of keeping us confused. Rather, it represents the efforts of infinite God to communicate with finite humans about truth and reality in the spiritual and physical realms. God knows that trying to figure out spiritual/physical reality using earthly wisdom is like plugging a pocket calculator directly into a nuclear power plant—the source overloads the receiver's capacity.

The trouble lies not with the way God has chosen to convey His message but with the way we humans try to grasp it. God speaks in figurative language and symbols to reveal spirit-realm/physical-realm realities, but we try to understand His meanings in purely physical/material terms.

Our Physical/Material Mindset

Jesus often encountered a physical/material mindset during His earthly ministry. He constantly spoke about the kingdom of God in very simple terms, using parables and metaphors such as water, seeds, coins, and fish. But the people who heard Him kept trying to interpret His parables and symbols literally instead of spiritually.

For example, Jesus explained the most basic spirit-realm/physical-realm reality—the new birth—to a searching Pharisee named Nicodemus. Unable to grasp Jesus' message, Nicodemus talked about re-entering his mother's womb and asked, "How can this be?" Jesus exclaimed, "I have spoken to you of earthly things and you do not believe; how then will you believe if I speak of heavenly things?"[1]

This kind of mindset—the so-called scientific approach—denies or ignores the dimension of the spirit and blinds us to the spirit-world realities of the Revelation. Once we accept that God is speaking in spirit-realm/physical-realm terms using symbols, the Revelation begins to open up its treasures to us.

Why Bother About Spirit-Realm Realities?

All this talk about the spirit realm might make you uncomfortable. The fact is that most people in our culture get up every morning and go

> **"This kind of mindset—the so-called scientific approach—denies or ignores the dimension of the spirit and blinds us to the spirit-world realities of the Revelation."**

through the whole day without the slightest thought of what is going on in the spiritual dimension. To them, angels, demons, and other spirit-realm beings are little more than eerie creatures in science fiction or horror movies. They may think of everything that lies beyond the material realm as paranormal—something we humans may someday be able to explain in purely scientific terms.

For such people, the supernatural is not a touchable, squeezable, graspable reality. Thus, the Revelation presents only a confusing set of riddles that have little meaning to their daily existence. Simply put, they can take it or leave it. If it enters their consciousness at all (perhaps through a television episode about the occult), it lingers only until their attention is redirected to something they find more interesting.

"Why even bother about the spirit realm?" they would ask if confronted with questions about it.

Here are four very important reasons why humans need to grasp spiritual reality.

(1) God is spirit. The conspirators have been doing a fairly good job of convincing most people—even Christians—to think of God only in physical terms. How? One way is by making an idol of the church itself—by letting the church, a human organization, usurp the rightful place of the Lord Jesus Christ as the focal point of worship and activity. Today, many Christians talk about doing the work of the church, being committed to the church, and making great sacrifices for the church. Some even act as if the buildings, rituals, and doctrines of their churches are sacred in themselves.

But Jesus said, "God is spirit, and his worshipers must worship in spirit and truth."[2] The Greek word translated as *truth* means unveiled reality, the reality pertaining to an appearance. Do you see the trap?

When we absolutize the church, we worship the appearance, not the reality behind it.

The Apocalypse, then, unveils the spirit-realm reality of Christ—here and now. God invites us to look beyond Jesus' earthly appearance to see Him in all His present, glorious reality. That is not pie-in-the-sky-by-and-by. It is at hand, right now.

That's what makes the Revelation message so vital for us today, in this present world. It lifts the veil and enables believers to get beyond Jesus' earthly ministry so that we can live daily in perfect fellowship with Him.

(2) Humans are spirit beings. Jesus made a very startling statement in one of His synagogue teachings: "Unless you eat the flesh of the Son of Man and drink his blood, you have no life in you."[3]

"This is a hard teaching. Who can accept it?" His disciples complained. It was so hard, in fact, that many of His disciples "turned back and no longer followed him."

When Jesus became aware that His disciples were grumbling about His statements, He explained, "The Spirit gives life; the flesh counts for nothing. The words I have spoken to you are Spirit and life."

Why is this such a hard concept for humans to grasp? It's because most of us do not recognize our spirituality. We can take in the idea that we have a body, a mind, and emotions, because we can prove them scientifically. But we can experience our spirits only through a new birth—through an awakening of our spirits to the realities of the spirit dimension.

The night before Jesus was crucified, His disciples demonstrated the complete lack of understanding of the spirit dimension typical of most humans. When He told them that His flesh was going to die, they protested vehemently. To them, His physical presence was everything. They wanted Him *with* them in His human flesh, but He longed to be *in* them in their spirits.[4]

Humanity has continually attempted to discredit and de-spiritualize the spirit-realm/physical-realm message Jesus gave to John through visual parables in the Revelation.

Because we are so attuned to the material world (our flesh), we long for a physical rapture, for a physical return of Jesus, for a visible New Jerusalem, for a physical wedding supper with Christ—someday,

"God has chosen human beings as the earthly seat of His kingdom. In humanity the spirit world (both good and evil) and the material world connect."

somewhere. The real message of the Revelation, however, is that we don't have to wait. Spiritually, we can dwell and dine with Jesus in His Holy City right here, right now.

"Yes, but we humans are also flesh and bone," you might protest, "and we live in a world of time, space, and matter." That brings us to the third reason we need to be concerned about the spirit realm.

(3) The kingdom of God is a spirit-realm kingdom. When the Pharisees asked Jesus when His kingdom would come, He replied, "The kingdom of God does not come visibly, nor will people say, 'Here it is,' or 'There it is,' because the kingdom of God is within [among] you."[5]

God has chosen human beings as the earthly seat of His kingdom. In humanity the spirit world (both good and evil) and the material world connect. The fact that the spirit realm is invisible doesn't mean that it doesn't exist; the spirit dimension is just as real as the physical world we experience through our five senses. Thus, when we deny or minimize the spirit realm, we simply diminish our ability to see it (through our spiritual eyes) and to operate in it. What's more, we will never be able to fully understand the physical world and to effectively rule and reign with Christ in it until we understand the world of the spirit.

It is crucial that we recognize how spirit-realm forces influence the behavior of both individuals and nations, and how they shape events in the material world. We must recognize that we can overcome and live victoriously in the material world only when we are energized by the Spirit of God within and among us.

(4) Spirit-realm reality is where the blessings are promised.
The temple rulers and teachers who constantly challenged Jesus refused to enter the spirit-realm kingdom of God, and they tried to keep
others from entering it as well.[6] How? By reducing everything to a
mere physical/material plane. They sought to obtain the blessings of
God by doing the works of the flesh.

Yet, the teachings of Jesus—especially the Revelation—repeatedly
promise God's blessings to those who enter the kingdom of God's
spirit realm and reign and rule with Christ. That's where the power is!
Jesus said:

- Blessed is the one who reads the words of this prophecy [the unveiling of Jesus] and blessed are those who hear it and take to
  heart what is written in it, because the time is near [at hand].[7]

- Blessed is he who stays awake [spiritually] and keeps his clothes
  [garments of righteousness] with him.[8]

- Blessed are those who wash their robes, that they may have the
  right to the tree of life and may go through the gates into the city.[9]

All of those promised blessings were at hand for first-century believers; they have been at hand for believers of all generations since;
and they are all available for believers today and in future generations.
But the key to receiving them is to enter, reign, and rule with Christ
in the spirit realm now—not to wait around for events that might happen someday.

Spirit-Realm Reality Can Only Be Received Spiritually

The Bible is a supernatural book, uniquely inspired by the Holy Spirit.
You simply cannot study it like any other. And, since it is a supernatural book, we can only receive its realities supernaturally, as they are
made alive to us by the Holy Spirit.

But how do we do that? Jesus gave us a simple formula to follow.
"Blessed are the *poor in spirit*," He said, "for theirs is the kingdom of
heaven."[10]

As we come in poverty of spirit, we recognize that the only hope
of solving mankind's two biggest problems—sin and death—lies in the
earthly ministry of Jesus Christ. In the Revelation we see Christ in all

His present, spirit-realm reality. No matter how intellectually brilliant we may be, we will not see the kingdom of God until we approach the Word of God in spiritual poverty. We are like the blind fools, the kingdom killers (the Pharisees)[11] of the gospel era.

"You diligently study the Scriptures because you think that *by them* you possess eternal life," Jesus chided the teachers of the law. "These are the Scriptures that testify about me, yet you refuse to *come to me* to have life," he lamented.[12]

If we read the Revelation with the eyes of the flesh, we can see only a physical Second Coming, a material global destruction, a geographical New Jerusalem, and a set of timetables. If, however, we approach it in poverty of spirit and allow the Holy Spirit to lift the veil by the Word of God, we can see and enter the spiritual dimension of God's kingdom.

Again, Jesus explains how to do that: "Unless one is born again, he cannot *see* the kingdom of God," He told Nicodemus.[13] That's the first step; we have to be born again to even *see* the kingdom of God. But He doesn't stop there. "Unless one is born of water and the Spirit, he cannot *enter* into the kingdom of God."[14]

So, the Spirit of God reveals the kingdom of God. Don't expect to comprehend with only your intellect; spirit-realm reality must be received spiritually, too.

Try as we may, we cannot figure out the mystery of spirit-realm reality by reducing it to a physical/material plane. But, if we are willing to come to the Bible in poverty of spirit and use the first key—recognizing that God uses figurative language to convey spiritual/physical realities and truths—the Revelation begins to open to us its bounteous treasures.

Key #2:
The Revelation Is Timeless

Most of us have been conditioned to put everything in the Revelation into a timeline and think of events as either past or future. There are two common approaches to fixing the dates and times of the Apocalypse.

- First, literary and form critics in most mainstream churches say that all the events in the Revelation are in the past. The entire message, they say, was written to encourage the saints of the first and second centuries who were under severe persecution by the Roman government. They say that, once Rome ended its persecution, the book lost all prophetic value, and its only value now is in the principles it contains.

- Second, the dispensationalists in most evangelical churches say that the events of the Revelation occur in stages. They may differ widely on the timelines of various stages but usually agree that part of the book depicts literal, historical events of the past; part deals with literal events in the present; but most of it deals with literal, future events.

In my estimation, these are both doctrines of men, not of God. The timelines on which they are based call for wild speculation as to which literal, historical events apply to which scriptural symbols. Tragically, they rob the Revelation of its present spirit-dimension/physical-dimension reality and its intended prophetic impact.

Careful study shows that the Revelation depicts time as ongoing, not in stages. Jesus told John to write down the entire vision. "Write [all of it], therefore, what you have seen [past], what is now [present] and what will take place later [future]."[15] The entire vision is past, present, and future. It is the timeless unveiling of Jesus Christ as He is, not a timetable of the future.

Through the Revelation, God is equipping believers of all generations with an understanding of how the world of the spirit operates. It is knowledge, revealed by the Word of God, of how the kingdom of God operates and how we can enter and live in it in this present world. This revelation, the highest form of knowledge and wisdom, is just as pertinent today as it was in the past and will be in the future.

Understanding Prophecy

Prophecy declares what we cannot know by natural means. It can either predict or it can speak forth the mind and counsel of God—past, present, or future.

The very spirit and life of all prophecy is Jesus. In fact, it is safe to say that all prophecy is the ongoing disclosure of Jesus. To see this is to understand prophecy; not to see it is to miss its richest meaning.

"My purpose," Paul said, "is that they may be encouraged in heart and united in love, so that they may have the full riches of complete understanding, in order that they may know the mystery of God, namely, *Christ, in whom are hidden all the treasures of wisdom and knowledge."*[16]

The Culmination of Prophecy?

Throughout His ministry, Jesus often drew parallels between His works and the works of the prophets—Isaiah, Elijah, Elisha, Noah, and so on. Like many of the prophets before Him, the Jesus of the Gospels is depicted as a suffering servant who is despised, rejected, persecuted, and eventually killed.

The Revelation depicts Jesus as the present-tense fulfillment of all prophecy.

- It is Jesus who stands among the lampstands and speaks with absolute authority to the seven churches of Asia.[17]

- It is Jesus alone who is worthy to break the seals of the seven scrolls.[18]

- It is Jesus who rides the white horse and defeats the enemies of God.[19]

- It is Jesus who shares the wedding supper with the overcomers.[20]

Perhaps the most profound truth in the Revelation is that Jesus freely receives worship—attesting to His deity.[21] This is not a new pattern. In fact, at least ten times in the New Testament people worshiped Jesus, and not once did He restrain them.

What is new is the degree to which He is exalted as "King of kings and Lord of lords."[22] Literally, every knee bows before Him and Him only, just as the Apostle Paul predicted.[23] He is the conquering "Lion of the tribe of Judah,"[24] He is in the midst of the majestic throne,[25] and He is the source from which the river of life flows.[26]

Yet, He has not lost any of His attributes as Savior. At least thirty times in the Revelation John calls Jesus the Lamb, and he often refers to the marks of death that Jesus still bears. Make no mistake about it; this is the same Jesus who died on the cross.

So there is really only one mystery in the book of Revelation—Jesus Christ, Himself—and He is fully unveiled. The veil is removed so that we can see Him in all His spirit-realm reality, the ultimate fulfillment of all biblical prophecy.

Thus, the Jesus of the Apocalypse is the same Jesus, but He is different from the Jesus of the Gospels because He is glorified. He is spirit and life to those who receive Him.[27] This is a profound mystery which we understand only by revelation, not by the reasonings of men.

Ongoing Disclosure Through the Testimony of Jesus

All this is not to say that we should restrict Jesus' activities and impact to some past or future date or limit them to the spirit realm. His presence visibly impacts the physical/material world right now, and it always will.

The Apocalypse reveals that "the testimony of Jesus *is* the spirit of prophecy."[28] *Testimony* literally means evidence given. It comes from the Greek *martyria* from which we get our word *martyr*. Therefore, the testimony of Jesus is not a biography; it is the ongoing disclosure of who Jesus is, as evidenced by His works—what He has done and continues to do, acting both alone and through His servants.

So Jesus Christ is revealed to us in the Apocalypse—crucified, resurrected, glorified, ruling, and reigning in both the spirit realm and the material realm—then, now, and forever.

"Behold *I am coming* soon! [suddenly, or quickly]"[29] Jesus said. The words *am coming* convey a continuous activity, so much so that some versions translate it simply as "I come." *Suddenly* or *quickly* implies that He just shows up without warning.

The whole context clearly supports the idea that the comings of Jesus do not represent a single event, far removed from the writing of the Revelation or confined to that timeframe. Let's look at three such statements.

First, John is instructed to "Seal not the sayings of the prophecy of this book: for the time is at hand."[30] As we saw earlier, *at hand* means graspable, squeezable, within reach, close enough to take hold of—not something that will happen over nineteen hundred years later. The instruction to keep the book open reinforces this concept. (We'll have much more to say about this in a later chapter.)

Second, Jesus says, "I am the Alpha and the Omega, the First and the Last, the Beginning and the End."[31] The ancient Greeks used the idiom *alpha to omega* to express completeness. The Hebrews expressed completeness as *from aleph to tau,* or *the first to the last.* These parallel our expression *from A to Z,* meaning everything, or all that happens from the beginning to the ending of a process.

Just as we do not mean to drop all that represent the letters between A and Z, Jesus is not implying that He was active at the beginning and will show up and be active at the end, but is inactive in between. He is both complete (needing nothing) and eternally present. He always has been, He is, and He always will be involved with humanity.

Third, the invitation "Come!" and "take the free gift of the water of life"[32] follows immediately after Jesus' announcement of what happens at His comings. The water of life was *at hand*: it was present then, it is present now, and it will continue to be present in the future.

We Are Active Participants in the Ongoing Testimony of Jesus

Christians of all ages who read, hear, and keep or obey the Apocalypse are repeatedly invited—even instructed—to participate fully in the ongoing testimony of Jesus.

But be forewarned—the job description given in the Revelation calls for living sacrifices (pure and spotless), living martyrs, who will live as Jesus lived and do what Jesus did. And doing the works of Jesus here and now can get you into big trouble. Why? The testimony of Jesus does not mean just talking; it means doing the works of Jesus. The Jewish and Roman rulers persecuted the saints, not merely because they spoke out for Christ, but because they backed up their words by healing the sick, casting out demons, and raising the dead. For that kind of testimony, many Christians throughout the ages have paid with their lives. In the Revelation:

- The white-robed saints are slain for the testimony of Jesus.[33]

- The two witnesses are killed by the beast and their bodies left lying in the streets because of the testimony of Jesus.[34]

- The dragon is enraged at the woman and goes off to make war against the rest of her offspring—those who keep God's commandments and hold to the testimony of Jesus.[35]

In the Revelation, then, the testimony of Jesus is not merely *the church's* verbal proclamation of the Gospel of Christ, although it certainly includes that. It is *Christ's ongoing disclosure of Himself* to and through all individuals who demonstrate His character and power. Christ reveals Himself to the world through His direct actions and through His saints as we do the works of Jesus.

When we accept the Revelation as the ongoing unveiling of Jesus Christ instead of trying to use it to predict the future, we can begin to unravel the mysteries of this great book.

If we in the church were to stop all the End Time speculation and recognize that everything in the Revelation was at hand in the first century, is at hand for us today, and will be at hand for future generations, we could usher in a Scripture-based, Revelation revival that would make the Protestant Reformation look mild by comparison.

But Doesn't the Revelation Predict the End of the World?

One of the most frequent questions people ask after I teach the Revelation as a timeless message about an ongoing reality is this: "Doesn't the Bible say that God is someday going to destroy the world and set up a new kingdom on the earth?"

The simple answer to that question is No! I've searched from Genesis through Revelation and cannot find any conclusive statement that there must be some future, climactic event that destroys the world and draws human history to a close in order to fulfill any unfulfilled prophecy.

People often interpret some isolated Scripture to support their final-destruction doctrine preference.° They might, for instance, take a verse out of context, such as, "Heaven and earth will pass away, but my words will never pass away."[36] "See," they'll exclaim, "that's a clear prediction that the earth is going to pass away!" They ignore Jesus' main point: that His words are more eternal than the heavens and the earth, and that He has just given (in the preceding verse) His word that the generation He's speaking to will not pass away until all the things he's predicting have happened.

Certainly, the Revelation has a dynamic, future dimension in the sense that it proclaims Christ as Lord of the past, Lord of the present,

---

° In a later chapter, we will explore in depth the so-called End Times scriptures.

and Lord of the future.[37] Yes, He has always been, He is now, and He will always be God. But nothing in the Bible indicates that He will have to do anything else to either prove or assert His sovereignty.

If we could just get our eyes and hearts off of what God may *someday do,* and grasp fully what He is doing and wants us to do *today,* we could live in the full reality of His kingdom right now.

How do we know all this? It's not some doctrine I have dreamed up, which leads us to the third key to unraveling the mysteries of the Revelation.

Key #3:
Let the Bible Interpret Itself

English poet Alexander Pope said, "A little learning is a dangerous thing." If that is true, then unbridled personal revelation is catastrophic. I cringe every time I hear someone say, "The Lord told me. . . ." People who cut loose from the Scriptures and live by their own visions and insights tend to see a demon behind every tree or to bend every truth to their own whims.

The foundation of all revealed knowledge is the Word of God, the Bible. True prophetic revelation is always anchored solidly in Scripture. In fact, most individual revelations come as spiritual insights into specific Scriptures. As we study the Bible in poverty of spirit, the Holy Spirit, the spirit of prophecy, reveals to us the spirit-realm/physical-realm realities it contains.

Here are some examples from the Revelation of how the Holy Spirit uses the Bible to interpret itself.

The Bible Interprets Itself Through Direct Statements

Again and again, Revelation states the "at hand" theme in simple terms—so simple, in fact, that people who won't take now for an answer read their own meanings into those statements.

Consider these statements from the first chapter:

- ". . . what must soon [not centuries from now] take place."[38]

- ". . . the time is at hand [not nineteen hundred years away]."[39]

- "Grace and peace to you from him who is, and who was, and who is to come . . . the [present] ruler of the kings of the earth."[40]

- "Look, He is coming [not just will come someday] with the clouds, . . ."[41]

These Scriptures overwhelmingly emphasize participating in the present reality of the kingdom of God.

Many of the strange symbols of the Revelation are interpreted by direct statements made in context. Those that are not have direct connections to symbols and statements elsewhere in the Bible.

Consider, for instance, these simple explanations:

- "The seven stars are the angels [literally, messengers] of the seven churches, and the seven lampstands are the seven churches."[42]

- "Each one [of the four living creatures] had a harp and they were holding golden bowls of incense, which are the prayers of the saints."[43]

- "The great dragon was hurled down—that ancient serpent called the devil, or Satan, who leads the whole world astray. He was hurled to earth, and his angels with him."[44]

As you can see, each of these symbols introduced in the Revelation is explained in context. If a symbol is not explained in its context, you can be sure it refers to something that is explained elsewhere in Scripture.

The Bible Follows Consistent Patterns

Everything in God's Word has a pattern, including prophecy. Jesus compared His comings, for example, to the comings of Elijah. Just as Elijah comes, Jesus comes. "And he [John the Baptist] will go on before the Lord, in the spirit and power of Elijah."[45]

After Jesus' transfiguration, one of His disciples asked, "Why then do the teachers of the law say that Elijah must come first?" And Jesus answered, "To be sure, Elijah comes [ongoing]. . . . Elijah has already come and they did not recognize him. . . . In the same way the Son of Man is going to suffer at their hands."[46]

"All the Prophets and the Law prophesied until John. And if you are willing to accept it, he is the Elijah who was to come."[47] He was the spirit of Elijah, not the man Elijah.

Thus, the comings of Jesus, just like the comings of Elijah, follow a definite pattern. As you read the Revelation, look for recurring patterns that are woven throughout God's Word.

Scriptures Confirm Each Other

No Scripture stands alone or contradicts any other Scripture. Thus, any interpretation of Scripture must be confirmed by other Scriptures. For instance, we've said that one way Jesus' ongoing testimony is manifested in all generations is by the saints who do "the works of Jesus." Is this a correct interpretation? Let's see if it is confirmed by other Scriptures.

First, it is clear from many accounts in the Gospels and Acts that Christians of the New Testament period did the works of Jesus.[48]

Second, nothing in Scripture declares that the works of Jesus were only for the so-called Apostolic Age.

Third, the New Testament constantly affirms that people of every generation are expected to do the works of Jesus.[49]

Therefore, we can conclude, since it is consistent with and confirmed by other Scriptures, that it is a valid interpretation.

Please don't misunderstand what I am about to say. I believe that the Bible is the inspired, inerrant Word of God. The problem is that the Bible was written in ancient languages. Therefore, it has to be translated into our language before it can have meaning to us for our daily lives. As a result, one of the burning controversies of our day rages around the question of whether the Bible should be taken *literally* or *figuratively*. I believe that God is much more concerned that it be taken *seriously*—that we take it to heart.

We don't need a dictionary or an encyclopedia or tomorrow's newspaper to interpret Bible prophecy. The Bible interprets itself. If we let the Bible interpret itself and study it diligently enough to know clearly what it says, we don't have to rely on other people to unlock the mysteries of the Revelation for us—we can unravel them ourselves.

Key #4:
Judge Any Interpretation
By the Fruit It Produces

Jesus warned that many false prophets would try to deceive the masses. He cautioned, "By their fruit you will recognize them."[50]

Earlier in the book, we spoke of how End Times doctrines create the negative fruits of conflict, anxiety, and confusion by arguing over precisely what may take place in the material world and when various events might happen. Receiving the full Revelation message as "at hand," however, produces the good fruits that come from entering and living daily in the kingdom of God.

Let's examine some of these fruits in the lives of individual believers.

Good Fruit: Worshiping God

When we receive the pertinent reality of the Revelation message, we can see Jesus in all His present glory and majesty. Seeing Him as *He is* creates a sense of awe and reverence that produces authentic and spontaneous worship. It removes any need to work up some emotional response or to go through some ritual. Like Saul on the Damascus road, we can only fall before His face in total surrender of our wills and respond to Him in love and adoration.[51]

The widespread emphasis on Jesus as friend in churches of our day leads many people to think of Him as a pal or a buddy. But one glimpse of the unveiled Jesus with a face beaming like the sun, eyes like blazing fire, and feet glowing like white hot brass,[52] and it quickly becomes obvious that this is no mere human friend.

The Apostle John knew the earthly Jesus. He shared His struggles, walked the dusty roads of Galilee with Him, leaned against His breast during the Last Supper, and saw Him crucified. He knew the Jesus of the Gospels intimately as friend, teacher, savior, and even resurrected Lord. Yet, when he came face to face with the unveiled Jesus in the Revelation, he was overwhelmed. "When I saw him," John exclaimed, "I fell at his feet as though dead."[53]

Once we have truly encountered Christ as He is today, no one will ever again have to tell us that we ought to worship God. We will worship Him as we partake of His reality.

Good Fruit: Godly Character

The unveiling of Jesus doesn't stop with feelings of awe and reverence. When we heed, keep, and obey the message of the Apocalypse, we find it profoundly impacting our daily lives. We develop godly character, not so much by our efforts but by our exposure to Christ.

As we enter into and live daily in a marriage relationship with Him, we begin to share His values, His traits, and His ways. I don't mean in any way to imply that we become little gods, as some teach today. The idea of our taking on the divinity of God came from Satan,[54] not from any word of the Lord in Scripture. Certainly, we are enjoined to rule and reign with Him: but there is never any doubt as to who is sovereign.

Instead we take on His character. John wrote in one of his letters, "We know that when he appears, we shall be like him, for we shall see him as he is."[55] This seeing Him and living in intimate, daily fellowship with Him has a way of removing all thoughts of being like anybody else but Him.

The End Times doctrines, which shove the reality of His appearing out into the future, tend to make the development of godly character a chore, a product of human effort. As we'll see in the next chapter, the Revelation makes it clear that His appearings (plural) are glorious present-tense realities that have a profound impact on those who receive them. They produce the fruit of godly character.

Good Fruit: Expansion of God's Kingdom

As we worship God and develop His character, we begin to do the works of Jesus. We actually become a part of the ongoing testimony of Jesus.

The first century apostles proved to the world that the Jesus they preached was alive, because they lived as He lived and did the same works that Jesus had done. This combination of proclaiming the gospel of Christ, living the life of Christ, and demonstrating the power of Christ led to the expansion of Christ's kingdom.[56] In the same way, when we grasp the present reality of the Revelation message today, we produce the good fruit of expanding His kingdom.

Worshiping God, developing godly character, and expanding His kingdom are the kinds of fruits God sought to produce by giving us the Revelation, not the fruits of anxiety and dissension over the future.

To Sum It All Up

Our difficulty in unraveling the mystery of the Apocalypse is not in the book's strange symbols and language. Rather, our problem is that most of us have been conditioned to think of the Revelation as a book about the future—not as the unveiling of Jesus Christ as a present, ongoing reality.

God does have something vital to say to us through the Revelation, but we can never grasp or understand it through a physical/material mindset. We must receive it as revealed knowledge through God's Word made alive to us by the spirit of prophecy, which is the ongoing testimony of Jesus. And that's where the promised blessings and power come from.

Remember and use these four keys to unlock the mysteries of this vital book:

1. The Revelation uses figurative language and symbols to reveal spiritual/physical realities.

2. In the Revelation, time is depicted as ongoing, timeless, not in stages.

3. Let the Bible interpret itself.

4. Judge any interpretation of Scripture by the fruit it produces.

Perhaps people have the most trouble grasping the fact that Jesus' "comings" are here and now. In our next chapter, let's look at what the Bible has to say about the so-called Second Coming.

5

WHY YOU DON'T HAVE TO WAIT AROUND FOR THE SECOND COMING

N ewspapers have a special name for their largest and boldest headline type—the type used only for the biggest stories they will ever be called upon to report. They call it *second-coming type.*

No idea has ever gripped the human imagination more firmly than the doctrine of a Second Coming of Jesus. Nor has any idea ever created more needless anxiety or spiritual poverty among Christians.

But try this headline as one worthy of the biggest and boldest second-coming type: *"Second Coming Exposed!"* In this chapter, that's exactly what we'll see. We'll discover from God's Word that the so-called Second Coming is a misnomer, a subtraction from the book of prophecy,[1] and a highly misleading doctrine. Some, I'm sure, will find this statement to be the most controversial of the book. Therefore, I feel compelled before continuing with this chapter to clarify an important point and to affirm to you my belief in a future, glorious coming of the Lord Jesus Christ. It will be a coming unlike any other. In the words of the Nicene Creed, "I believe . . . He shall come again with glory to judge both the living and the dead; Whose kingdom shall have no end."

However, in this chapter, I will deal more with the presence of Jesus actively working and coming in our midst in the here and *now!* I want to move the reader who might be waiting only for the Second Coming to see, through God's Word, the full, glorious, and very present reality of Jesus' comings in everyday life. Hopefully, this will clear up any misconception and open the way for us, as Christians, to unite in doing the works of Jesus. Let us stop limiting His comings to merely a past event or a future hope!

Of course, it's not what John Noē (or any other human) says about the coming of Jesus that counts, but what the Word of God says about it. So let me urge you to get out your own Bible and test everything you read in this chapter—and everywhere else.

Second Coming Does Not Fit The Terminology of the Scriptures

Do you know what the Bible actually says about the Second Coming? Nothing! Nowhere does the Bible use the term *Second Coming*. The idea that Jesus is off somewhere waiting to come back at some future time, the idea of limiting the comings of Jesus to only two, is man's, not God's. And, as we shall see, it is neither the teaching nor the pattern of the Scriptures.

God's Word, both Old and New Testaments, does clearly teach that there are *many comings* of Jesus, and it promises *innumerably more comings*. Jesus' comings were at hand for first century believers; they have been at hand for believers ever since; they are at hand for believers today; and they will continue to be at hand in the future.

Does all this imply that there may be no final coming? No. It means simply that between now and that Jesus is coming and shall come many times.

I recently asked a seminary professor of eschatology to show me a Scripture to support the idea of a single, future Second Coming. Together, we examined all the classic Second Coming Scriptures, one by one. Each of them was pertinent and fulfillable for first century believers and nowhere limited to a single future event. "I agree . . . I agree . . . I agree," he said on each of them. "But," he lectured me, "I still believe Jesus has left this world, hasn't come back yet, and there will only be one coming—the final Second Coming."

With all due respect to this precious man of God, such a response is an emotional reaction which grows out of a lifetime of doctrinal conditioning—not out of the Word of God.

"Do you know what the Bible actually says about the Second Coming? Nothing! Nowhere does the Bible use the term *Second Coming.* The idea that Jesus is off somewhere waiting to come back at some future time, the idea of limiting the comings of Jesus to only two, is man's, not God's."

What's at Risk Here?

What's involved here is much more than semantics or a doctrinal dispute over some insignificant issue, like the ancient squabble over how many angels can dance on the point of a pin.

The comings of Jesus represent a crucial and glorious spirit-realm/physical-realm reality for every generation. The comings (plural) of Jesus are countless. They take many forms, producing both exciting and life-changing results in the individuals who receive them; and they are essential to the expansion of God's kingdom in this age.

Oh, the conspirators would love to keep people busy looking for just a single Second Coming, somewhere up in the sky, off in the future. Why? Because it distracts them from tapping into the spiritual dynamite[2] of the kingdom of God, from worshiping God in all His unveiled reality, and from doing the works of Jesus in the full power of His Spirit, today.

It's Time to Flip the Switch

What saddens and troubles me deeply is that Jesus is not off somewhere waiting to come back. He is coming right now, and millions of

Christians don't even know it. He is in the comings business; He is among the churches; He is active and involved[3]—but most churches don't recognize His comings. What a tragedy!

Too many people remind me of a modern parable about a man who bought a new personal computer in the *hope* that it would open up a whole new career for him. Wanting to get the full benefit, he started attending seminars and reading every book he could find on computers, disk operating systems, software, and programming. After many fruitless, frustrating hours sitting before a blank screen and wondering why nothing was happening, he picked up the owner's manual and began to read. There, on page one, he found his problem. The instructions said, "First, make sure your computer is plugged into a power source, then turn on the switch."

My friend, it's time for us to quit chasing after the doctrines of men and to start reading God's owner's manual, the Bible! We need to make sure we are plugged into the ultimate power source, Jesus, and then turn on the switch, our own spirit.

We don't have to live on a *hope* that Jesus is going to come back someday, snatch us out of this troubled world, and set us free from the shackles of our flesh. This is Gnosticism, not Christianity. Hope is for those who have not yet received something they desire. We can live in the *reality* that Christ has already come, that He is coming—right now—and that He will continue to come.[4] But to live in the fullness of that reality, we have to break the shackles of our physical/material mindset, which demands only a physical/material Second Coming, and receive His comings as both spirit-realm and physical-realm reality—here and now.

Is that a second-rate option? No! A thousand times, no! The spirit realm is as real as this book you now hold in your hands. It may even be more real, because it is eternal.

We can catch a glimpse of just how real the spirit realm is by studying Jesus' post-resurrection appearances.[5] He walked through closed doors as if they were not there. But, lest anyone think Him a ghost, He eats bread and fish. The implication is obvious—He is more real than the door or the bread or the fish.

Now how do we know that the comings of Jesus are a present-day, spirit-realm reality—not just some major news event waiting to happen someday? Because God's Word tells us so.

"The Bible contains many references to many different comings of Jesus, but none to a single Second Coming."

Second Coming Does Not Fit the Teachings of Jesus

The Bible contains many references to many different comings of Jesus, but none to a single Second Coming.

It's amazing, when you stop to think about it. Many people who focus on a single, future Second Coming, support their doctrine by saying you have to take the Bible literally. Yet, if you take it literally, it still does not predict a single, future Second Coming. (After all, the Bible never uses this terminology.)

The truth is that very few, if any, people take the Bible literally across the board. How many people do you know, for instance, who read the Old Testament in Hebrew and the New Testament in Greek? Most people read translations; and, since it is impossible to translate literally from the ancient languages, any translation *is*, to some extent, an interpretation.

Or, how many people do you know who are walking around half-blind because they've gouged out their right eye,[6] or one-handed because they've cut off their right hand?[7]

Why is it that so many people can readily accept as figurative such metaphors as the gouging out of eyes and the cutting off of hands but insist on taking literally all Jesus' references about His comings? Why do we readily accept such terms as *born again* or *the bread of life* or *living water* as symbols, yet refuse to accept *come again* or *wedding banquet* or *comes in glory* as symbols illustrating spirit-realm/physical-realm realities?

Why did Jesus use physical/material symbols to convey spirit-realm/physical-realm realities? Because we humans have no frame of reference to enable us to understand the realities of the spirit realm. We can only relate what we don't know to what we do know.

The Classic Second Coming Scriptures

With those thoughts in mind, let's look at a few of the most common Scriptures people traditionally use to support a single Second Coming doctrine.

John 14:18–21. Verses 18–19: "I will not leave you as orphans; I will come to you." (Come to whom? The disciples with whom He's talking at the Last Supper.) "Before long, the world will not see me anymore, but you will see me. Because I live, you also will live."

Verse 20: "On that day [the day I come to you] you will realize that I am in my Father, and you are in me, and I am in you [in spirit]."

Verse 21: "Whoever has my commands and obeys them, he is the one who loves me. He who loves me will be loved by my Father, and I too will love him and *show [or manifest] myself to him*" (emphasis added).

This promise for a spiritual/physical coming is addressed to individuals. And Jesus fulfilled that promise within a few days; He came to those very same people.[8]

Acts 1:3–11. Verse 3: "After His suffering, he showed himself to these men and gave many convincing proofs that he was alive. He appeared to them over a period of forty days and *spoke about the kingdom of God* " (emphasis added).

Verse 6: "So when they met together, they asked him, 'Lord, are you at this time going to restore the kingdom of Israel?'" They were thinking about a physical/material kingdom. And Jesus did not answer their question directly.

Verse 7: "He said to them: 'It is not for you to know the times [plural] or the dates [or seasons] the Father has set by his own authority'" (emphasis added). Why does Jesus use the plural forms of *times* and *dates?* Because there are many times and dates. This is significant because it expresses the ongoing, countless fulfillment of this prophecy.

Verse 9: "After he had said this, he was taken up before their very eyes, and a cloud hid him from their sight." I believe that was the same cloud that was in the temple, that the Jews in the wilderness followed by day, and in which Moses and Elijah appeared in the

Transfiguration. It is a glory cloud, a cloud that is filled with perfected saints and angels.

Verse 11: "'Men of Galilee,' they said, 'why do you stand here looking into the sky? This same Jesus, who has been taken from you into heaven, will come back in the same way you have seen him go into heaven.'" The Greek word for *will come* actually means *comes or goes*. The word we translate *way* refers to *means* or *manner*, not a place or a form. Jesus comes and goes in and out of the spirit realm, manifesting Himself in the physical realm. That's the means and manner of His comings. The place and form vary. Remember, biblical Greek is a much more elaborate language than modern English. It may take six or seven words in English to convey the many meanings of one word in ancient Greek. It's also important to note that Jesus comes in the clouds.[9] But, as we will explain in our next chapter, these are not physical clouds. He comes in a spirit-realm cloud.

Matthew 24. Verse 3: Jesus had just predicted the destruction of the temple: "There will not be left here one stone upon another, that will not be thrown down" (24:2, RSV). "'Tell us,' they [His disciples] said, 'when will this happen, and what will be the sign of your coming and of the end of the age?'" Note that Jesus was talking about the physical destruction of the temple, but the disciples were asking about the end of the age and the signs of His coming.

In the verses that follow, Jesus talks about things like the sun being darkened, the moon not giving its light, and the stars falling from the sky. But now He is using figurative language to describe the ongoing fallen state of the world.

Verse 33: "'Even so when you see all these things, you know that it [or He] is near, right at the door'" (not nineteen hundred plus years away).

Verse 34: "'I tell you the truth, *this generation* will certainly not pass away until all of these things happen'" (emphasis added). Jesus was not talking about some future generation, because the pronoun *this* has no antecedent. None of the preceding verses ever mentioned a future generation. Jesus is speaking in the first person to *His* generation. Therefore, *this generation* simply refers to the people of that time. How the conspirators have distorted these words! Jesus frequently spoke of His contemporaries as *this generation*.[10]

The temple was destroyed in A.D. 70, and the very people with whom Jesus was talking went through great tribulation (literally, *trouble*). All these things happened, and they continue to happen today.

Let's just take Jesus at His word and not try to push all these things off on some distant, future generation, as the conspirators do, since they cannot explain these happenings then and there in physical/material terms.

Space will not permit us to cover all the so-called Second Coming Scriptures. We will look at others in later chapters (especially those that have to do with a rapture). But I hope by now you are beginning to see that the only way you can get a single Second Coming out of such Scriptures is to think of their symbols in purely physical/material terms. If you search the comings Scriptures for what they really say, you will readily see that limiting the comings of Jesus to a single, future Second Coming does not fit the teachings of Jesus—nor any other Scriptures, for that matter.

Second Coming Does Not Fit
The Pattern of the Scriptures

Here's a real shocker of a headline that certainly deserves the use of second-coming type: "Second Coming Reported in Ancient Religious Courtroom!"

Far-fetched? Think about it! If you call the babe in the manger the first coming of Jesus, that means the Second Coming is already over. It happened when Jesus appeared to Stephen during his trial before the Jewish Sanhedrin.[11] Or it happened when He appeared to Saul on the road to Damascus,[12] or to John in the Revelation.[13]

The comings (appearings) of Jesus run like a thread through both the Old and New Testaments. He usually comes to individuals; He comes suddenly, unexpectedly, and usually unannounced; He comes to bring aid, to judge, to assign a task, or to proclaim a message. Often, His appearings are recognized only by the person for whom they are intended. His appearings produce a profound, life-altering impact upon those who receive them, and in turn upon people and nations who are then touched in ministry.

"If you search the comings Scriptures for what they really say, you will readily see that limiting the comings of Jesus to a single, future Second Coming does not fit the teachings of Jesus—nor any other Scriptures, for that matter."

Consider, for example, a few of the comings of Jesus referred to in the Old Testament:

- Exodus 3:2–14: He appeared to Moses in the burning bush. In verse 6, He identified Himself as the God of Abraham, Isaac, and Jacob. Jesus alluded to this in John 8:58 when He said, "Before Abraham was, I AM." The eternal "I AM" of Exodus 3:14 is the same identification He gave for Himself in Revelation 1:8, when He described Himself as "the Alpha and the Omega . . . who is, and who was, and who is to come, the Almighty."

- Exodus 17:1–7: Jesus was the rock which Moses struck, and from which the life-giving water flowed. How do we know this? Paul told us in 1 Corinthians 10:4, ". . . that rock *was* Christ." Notice Paul didn't say the rock represented or symbolized Christ, but *was* Christ.

- Daniel 3:24–27: Jesus appeared in the fiery furnace with the three young Hebrews. "Did not we cast three men bound into the midst of the fire?" King Nebuchadnezzar asked (v. 24, KJV). "Lo, I see four men loose, walking in the midst of the fire . . . and the form of the fourth is like the Son of God" (v. 25, KJV). I believe that fourth man represents another coming of Jesus.

Again, space will not permit us to explore in detail all the comings of Jesus in the Old Testament, but there were many more. I encourage you to study all the Old Testament appearances (theophanies) of Jesus.

New Testament Patterns of Jesus' Comings

The Apostle Paul recapped many post-Resurrection, pre-Ascension comings of Jesus in his first letter to the Corinthians.

- First Corinthians 15:5–8: "and that He [Christ] appeared to Peter, and then to the Twelve. After that, He appeared to more than five hundred of the brothers at the same time, most of whom are still living, though some have fallen asleep. Then he appeared to James, then to all the apostles, and last of all He appeared to me also, as to one abnormally born."

That's a lot of comings. Some were private, but some were public.

There are also many post-Ascension comings of Jesus in the Scriptures. First, let's examine a few that we can definitely identify:

- Acts 7:55: "But Stephen, full of the Holy Spirit, looked up to heaven and saw the glory of God, and Jesus standing at the right hand of God."

That's a coming of Jesus. It's one of the appearings Jesus taught about. It fits the pattern.

- Acts 9:4–5: "He [Saul] fell to the ground and heard a voice say to him, 'Saul, Saul, why do you persecute me?' 'Who are you, Lord?' Saul asked. '*I am Jesus,* whom you are persecuting'" (emphasis added).

That's another coming of Jesus.

- Acts 10:13–15: "Then a voice told him, 'Get up, Peter. Kill and eat.' 'Surely not, *Lord!*' Peter replied. 'I have never eaten anything impure or unclean.' The voice spoke to him a second time, 'Do not call anything impure that God has made clean'" (emphasis added).

Again, that's a coming of Jesus.

- Acts 22:17–18: "When I [Paul] returned to Jerusalem and was praying at the temple, I fell into a trance and saw the Lord speaking. 'Quick!' he said to me. 'Leave Jerusalem immediately, because they will not accept your testimony about me.'"

If your doctrine demands it, you can call that a vision. I'm comfortable calling it a *coming* of Jesus.

- Acts 23:11: "The following night *the Lord* stood near Paul and said, 'Take courage! As you have testified about me in Jerusalem, so you must also testify in Rome'" (emphasis added).

Yet another coming.

- Revelation 1:17: "When I saw him, I fell at his feet as though dead. Then he placed his right hand on me and said: 'Do not be afraid. I am the First and the Last.'"

Jesus appeared to John.

When you consider symbolic names that refer to Jesus, you will find other New Testament appearings: to Philip (Acts 8:26), to Cornelius (Acts 10:1–6), and again to Peter (Acts 12:7).

As you can see, the Scriptures promise and record many comings. Nowhere do they limit Jesus to a single Second Coming event.

So Why Does It Matter, Anyway?

"Why does it really matter if you're right?" a student in one of my Bible studies once asked me.

First, it matters because the conspirators use a single Second Coming to hold people in bondage to an earthly Jesus. The message of the Revelation is that, in the unveiled Christ, you are free from the limitation of just knowing *about* Him in the past or somewhere out in the future. We can know and fully experience Him now, in the present.

"The conspirators use a single Second Coming to hold people in bondage to an earthly Jesus."

Second, it matters because much of the church in general doesn't know what is going on in the spirit realm. Jesus comes, and most of His church doesn't even know it. He comes in many countless ways—in judgment, in comfort, in revelation—but He comes.

Third, it matters because the world of the spirit has authority over the world of the flesh. Most Christians are so bound up by religious, worldly teachings that the idea of operating in the spirit realm is foreign to them.

We've got to learn how to operate in the spirit realm before we can bring the world the testimony of Jesus by doing His works. It is one thing to preach against the new age movement for operating in the realm of the supernatural. It is quite another to bring the supernatural into the church, where it belongs.

Jesus is in the spirit realm in a resurrected body that's just as real as human flesh—but it's also different. We can't think of Him merely as earthly flesh; we have to think of Him in all His spirit-realm reality. We will never be able to operate in the power of God's Spirit until we start thinking and believing spiritually.

The Comings of Jesus Are a Present Reality

The comings of Jesus are an ongoing reality. He comes to individuals. "Whoever has my commands and obeys them," Jesus said, "he is the one who loves me . . . and I too will love him and *show myself to him.*"[14]

All Bible prophecy is and can be fulfilled in each individual. "Christ was sacrificed once to take away the sins of many people; and he will appear a second time, not to bear sin, but to bring salvation to those who are waiting for him."[15] The context clearly shows that this is a spiritual coming for those who receive Him as Savior.

Today, Jesus appears physically to many people. A number of people in recent history, many of whom are alive today, have publicly testified to having direct encounters with Jesus. Some of these comings have been visual, some audible, some bodily. Most are private, but some are public. All of them, however, are personal and real.

Jesus said the kingdom of God is both in you and among you.[16] The word *Apocalypse* itself is a transliteration of the Greek word *apokalypsis*, which not only means an unveiling or an uncovering but also the manifestation, the coming, the appearing of Jesus Christ—*to you!* The book of Revelation is written to *individuals.* That's why Jesus said after each of the messages to the seven churches, "Let *him* who has ears hear."[17] Throughout, the Revelation admonishes and blesses—not a group getting ready to go on a giant space trip—but individuals living in this world, then and now. The book of Revelation itself was designed to let Christ appear to you as He appeared to John. Yet most people see only beasts, plagues, earthquakes, locusts, and torment.

His Comings Are Continuous

"Now the dwelling of God is with men, and he will live with them," says the Revelation.[18] When? "Seal not the sayings of the prophecy of this book: for the time is at hand," answers the messenger.[19]

Traditional teaching says that at hand and near could be thousands of years down the road. Many argue that God is not bound by time, as humans are, and that with Him a thousand years are as a day. Yet the opening verse of the book clearly says that it was not written *to God*; it was written *to man*. It's purpose is to show us, His servants, what is *at hand*—then and now.[20]

Do you think it possible that first-century Christians were mistaken in their firm expectation that the coming of the Lord was at hand (imminent) during their lifetime? Has history proven them wrong? Were they misled or deluded? One can't help but wonder—if they were wrong on this important fact of the faith, were they perhaps wrong on other facts, too?

On the contrary, the book contains promises of His comings to the individual and instructions for its readers to carry out continuously— not because of some future event, but because of the countless, ongoing comings of Jesus.

He Comes in a Variety of Ways

Over the centuries, many artists have attempted to depict Jesus as He appeared in the Gospels. But why don't we often see a picture of Jesus as He appears in the Revelation? Because the conspirators have conditioned us to picture only an earthly Jesus.

It may come as a shock to some people, but the Jesus who comes is totally beyond human control. He comes when, where, and how He pleases.[21] In the Revelation, He shows up in many different ways: as an awesome, human-like being with a sword coming out of His mouth; as a lamb with scars on it; as a conquering warrior on a white horse; as an all-pervasive light.

There is nothing we can do in our own strength to bring about His comings. We can't meditate Him down from heaven or visualize His comings into reality. He chooses when and how to manifest Himself to us.

The point of this chapter is not so much *how* He comes but *that* He comes mostly to individuals—if we will only break the shackles of traditional eschatological, or End Times, doctrines and receive Him as He chooses to come. Remember, the idea that Jesus is off somewhere waiting to come back at some future time or limiting the comings of Jesus to only two is not the teaching, the pattern, or the terminology of the Bible. As the first line of the classic church hymn, "The Battle Hymn of The Republic" says: "Mine eyes have seen the glory of the coming of the Lord." Have yours?

Come, Lord Jesus, *now*!

A Simple, but Profound, Formula

If you are like most of the people I meet, it's not easy to shake off the religious conditioning of a lifetime. "This is really great!" many people respond. "It certainly makes the Word of God come alive, *but . . .*"

How can you break away from all the traditions you've been taught about the so-called End Times and begin to discover the present realities of God's Word? The Bible gives us a very simple but profound formula:

> My son, if you accept my words
> and store up my
> commands within you,
> turning your ear to wisdom
> and applying your heart to
> understanding,
> and if you call out for insight
> and cry aloud for understanding,
> and if you look for it as for silver
> and search for it as for hidden treasure,
> then you will understand the

fear of the LORD
and find the knowledge of God.
For the LORD gives wisdom,
and from his mouth come
knowledge and understanding.[22]

"The purpose of Jesus' countless comings is not to get you out of this world, but to empower you, with a prophetic foundation, to operate in spirit-realm authority."

Most people have little or no direct knowledge of the Bible—especially of biblical prophecy. All they know is what other humans have taught them. Thus, they are like the people to whom Isaiah was sent: "ever hearing, but never understanding . . . ever seeing but never perceiving."[23] Here are four ways to discover the reality of Jesus' comings:

1. If you're not already doing it, begin to study your own Bible diligently. Look up the so-called Second Coming Scriptures and study them carefully. Study the whole context of each verse. Use a good concordance to look up references and see how they relate to all other Scriptures.

2. Recognize that the purpose of Jesus' countless comings is not to get you out of this world, but to empower you, with a prophetic foundation, to operate in spirit-realm authority. The way of escape from sin and death and from the evil forces of this world is within the kingdom of God, not in outer space.

3. Recognize that, in biblical prophecy, we are talking about spiritual/physical realities, just as we are with terms like *the bread of life* or *living water* or *salt and light*. We're talking about getting beyond Jesus' earthly ministry into the unbridled reality of His Spirit.

4. And finally, open your spirit and heart to His comings in your own life. One of the most pathetic pictures in the Revelation is of Jesus standing outside the doors of the hearts of churches and individuals—trying to get in.

Countless people are sitting around in churches, in prophecy conferences, and in front of their televisions frantically asking, "When is Jesus coming back?"

"Here I am!" Jesus calls out. "I stand at the door and knock. If anyone hears my voice and opens the door, I will come in and eat with him, and he with me."[24] This is a promised, personal, individual, actual coming of Jesus for all believers who will hear and open their heart's door.[25]

"Yes, I read that," the end-timers say impatiently. "But don't bother me. . . . I've just read about another sign in the Middle East. . . . I'm trying to find out—When is Jesus coming back again?"

Don't be like that! Stand up in your spirit, and go answer the door! Jesus will come in and eat with you—and He'll bring the feast. You have His word on it! Say, like John after he had seen Jesus in all His unveiled glory, "Amen. Come, Lord Jesus."[26]

Oh! One more thing: you don't have to wait around to be raptured, either. Let's talk about that in the next chapter.

6

HOW YOU CAN BE RAPTURED RIGHT NOW

C aught up . . . in the clouds to meet the Lord in the air."[1] What
does it mean?

To millions, it means Rapture mania—a near-frantic preoccupation with the idea of Christians being physically whisked away from
planet Earth, en masse, on a gigantic flight through outer space.

You can read it on the bumper stickers:

- "In case of Rapture, this car will be unmanned!"

- "Rapture: The only way to fly!"

- "He's coming to take me away! Ha! Ha!"

You can see it in print:

- Books: *88 Reasons Why the Rapture Will Be in 1988*

- Articles: "We don't want to delay the Rapture—We need your fi-
nancial support, NOW!"

- Tracts: "We're in the RAPTURE Generation!"

You can see and hear it broadcast:

- On Television: "Folks, this could be our last broadcast! The Rapture is *that* close!"

- On Radio: "This program is taped, so I may already be in heaven by the time you hear it! We're talking Rapture, people! We're talking any day . . . any minute! Are you *reeaaddyy?*"

You can hear it in the gospel songs:

- "I want to hear that trumpet sound,
  I want to feel my feet leave the ground!"

- "Some glad morning, when this life is o'er,
  I'll fly away!"

- "Oh, I'm gonna' take a trip,
  In the old gospel ship!"

And, it's not just a small lunatic fringe hyping the idea of a Rapture. You'll hear sermons and teachings about it in some of the biggest churches in the world. It's being taught in many major seminaries, and it appears in the literature of some of the largest denominations.

A Touchy Subject

In fact, the idea of a one-time, physical, corporate Rapture is one of the touchiest doctrines to question. Oh, it's all right to argue about *when* it will occur. If you're a post-tribber, you might get shouted down by an audience of pre-tribbers, or vice versa. But they won't call you a heretic—they'll just say you're ignorant about the Bible.

Yet millions of people are questioning all the Rapture mania, and masses are simply confused. Their heads say it must be true, because they've been conditioned all their lives to believe it. Their emotions say there's got to be some way to get out of this world without dying. But deep within them there's a nagging feeling that something doesn't quite fit—especially in light of all the recent failures to predict when it will happen.

So, not knowing exactly what to make of it all, some just refuse to think about it. They are sincere, honest people who plod along, day after day, doing the best they can and hoping everything will come out all right in the end. Others continue to hope for the Rapture. But, as Proverbs says, "Hope deferred makes the heart sick."[2]

What Did God Mean by It?

Certainly God could speak a few specks of dust off this earthly mass, which He originally spoke into existence, at any time He wished. But He hasn't. And, of course, removing a group of believers through a Rapture is a possibility. But this has not happened throughout church history nor

---

"Yet millions of people are questioning all the Rapture mania, and masses are simply confused. Their heads say it must be true, because they've been conditioned all their lives to believe it. Their emotions say there's got to be some way to get out of this world without dying."

---

today. So *what else* might God have had in mind when He inspired Paul to write in 1 Thessalonians the words "caught up in the clouds to meet the Lord in the air" (4:17) nearly nineteen centuries ago?

I believe He had something in mind far more pertinent and glorious than snatching His church out of the world before He wreaked havoc upon the earth. After all, where's the victory in a great escape?

I believe that the Jesus of the Gospels demonstrated that He was far more than a political messiah. His empathy with the masses, His aloofness from governmental structures, and His willingness to die indicated that He wanted to accomplish something far superior to a global political revolution.

No, I believe that God has something far more wonderful and exciting in mind. Think about the Bible as a whole, not just as a few isolated statements.

Scripture emphasizes a triumphant God who enables His people to triumph as well. God's people do not run away or get rescued. Exodus, for example, tells much more than the story of Moses rescuing

God's people from bondage in Egypt. Rather, it emphasizes God's efforts to purify His people and create godly character within them while leading them to the Promised Land, which they would win by His power. Jesus conquered death by dying, not by climbing down from the cross or by calling angels to rescue Him. He conquered sin by facing temptation head on and refusing to give in, and by taking sin's awful guilt upon His own shoulders.

That's the spirit of the Scriptures—facing up to sin, death, and evil in this world—and conquering them.

I'm not trying to take away anybody's blessed hope of getting out of here alive or destroy anybody's dream of a perfect world system. But you'll discover in this chapter that you can enter Christ's realm right now—without His having to come back and take you away. There is a realm, an intimacy, to which God invites His saints. Through this inner reality, we can share in His death, His resurrection, and His triumph over evil in this world. And our feet never have to leave the ground.

Putting the Rapture Theory into Perspective

Before one too readily subscribes to the Rapture theory, it is important to put this doctrinal teaching into perspective. When, where, and by whom was it introduced in church history? Does this idea reflect the best Christian thinking down through the ages? Is it part of the Christian tradition? Who has championed this idea?

Many Christians who have grown up in America in the last half-century have never heard any teaching other than a secret Rapture of the saints prior to, or in the midst of, a seven-year tribulation period. But I wonder if you know the history and the story behind Rapture teaching? People who hold it as their doctrine seem to assume that it has always been taught in the church. It has not.

This new theory began in 1830 and departed dramatically from the historic position of the church. It had never been heard of before. The church had never considered the hope of a bodily removal prior to that. So how did it all start?

The answer is most interesting. In about 1830 a group of people who had become known as the Plymouth Brethren, under the direction of J. N. Darby and others, began to hold what they called Pro- phetic Conferences. Supposedly, during one of those conferences an utterance came forth as a prophetic message from the Lord. A young Scottish woman named Margaret Macdonald received a private vision,

---

"I wonder if you know the history and the story behind Rapture teaching? People who hold it as their doctrine seem to assume that it has always been taught in the church. It has not."

---

a revelation, that only a select group of believers would be removed from the earth before the days of the Antichrist; but she also saw other believers enduring the tribulation.

Church scholars have called this vision into serious question. You can read it in Dave McPherson's book *The Incredible Cover-Up*. Whenever someone comes up with a new doctrine or insight, revelation, or practice (including what you are reading in this book), we have the right and obligation to check out its validity.

This Rapture teaching began as a result of one woman's private vision and charismatic utterance. Darby became the main spokesman for this view. It spread slowly until the early twentieth century, when the second edition of the *Scofield Reference Bible* in 1917 and the End Time dispensationalism charts in *Dispensational Truth* by Clarence Larkin in 1918 accepted the theory as truth, included it in their works, and popularized this view in the thinking of millions. It has become so deeply entrenched since then that many pastors and Christian leaders assume it is an essential teaching of church history extending back to apostolic times. Again, it is not.

One of the consulting editors of the *Scofield Reference Bible*, W. J. Eerdman, who served and accepted Darby's view, subsequently re- futed it. In a tract entitled *A Theory Reviewed*, he wrote, "Better the disappointment of truth than the fair but false promises of error."

This Rapture scheme, though popular in recent years, has shallow roots in historic Christian interpretation of the Scriptures. At present it is collapsing under the weight of criticism from Bible-believing seekers of truth. So *what else* might God have had in mind when He inspired Paul to write, "Caught up . . . in the clouds to meet the Lord in the air"? Let's take a closer look.

The Rapture Doctrine: An Idea of Man or a Truth of God?

All this is not some new doctrine I've dreamed up. It is far more in tune with the spirit and the teachings of Scripture than the idea of a physical, corporate, one-time removal of the church from the world.

Count on it! Anything that gets your mind and heart off what God wants to do in your life, and through you in the lives of others—the furthering of His Kingdom—is a deception.

I believe there are at least ten fallacies in the bodily-removal, Rapture doctrine.

(1) The word *rapture* does not appear in Scripture. Both the word and the concept of a physical removal of the church are not historic teachings of the church.

(2) Paul wasn't the first to teach the idea of a gathering. He even referred to the Lord's own word[3] on the subject, when Jesus spoke of sending His angels to "gather his elect."[4] But notice that Jesus said, "*This generation* will certainly not pass away until all these things have happened" (emphasis added). As we saw in the preceding chapter, *this generation* clearly means the people who were standing before Him.

(3) In Paul's often-quoted "caught up in the air"[5] statement, the Greek word for the *air* the saints are caught up into means the unconscious breathing air—not the atmosphere. There's a big difference! This is a technical and very important distinction. I'll explain it in more detail later in this chapter.

(4) The great escape idea is contingent upon the limiting assumption of a single Second Coming of Jesus. As we showed in the last chapter, the Scriptures make it clear that His comings are many (countless), and that He comes *to* us; we are not jerked *out of* the world to Him.

(5) The idea of a future, single-event, raptured church overlooks the fact that immediately following the famous Rapture passage (1 Thessalonians 4:13–18), Paul continues, "Now, brothers, about times and dates . . ." Times and dates for what? What he just finished telling them about: being caught up. Notice the plural use of times and dates. Why plural? Because they are countless, ongoing fulfillments here, too.

(6) Paul further describes in 1 Thessalonians 5:1–2 how the day (singular) of the Lord will come like a thief in the night. Don't forget that there are many days of the Lord, not just one (Luke 17:22, 26). This again demonstrates the many individual fulfillments of Paul's often quoted "caught up in the air"—such as the unique experiences that happened to John, Paul, Peter, and Philip.

(7) A bodily Rapture doctrine depends upon a physical/material interpretation of the main Rapture passages. Yet this approach of bending the spirit of Scriptures to conform to doctrines that bind up the kingdom of Heaven drew Jesus' angriest responses to the Scribes and Pharisees of His day.[6]

(8) A physical, corporate, one-time removal of the church focuses attention on *when*, rather than *what* and *how*; and it breeds enormous confusion. Rapture proponents overlook the fact that Jesus warned against speculating about dates and times and told His disciples to concern themselves instead with what they were to do and how they were to do it.[7]

(9) The physical, corporate Rapture idea depends upon a chronological interpretation of the Scriptures. For example, in Revelation 4:1, *after this* is often taken to mean after the so-called church age. Yet the context makes it clear that the first *after this* means next in the vision, and the second *after this* means after opening the door to the spirit realm. As John looks through the door, he is able to see into the spirit realm. This demonstrates a spiritual Rapture, not being jerked out of the world.

(10) Since there is no direct teaching to support it, the physical Rapture doctrine grows out of deductive reasoning, or inference.* This reasoning goes something like this: Since sin and death exist in the material world, God must snatch His saints out of it, destroy it, then

---

* Later in this chapter I'll show you how our Western materialistic mindset causes us to read the so-called "Rapture passages" in literal, physical terms.

create a new and sinless world. Forget about God loving the world enough to give His only begotten Son for it.[8] Forget about Jesus' prayer for God to keep His people in the world to carry on His work, not take them out of it.[9] Those Scriptures, according to the Rapture doctrine, are *not* to be taken literally; but the ones about a snatching away *are* to be taken literally.

So the idea of a one-time, future, physical removal of the church is a flawed doctrine of man, based on a pick-and-choose approach to interpreting isolated Bible passages. It is not a reality of God that reflects the terminology, teachings, and patterns of the Bible as a whole. It is a tool of those who conspire against the Apocalypse. God has chosen to leave His people in the world. He has not, and probably will not, take them out of it, though He could.

Please Hear What I'm Not Saying

Does this mean that I think all those who believe in and teach the Rapture are evil people who are viciously deceiving themselves and others? Certainly not! I'm not saying they are evil any more than our Lord was saying that Peter was literally Satan when He rebuked Peter for trying to dissuade Him from going to the cross.[10] I believe that many (perhaps most) of them are sincere Christians who honestly believe that they are teaching the Word of God.

I am attacking, however, the same fleshly mindset that caused Peter to recoil in horror at the thought of his Lord dying.

Flesh Wants an Easy Way Out

It's easy to see why the idea of a great escape is so believable and appealing to the flesh in us. There are two strong reasons people grasp at any hope of avoiding a trip through a dirt grave to reach heaven.

First, the high emotionalism associated with the Rapture grows out of a very human desire—a compelling drive to survive. Most Christians are afraid of dying. Oh, we'll talk about going to a better place and say we long to see Jesus face to face. But let us get a sharp pain in the chest, and we'll spend more money trying to stay alive than we'd ever give to the Lord.

> ## "God has chosen to leave His people in the world. He has not, and probably will not, take them out of it, though He could."

Couple the survival instinct with a deep belief that this world is an evil place that is beating us up, and the idea of a Rapture offers the easiest of all possible alternatives—a way to get out of this evil world as soon as possible, without dying.

Second, the physical and corporate aspects of the Rapture idea appeal to us because we have grown up with a Western world view. We live in the Western hemisphere, and that has influenced the way we view the world and our role in it.

Our Western world view tends to be materialistic and scientific. It operates on a basic assumption that there is a scientific framework which assumes order, control, and material existence as reality. What we can see and test is real; what we can't is not real. Thus, we've been conditioned by our culture to think of everything as literal, physical, and scientific—versus figurative, spiritual, and faith-centered. Yet, the Bible is written with a Middle Eastern world view—looking at reality spiritually, poetically, or symbolically.

The problem all this creates is that we tend to view spiritual reality as *inferior* to physical and material reality. "If you start spiritualizing this and that from the Bible," one Rapture teacher said to me, "pretty soon you have nothing left!"

But I didn't start it—God did. He breathed His own life into human nostrils, and man became a living being.[11] Until then, man was nothing but a dead lump of clay. Life itself is spirit—the very Spirit of God Himself.

The bottom line is this: we will never be able to grasp the glorious truth of being "caught up . . . in the clouds to meet the Lord in the air"[12] until we throw out the notion that saving our flesh is what matters most to us and to God. With this in mind, let's look more closely at the key Rapture passages.

The So-Called Rapture Scriptures Speak Of
Present-Day, Spirit-Realm/Physical-Realm Reality

The scriptural passages that speak of being caught up *do not* just describe a possible physical removal of a group of believers from planet Earth as a one-time, future event. Instead, they may also speak of an ongoing, spiritual/physical reality—we are caught up, in the Spirit, in Christ. Perhaps this is the most relevant fulfillment of this prophecy—attaining the fullness of Christ in our individual lives.

We know very little today about being in the Spirit, if the truth be known. Satan has taken this truth right out of the church at large, possibly leading us instead to believe a fairy-tale—something about a giant space trip!

Yet, you can find believers throughout the history of the church who knew what it meant to be visited by God—to be gathered, or raptured, into the presence of the Lord. This is not something ordinary; but it can and should be part of any believer's growth in Christ. Each of us should desire to experience it while our feet are still planted on earth. Anything less just leads us to slothfulness.

Our present society does not understand or accept the idea of getting caught up into the spirit realm—being raised up into the great cloud of witnesses that surrounds us.[13] These witnesses include thousands of angels in joyful assembly, the church of the firstborn, God, the spirits of righteous men made perfect, and Jesus.[14]

But we don't get into the spirit realm by getting out of ourselves and going someplace. Rather, we enter our own spiritual dimension. Has the church lost this vital, life-giving concept?

This spirit-realm/physical-realm reality does not deny a life after death for Christians. On the contrary, it means that, for overcomers, life after death simply continues the resurrected life of ruling and reigning with Christ, which we can enter into here and now. John called this the first resurrection.[15] It was not a one-time event, but a spirit-realm/physical-realm reality—obeyable, heedable, and keepable for all who would partake. After all, didn't Jesus say, "I am the resurrection and the life"? The resurrection is a Person, not just a single historic event.

1 Thessalonians 4:13–18

The Scripture most commonly used to support the physical-removal Rapture idea is 1 Thessalonians 4:13–18.

> Brothers, we do not want you to be ignorant about those who fall asleep, or grieve like the rest of men, who have no hope. We believe that Jesus died and rose again and so we believe that God will bring with Jesus those who have fallen asleep in him. According to God's own word, we tell you that we who are still alive, who are left till the coming of the Lord, will certainly not precede those who have fallen asleep. For the Lord himself will come down from heaven, with a loud command, with the voice of the archangel and with the trumpet call of God, and the dead in Christ will rise first. After that, we who are still alive and are left will be caught up with them in the clouds to meet the Lord in the air. And so we will be with the Lord forever. Therefore encourage each other with these words.

It is quite possible that Paul, anointed by the Holy Spirit, wrote down things he didn't fully understand, because the Revelation had not been given at the time of his writings. That's not to take away any of the validity of Paul's message any more than it is to say that the Old Testament prophets did not understand all they wrote down about the coming of the Messiah.

There are many examples throughout Scripture in which writers described coming events for which they had no frame of reference. For instance, Isaiah, Ezekiel, and Daniel all spoke of Jesus from the limited Old Testament perspective. They had not had the privilege of reading the Gospel narratives, as we have today.

Our real problem in grasping scriptural truths and realities, however, seldom stems from the limited historical perspective of its writers. Our problems most often stem from the limiting biases and doctrines that influence the way we interpret specific passages. The Gospels give many accounts of temple leaders who, having read the Scriptures, attacked Jesus because they had drawn diametrically opposed conclusions to His.[16]

Let's look at some of the key concepts in 1 Thessalonians 4:13–18. As we examine their meanings and some of the original language, we can readily see how End Times doctrines have been distorted.

"Caught up . . . in the air." We are caught up, yes, but to where? Are we caught up in a ring around the world, some of us going up and others down? How confusing! The clue is found in the word *air.* Notice we are not gathered up around the throne, but in the air.

Lets look at the meaning of the Greek word used for *air.* In the Greek language, words convey much more accurate and detailed meanings than do our English translations. There are two Greek words which the New Testament translates as *air.* The first one is *ouranos,* or atmospheric air,[17] where birds fly (or higher). This is *not* the word Paul uses in the Rapture passage. Paul uses the word *aer.* In contrast to the more common type of air used throughout the New Testament, *aer* means the internal breath. It comes from a verb which means to breathe unconsciously. This usage suggests that we breathe so naturally we don't even have to think about it—we just do it.

First-century Christians knew immediately what Paul meant by the word *aer.* He used the same word in Ephesians 2:2 to symbolize the spirit realm—"the *kingdom of the air.*" Revelation uses the same word to describe the air into which the seventh vial is poured out.[18] Jesus also used a derivative of it in answering His disciples' question, "Where, Lord?" He had just described two people in one bed; one would be taken and the other left. Two women would be grinding grain together; one would be taken and the other left. He said, "Where there is a dead body, there the eagles (*aetos*) will gather."[19]

And where is all this? It's in the spirit realm—inside us and among us, where the kingdom of God exists. And just like the air we breathe, it's not only inside us, but also around about us. This is not the same air where birds fly, and it is not what most people think about when they contemplate a Rapture flyaway through the sky into outer space.

The thought Paul expressed in the Thessalonians passage is that we are to be caught up into the spirit realm, not physically removed from the earth. Being "caught up . . . in the air" is an inner spiritual/physical reality, not a physical removal.

"With them in the clouds . . ." In prophecy, clouds symbolize humans, spirit-realm beings, and those who have died in the Lord[20]—not atmospheric clouds. Hebrews 12:1 speaks of our being "surrounded by . . . a great cloud of witnesses," the saints who have died in the Lord. Jude 12

describes "godless men, who change the grace of our God into a license for immorality and deny Jesus Christ" as "clouds without rain."

Paul's message is that, as we are caught up in the spirit realm, we become a part of that great cloud of witnesses.

"To meet the Lord . . ." Our feet never have to leave the ground for us to meet the Lord. In the Spirit, we meet (literally, have *a friendly encounter with*) Christ and are transformed into the fullness of His reality. As we are caught up in the spirit realm, where Christ is, we unconsciously do the things of the Lord without ever having to think about doing them. He becomes our new reality.

"Asleep in him . . ." Acts 7:60 says that Stephen fell asleep. He physically died, in Christ, and went to heaven. The *asleep* are the physically dead who have died in Christ. Paul comforts his hearers by assuring them of what happens to believers who have died physically. But there *is more.*

"The dead in Christ . . ." This could be those described above who were asleep, or it could refer to another group. Jesus said in John 5:25, "A time is coming and *has now come* when the dead will hear the voice of the Son of God, and those who hear will live" (emphasis added). Proverbs 21:16 says, "A man who strays from wisdom comes to rest with the dead." These passages refer to those who are physically alive but spiritually dead. They are not reigning and ruling as part of the first resurrection. They are saved, heaven-bound saints, but other than that they are dead spiritually.

"We who are still alive . . ." These are the people who have experienced the first resurrection[21]—those who have come alive in Christ and are also physically alive.

"Encourage one another . . ." Being caught up in the Spirit is not simply a gleeful escape from physical/material reality. The Spirit changes, equips, and empowers us for ministry and for spiritual warfare. It does not make us disappear. Disappearance is *not* where the power is. Anything Jesus did in His earthly ministry, we can do now. We receive levels of authority and blessings to the degree that we are caught up. First-century believers expected this kind of empowerment in their own lives. Were they mistaken? Misled? Under a delusion? If it didn't happen then or hasn't happened for over nineteen hundred

years, could they also have been wrong about other aspects of their faith? Of course not!

Note, again, the next verse in 1 Thessalonians 5:1 referring to times (plural) and dates (plural). There have been, are, and continue to be many fulfillments of this important passage in the lives of individual believers throughout the history of the church. Are you a part of this marvelous truth and fantastic promise? Maybe, now that you see a greater application than you previously saw, you soon will be.

1 Corinthians 15:51–57

Could this classic Rapture passage also have been fully pertinent for the believers hearing Paul's words in the first century? Or is it yet unrealized in its fulfillment, even to us today? Indeed, this whole chapter was intended to have a very practical fulfillment for its first hearers and for us today. It has been pushed out into the future because we haven't been able to explain a present fulfillment.

In the verses preceding 1 Corinthians 15:51–57, Paul explains that death came through Adam, and the resurrection of the dead came through Christ. Again, he speaks of people being asleep and alive. Then he says, in verse 23, that all will be made alive, "but each in his own time: Christ the first-fruits; then when he comes, those who belong to him." *Each in his own time* (order, or turn) clearly means that being made alive is not a one-shot, corporate deal, but an ongoing, countinual reality for individuals.

Now let us look at verses 51–57.

> Listen, I tell you a mystery: We will not all sleep, but we will all be changed—in a flash, in the twinkling of an eye, at the last trumpet. For the trumpet will sound, the dead will be raised imperishable, and we will be changed. For the perishable must clothe itself with the imperishable, and the mortal with immortality. . . .
>
> Then the saying that is written will come true: "Death has been swallowed up in victory. Where, O death, is your victory? Where, O death, is your sting?"
>
> The sting of death is sin, and the power of sin is the law. But thanks be to God! He gives us the victory through our Lord Jesus Christ.

"We will all be changed . . ." Paul was talking about a coming reality in everyone's life. He does not say *removed*, but *changed*—transformed into the likeness of Christ. This change is miraculous, it is effected by Jesus Christ, and it occurs "in a flash, in a twinkling of an eye," instantaneously. When the revelation of the unveiled Christ hits us (remember, each in his own order), it is like a spiritual lightning bolt. Suddenly, the Bible becomes a new book to us, and the world of the spirit opens up.

"At the last trumpet . . ." When will all this occur? Let's locate the last trumpet in Scripture. It's the seventh trumpet in Revelation 10 and 11. In prophetic symbolism, an angel sounding a trumpet represents a

---

"When the revelation of the unveiled Christ hits us (remember, each in his own order), it is like a spiritual lightning bolt."

---

voice, or message, from God. And what is the message of the last trumpet? It is the message of the seventh trumpet from the heavenly host proclaiming, "the kingdom of the world has become the kingdom of our Lord and of his Christ, and he will reign for ever and ever."[22]

As we have seen in earlier chapters, Revelation unveils Christ in His Alpha and Omega form. The last trumpet has already sounded in reality, but not everyone has received it. It continues to sound for individuals as they personally receive the revelation of Jesus Christ. The sounding of the last trumpet does not tell people to leave, but to get ready to reign on earth in this life. "And you *have made them* to be a kingdom and priests to serve God, and they will reign on earth."[23] This is the same trumpet Jesus referred to when He said, "And He will send forth His angels with a *great trumpet and they will gather* His elect from the four winds, from one end of the heavens to the other."[24]

When we receive the unveiling of the Lord Jesus Christ, we are changed instantaneously into kings and priests to rule and reign in the kingdom of God. Quit trying to put this all off into the future. This is a powerful spiritual/physical reality, available then and here and now.

"The dead will be raised imperishable . . ." Who are these dead? They are those who are physically alive, but not reigning and ruling with Christ. As Paul said, "I want to know Christ and the power of his resurrection . . . and so, somehow, to attain to the resurrection from the dead."[25] When? In his earthly life. That is why he also said, "Wake up, O sleeper, rise from the dead, and Christ will shine on you."[26]

Earlier in this chapter, Paul had said, "Flesh and blood cannot inherit the kingdom of God, nor does perishable inherit imperishable." We keep trying to drag the flesh into the kingdom, but the flesh is what holds us back from inheriting the kingdom.[27] Our flesh is perishable, but our spirit is imperishable. It is eternal. "For you have been born again, not of perishable seed, but of the *imperishable*, through the living and enduring word of God."[28]

When we receive the revelation of the last trumpet, the message, we are changed (transformed). We suddenly realize that we are *eternal*. Our bodies even change as we offer them to God as instruments of righteousness instead of wickedness.[29] Of course, our physical bodies may die and be resurrected later, but our spirits will live forever.

The reality of the trumpet revelation is that, if we have been made alive in Christ, we *are now immortal*.[30] When we fully realize our immortality, we are changed. We look at everything differently; we don't get all worried about earthly things; we think and operate on a different plane. We are caught up.

"Death has been swallowed up in victory . . ." Christ, by His resurrection, has destroyed death as a universal fact. It's a done deal.[31] As we are resurrected in Him, individually, death is destroyed for us.[32] We no longer live after the flesh, but after the spirit. The reason most Christians are scared of death is that they have so little experience with the spirit dimension. It's actually a fear of the unknown. When you get caught up in the Spirit and live in the Spirit, death loses its sting. It's no big deal. But, if you haven't, death still holds its sting for you.

"The sting of death is sin . . ." Adam was afraid of meeting God, and he hid from Him.[33] Why? Because he had sinned. The result of his sin was death. Paul said, "For as in Adam all die, so in Christ all will be made alive."[34] When we are dead in sin, all we know is the

flesh. The idea of losing that flesh is frightening, because we feel it is all there is of us. So we hang on to it. We try to make our flesh safe, secure, happy, and comfortable—because we think it's all we have. But, when we are made alive spiritually in Christ, we discover that our flesh is no longer our problem, nor our treasure. We crucify it so we can be raised spiritually in Christ, in the power of the resurrection. When that power takes over, the power of sin over us is gone. We can let the flesh go and live the resurrected life of Christ. We can walk supernaturally, unconsciously in the Spirit—now, in this life, on this earth.

"The power of sin is the law. . . ." Many of us keep trying to earn immortality by doing good things, by obeying the law. We've got this image from the Dark Ages of Saint Peter standing at the gates, weighing our good deeds against our bad deeds. If getting into heaven through the works of the flesh were possible, Christ's death on the cross would have been unnecessary. New Testament reality is that the power of sin—the flesh's inability to fulfill the law—is broken by the *fact* of Christ's death and resurrection, and it is broken *in us* by our resurrection in Christ. We are freed from doing the works of the flesh so that we can do the works of Jesus by the power of His Spirit.

"But thanks be to God! He gives us the victory through our Lord Jesus Christ." He gives—present tense—not will give someday. And, it is a great victory, not a great escape.

Please note the major difference in human priorities and God's priorities. Human beings think mostly in terms of surviving and staying physically healthy, prospering materially, being emotionally happy, and perhaps being morally good. God's priorities are that we worship Him in spirit and truth, develop godly character (purity of heart), and that we rule and reign spiritually and physically with Him in His kingdom. Oddly enough, when we order our lives after God's priorities, we get more than we ever dreamed possible. We don't just survive, we become immortal; we don't just prosper materially, we gain the riches of Christ. We don't just have happiness, which can be destroyed by circumstances; we have His joy, which cannot be touched by circumstances. We are not just good; we are empowered to do the works of Jesus. That's a very, very good trade.

2 Thessalonians 2:1–4

One other key Scripture used to support the idea of a corporate/physical Rapture is 2 Thessalonians 2:1–4. Let's examine it briefly.

> Concerning the coming of our Lord Jesus Christ and our being gathered to him, we ask you, brothers, not to become easily unsettled or alarmed by some prophecy, report, or letter supposed to have come from us, saying that the day of the Lord has already come. Don't let anyone deceive you in any way, for that day will not come until the rebellion occurs and the man of lawlessness is revealed, the man doomed to destruction. He opposes and exalts himself over everything that is called God or is worshiped, and even sets himself up in God's temple, proclaiming himself to be God.

"... *saying that the day of the Lord has already come [past]* ... *that day will not come until* ..." This passage implies that someone was circulating a letter under Paul's name stating that the day of the Lord had already come and gone. But the message of Revelation is that the day of the Lord has come, it is coming, it will continue to come. It is ongoing. The fact that it has come is not the end of it. So Paul is saying, don't let anyone deceive you and say that it has come and is not going to come again.

Note: Those who hold to a literal, physical interpretation of this Scripture either overlook entirely or dismiss Jesus' statements in Matthew 16:27–28: "For the Son of Man is going to come in his glory with his angels. . . . I tell you the truth, *some who are standing here will not taste death* before they see the Son of Man coming in his kingdom" (emphasis added). In the next few verses, we learn that some who were standing there (Peter, James, and John) saw Jesus transfigured. They experienced the glorified Christ—this was their day of the Lord.

"... *man of lawlessness is revealed* ..." Who, or what, is the man of lawlessness? It is the flesh; it is self-righteousness; it is the sinful nature of human beings. And where is God's temple? It is in us. We are God's temple. Paul, in Romans 7:14–25, explains how it works: "... the law is spiritual but I am unspiritual [flesh], sold as a slave to sin [my sin nature]." He speaks of how his flesh wages war against his spirit, making him a prisoner and keeping him from doing what he knows is right. "What a wretched man I am!" he exclaims in verse 24. "Who will rescue me from this body of death?" Then, in verse 25, he

"God's priorities are that we worship Him in spirit and truth, develop godly character (purity of heart), and that we rule and reign spiritually and physically with Him in His kingdom."

rejoices. "Thanks be to God—through Jesus Christ our Lord!" The day of the Lord is eternal. It is the day (or instant) in which the flesh of each individual is revealed to him, and he is transformed into the spiritual likeness of Christ.

Space will not permit us to examine all the Scriptures that are used to defend the idea of a one-time, corporate, physical Rapture. But I hope you can see two points that are clear. First, if we try to interpret these passages literally and physically, we will raise more questions than we can answer. And second, when we accept their language as figurative and symbolic (as all prophetic language is), we can easily understand them. They stand in complete harmony with both the spirit and the essence of all other Scriptures.

Of course, I discovered a long time ago that there is no reason to teach this until an individual is ready to receive it. Only the Holy Spirit can prepare you. If you are ready to receive it as light and life, let's move on to the next major point.

How You Can Live in Raptured Reality—Now

The Revelation message challenges us to overcome—to be transformed into spiritually liberated, energized, and controlled kings and priests—so that we can rule and reign with Jesus in His kingdom—now!

Many Christians are trying to escape a physical grave, and they are already in a spiritual grave. Jesus said, "Woe to you [Pharisees] because you are like unmarked graves which men walk over without knowing it."[35] Religious bondage can do that to you.

So, the first hurdle is to quit trying to escape death by getting out of this world alive through some future, bodily Rapture.

The essence of being caught up in the air to meet the Lord and being changed in the twinkling of an eye is this: one must be *in Christ*. How do you know when you are in Christ? You will walk as Jesus did[36] and do the works that He did.

Those Mansions Are Not in the Sky

The night before He was crucified, Jesus told His disciples, "There are many rooms [dwelling places] in my Father's house. . . . I am going there to prepare a place for you. . . . I will come back and take you to be with me that you also may be where I am. You know the way to the place where I am going."[37]

Many have built elaborate doctrines about the location and nature of the so-called mansions in the sky. Some have even worked out formulas to determine the relative size and location in heaven for each saint's mansion.

The idea of physical mansions is totally inconsistent with the tone and character of the remainder of the Upper Room discourse.[38] Notice how Jesus responded when Thomas asked a physical/material kind of question: "Lord, we don't know where you are going, so how can we know the way?" Jesus replied, "*I am the way*—the truth and the life" (emphasis added). Thomas was looking to go away to a physical/material place, but Jesus' response made it clear that He was speaking about a spirit-realm reality.

Where was Jesus talking about taking us? To where He is! And where is He? He's inside us, in the place of the spirit—that place of the internal, breathing air.

But it goes deeper than having Christ in our hearts. Later in this same discourse, He characterized Himself as a vine and His disciples as branches.[39] "If a man remains in me and I in him, he will bear much fruit." Then He added, "Apart from me you can do nothing."

"Christ *in you*," said Paul, is "the *hope* of glory."[40] It is only a hope because you don't yet possess the fullness of Christ's unveiling. *You in Christ is glory.*[41] When we are caught up in the spirit in Christ, and He shows us Himself as He is today, we are transformed into His likeness and are equipped to live victoriously and to minister in His power—to do the works of Jesus. In that dwelling place, we can live in

> **"Many Christians are trying to escape a physical grave, and they are already in a spiritual grave. . . . The first hurdle is to quit trying to escape death by getting out of this world alive through some future, bodily Rapture."**

such fellowship with Him that we don't have to consciously think about what we are doing or not doing. His presence becomes as natural to us as the air we breathe.

Is it hard to enter into that kind of raptured relationship? Well, yes and no. It is hard because the flesh does not die easily or willingly. All we have to do is read Romans 7 to see how our flesh struggles to keep from being crucified.

But it is easy because it is what God wants most to happen, and it is something He does for us individually. Our part is to yield ourselves completely to Him in love and receive His revelation. "If anyone loves me," Jesus said, "he will obey my teaching. My Father will love him, and we will come to make our home with him."[42]

And how do we obey His teaching? Jesus answered, "But the Counselor, the Holy Spirit, whom the Father will send in my name, will teach you all things and will remind you of everything I have said to you."[43] The tough part is that we have to shake off the teachings of man—as good and sincerely motivated as they may be—and respond to God's Word, illuminated by His Spirit.

The hour of temptation is that point in time when we are about to go into the spirit realm—to operate in the Holy Spirit, to learn, to minister in the Spirit—but our flesh pulls us back. We still want to get out of this world. Psychologically, that appeals to our flesh. We want to get out of here and let Jesus come back to take care of the mess in this world. But His plan is for us to become an integral part of His kingdom, to rule and reign with Him as kings and priests, to play a vital role in changing the world.

"They came to life and reigned with Christ. . . . This is the first resurrection. Blessed and holy are those who have part in the first resurrection. The second death has no power over them."[44]

Jesus is the resurrection and, when we are in Him, we reign and rule; we have life. We can choose to partake of the first resurrection— *right now!*

Before You Read On

In the remainder of this book we will talk more about the specifics of how we experience all this. But don't get caught up in the how-to's. Stop! Right now, before you read on, yield yourself totally to Jesus! If you have not been born again, repent and ask Him to come into your life and to show you His kingdom. If you have been born again and have not yet entered His kingdom, open yourself to receive the Revelation and get caught up in His Spirit to rule and reign with Him.

Can you blindly trust the teaching of this chapter? Absolutely not! I am not trying to change your mind; I'm trying to open your eyes and heart to all the wonderful things God has for you *now*. If I can change your mind, then someone else can change it back. But, if the Holy Spirit changes you, you are changed for good.[45]

Study this for yourself in the Word of God. As you study, ask the Holy Spirit to guide you into His truth. You can trust Him. Jesus said His Father would not give you a serpent. I can tell you from personal experience that He won't give you a dragon or a beast or an antichrist or anything else that Revelation talks about. He will give you His kingdom.

And, speaking of beasts, we'll take a look in our next chapter at how Jesus enables us to tame the beasts that rage within us.

7

HOW YOU CAN CONQUER THE AWESOME CREATURES OF THE APOCALYPSE

The conspirators love to terrify people by all their talk about the beastly creatures of the Apocalypse. Who of us has not heard spine-tingling tales describing awesome physical displays of God's wrath? Countless sermons, books, movies, and dramas have played on such vivid, literalistic themes.

- The ruthless "four horsemen of the Apocalypse"
- Devastating earthquakes, famines, and plagues that leave men gnawing their tongues in agony
- The sun, moon, stars, and waters turning into blood
- Giant locusts with stingers in their tails
- A great red dragon chasing an expectant mother
- Multiheaded beasts, one inflicting his dreaded mark on unsuspecting humans
- The "great white throne of judgment"

- The cataclysmic "Battle of Armageddon"

- The seductive, but deadly, Harlot

- The fiery-tailed dragon being cast down to earth

- The beguiling and enslaving Antichrist deceiving all the nations

- Merchants and kings lamenting the fall of evil Babylon after being rebuilt in the Mideast.

What do all these things mean? Are they God's way of showing us how vindictive He can be when He doesn't get His way? Were they written to give us a countdown to doomsday?

No, these are all visual parables about the spirit-realm activities behind the material world and the false religious system. To reduce them to single physical events and push them out into the future is to miss their vital message for individuals and for God's true church. It's a message the conspirators don't want Christians to receive.

In this chapter we will strip away some of the mythology surrounding the creatures and events of the Revelation and clarify, from the Scriptures, the spiritual and material significance of such symbols.

Whole books could be (and have been) written about each of the subjects listed above. Obviously, we cannot explain in one chapter all the mysteries of apocalyptic imagery—mysteries which have confounded theologians for two millennia.

In fact, an understanding of these visions and images does not come simply through explanation, but by revelation.[1] I can show you how the fallacy of reducing all the symbols to physical and material creatures and events serves only to limit one's understanding of the spiritual realities God has revealed through them. Only the Holy Spirit, however, can make them come alive for you.

I hope that this chapter (and this whole book) will stimulate your hunger and thirst for a greater personal revelation of Jesus Christ and for the realities of your own spirit dimension.

Needed: A Major Paradigm Shift

As we've seen in previous chapters, the Revelation is at hand; it is ongoing. It is continually being fulfilled. It cannot be bound by, nor does it predict or specify, actual historic or future events. Instead, the

Revelation was *written to and is fulfilled entirely inside individual believers and the church.*

To grasp that concept requires a major paradigm shift. A paradigm is a controlling idea or a way of thinking about a subject. The historic/future, physical/material paradigm has been deeply ingrained in most of us. We have been taught and have believed End Times doc-

---

"The Revelation was written to and is fulfilled entirely inside individual believers and the church."

---

trines for so long that any other way of thinking about the Revelation seems wrong—perhaps even demonic. This paradigm is very difficult for most of us to change.

Yet, the unexpected manner in which Old Testament messianic prophecy was fulfilled by Jesus' birth in a manger should serve as a warning to believers today. Back then, temple theologians had drawn up elaborate scenarios of the coming Messiah as a political liberator of the nation of Israel. When He didn't arrive on the scene like they thought a future monarch should, or lead a rebellion against Rome, they rejected Him. They even accused Him of blaspheming God and charged Him with doing His mighty works by the power of Satan.[2] Challenging conventional theology is, and has always been, considered heresy.

People today who are looking only for a one-time, future coming of Jesus and the establishment of a political kingdom on planet Earth are making the same mistake that the first-century theologians made. Jesus comes! He is in the comings business! The unfolding of His kingdom is within and among all Christians who sincerely seek the fullness of Christ in their daily lives. The Revelation is not a literal, materialistic book any more than Jesus' kingdom parables are literal and materialistic.

Rather, the visual parables of the Revelation provide believers with a spirit-dimension perspective of our present struggles. They empower us with valuable, revealed knowledge, and equip us with insights into how we can overcome evil in both the spirit realm and the material world.

God wants us to know about and understand the invisible spirit realm and how it interacts with the visible material realm. And He wants us to know how to overcome evil spirit-realm forces. If we don't overcome in the spirit dimension, we are destined to fail in both the spirit world and in the physical/material realm; and many have.

If you long for the full manifestation of Christ, eventually you have to end up in the book of Revelation. It is the ultimate wisdom of God to reveal Himself—internally and spiritually—to those who have spiritual ears to hear. Virtually all spiritual truths come to fruition in the book of Revelation. Clearly, a correct view of Revelation is essential to biblical Christianity.

Therefore, to remain ignorant, confused, or fearful in this area of faith is a very serious matter. Christians today need to properly teach and understand the messages of the Revelation, perhaps more than any other message.

The claims I'm making are not the idle speculations of an overactive imagination. They are, in fact, more consistent with scriptural prophecy (not only with the Revelation but with every book of the Bible) than are the End Times doctrines. Let's look more closely at some examples of how the Revelation unveils Jesus Christ and what must soon happen.

Have You Eaten Any Good Books Lately?

In the midst of the unfolding drama of the seals, trumpets, and vials, the angel of the Lord instructed John to *eat the scroll*.[3] Why? To internalize God's message. Why was it to be internalized? Because that's where the action was going on—inside John. The vision was an up-to-the-minute report of spirit-realm activity taking place within the writer.

God wanted John to realize that the spirit-realm activities he was witnessing were significant and applicable to him. Further, they were simultaneous and timeless, not chronological and predictive. The prophetic messages of the letters to the seven churches, the breaking of the seals, the sounding of the trumpets, and the pouring out the contents of the vials (bowls) were all at hand.

Yet God did not intend the prophetic messages contained in the scroll (or book) for John alone. Immediately after he ate the scroll, the angel told him, "You must prophesy again about many peoples, nations, languages and kings."[4] When you couple that statement with the angel's instructions to John, "Do not seal up the words of the prophecy of this book, because the time is near [at hand],"[5] it becomes quite clear that the message is for all people, everywhere, of all times.

Also, the frequent use of personal pronouns in Jesus' statements throughout the book of Revelation shows that the prophetic symbols represent the continuous unveiling of Jesus Christ within the individual believers.

Thus, the unfolding spirit-realm drama of the Revelation symbolizes Christ's ongoing judgment of the evil forces that seek control in our lives. These awesome creatures and descriptions provide a parabolic glimpse into the same gripping human struggle against sin that Paul so vividly described in Romans 7:7–24a, and the glorious victory he proclaimed in Romans 7:24b–8:39.

So the action is inside us. The Lamb stands up inside us.[6] The seven seals are opened inside us.[7] The seven trumpets (messages) sound inside us.[8] And the seven vials are poured out inside those who reject one or more of the messages to the seven churches.[9] These seven seals, messages, and vials all work together inside every believer concurrently, not sequentially, to effect an ongoing, dynamic fulfillment—not a global timetable or merely a serialized unfolding of the future.

To clarify that the prophecy was for all people of all generations, John was "given a reed like a measuring rod and was told, 'Go and measure* the temple of God and the altar, and count the worshipers there.'"[10] What is the temple of God? The New Testament states emphatically that we, God's people, are His temple.[11]

Of course, most Scripture has more than one level of fulfillment. The Revelation is fulfilled on the individual, personal level; and it is also fulfilled collectively among the body of believers. Jesus said that

---

* In prophetic Scripture, "measuring" is a symbol of God's judging human beings against His standards, and His measurement can bring deliverance or punishment. See Daniel 5:27, Zechariah 2:2, and Jeremiah 65:7b.

this is where the kingdom of God is located—both within and among believers. This gives substance and relevance to the Revelation here and now. And that's where the apocalyptic action is—inside us and among us—in God's kingdom.

So the judgments are pronounced first within the individual, then through the individual to the church. We receive the prophetic message (the sounding of the trumpets), then we become messengers to carry the prophetic word to other people within the church who either receive or reject it.

Sweet and Sour

John found, just as the angel predicted, that when he ate the scroll it tasted sweet, like honey in his mouth, but it turned his stomach sour.[12] That's the way it is when we receive the unveiling of Christ's spirit-realm/physical-realm reality. It tastes sweet, precious, and glorious. We long to have everything God has for us.

The conflict arises, however, when the light of God's truth starts revealing the evil spirit-realm forces at work within us; and His sword begins to war against everything in us that is not consistent with His character. What was sweet to our taste turns sour in our inner beings. Our inner-man becomes a battleground in which with Christ we fight against the evil, spirit-realm forces.

God is most interested in our inner character, so He judges, by His Word, the spirit-realm evil that lurks in our hearts. If we overcome evil in our inner-selves, if we press through to victory, we can go on to rule and reign with Christ in His kingdom. We wear the white robes of righteousness. God's seal of ownership is stamped upon our foreheads. And we sit with Him on His throne.[13]

Revelation emphasizes strong inner character because it is one of the major secrets of the kingdom of God. Jesus continually taught that wealth, fame, social standing, and political clout meant nothing in His kingdom. Rather, building and maintaining strong inner character would reap the full benefits of God's kingdom. Without strong inner character, even the strongest and most powerful human beings cannot stand against evil spirit-realm forces; yet, with strong inner character,

"Jesus said that this is where the kingdom of God is located—both within and among believers. This gives substance and relevance to the Revelation here and now. And that's where the apocalyptic action is—inside us and among us—in God's kingdom."

even the most frail human saints can reign and rule over Satan and all his cohorts.

Once we are able to reign and rule over spirit-realm forces within us, we hear God's trumpets calling us to action; and we go forth to reign and rule among the churches and in the material world. That, in a nutshell, summarizes the Revelation message and the message of Jesus.

Let the Revelation Show You How the Spirit Realm Operates

Popular theology seeks to interpret prophetic symbols and terms in light of their present-day associations, and in light of what the theologians expect to occur in the future. It's like figuring out what you believe is going to happen, then interpreting the symbols to meet your expectations.

Yet, careful examination of the symbols in Revelation quickly reveals that they were formed by looking backward, not forward. They were deeply rooted in the other sixty-five books of the Bible, especially in the Old Testament, not in today's dictionaries or newspapers.

Look, for example, at the dominant symbolic role the number seven (and variations of it) plays in the Revelation. The book contains seven visions, seven worship scenes, seven spirits who worship before God, seven candlesticks (representing seven churches which receive seven letters), seven seals on the scroll of the Lamb, seven trumpets (sounded by seven angels), seven bowls (or vials) of wrath that are poured out by seven angels, and a beast with seven heads.

Many eschatologists (End Times theologians) try to fit all these sevens into timeframes and use them to predict actual future events. Some even try to add the two three-and-half-year periods that are mentioned[14] to predict an actual seven-year tribulation period. Then they argue endlessly over whether the Second Coming of Christ will occur before, after, or during that tribulation period.

Yet John bases his usage of the number seven on the prophetic symbolism the first-century Christians attached to the number. To them, it represented perfection or completion; especially when associated with God. The number seven had also appeared numerous times in the Old Testament, and the ancient prophets used it—most often to express the completion of God's plans or judgments.

It doesn't take much spiritual insight, then, to see that the Revelation is concerned with *perfection, maturity, completion, or reaching the goal God intends for each believer's life*—not with predicting times and dates, or even events. And, since the writer paid so much attention to the spirit realm, it is clear from the context that he is talking about *spiritual maturity or completion* for the individual—not about the end of the world.

Oddly enough, many people who encounter the idea that the sets of sevens of the Revelation are internal, spiritual, and concurrent (instead of global, material, and sequential) reject it. They say it just doesn't seem right. But God's Word cautions, "There is a way that seems right to a man, but in the end it leads to death."[15] I'm not suggesting that anybody who disagrees with me on this point is doomed. It may very well be, though, that pushing all prophecy out into the future as literal and physical could, and does, cause many Christians to remain dead in Christ.

But please don't take my word for it—or anyone else's word. Search God's Word for yourself. The Bible itself is the final arbiter of all ideas about Scripture.

Recurring Spirit-Realm Themes of the Revelation

Despite all the criticisms that scholars have leveled against it, the Revelation is a divine masterpiece, a literary symphony of magnificent proportions. It is the crowning glory of the entire Bible, the point where all scriptural truths come together.

"Despite the fact that the beastly creatures get most of the coverage in books, magazines, and the press, Jesus Christ is the central figure of the Revelation."

Like any great symphony, it contains recurring motifs, or themes, which run like golden threads through the whole work. Let's examine some of those recurring themes and see how you can apply them to your own daily life.

Christ Is Worthy to Be Worshiped and Is Given Full Authority In God's Kingdom

Despite the fact that the beastly creatures get most of the coverage in books, magazines, and the press, Jesus Christ is the central figure of the Revelation. The whole book is the revelation God gave to Him and He gave to His true church.[16] It is Christ who receives the worship of John,[17] the angels,[18] the four living creatures,[19] the white-robed saints,[20] the twenty-four elders,[21] and eventually the whole world.[22]

He is declared worthy to receive worship, honor, power, and glory,[23] and He alone is worthy to open the seals.[24] He is given the keys of David,[25] the keys of hell and death,[26] the keys to the bottomless pit,[27] and the keys to the book of life.[28]

He stands in the center of the throne of God;[29] He sits on the conqueror's white horse;[30] His seal of authority is placed on the forehead of the numberless saints;[31] He is given the power to judge;[32] He is called Lord of lords and King of kings;[33] He is the Bridegroom who receives His bride at the wedding supper;[34] and He is the light of the new heaven and new earth.[35]

Are you beginning to get the picture? It is Jesus who plays the starring role in the drama of the Revelation—not the Antichrist, or the beasts, or the great harlot, or Babylon, or Israel, or Russia, or China, or anyone else.

Take the supernatural, spirit-realm reality of Jesus Christ out of Revelation (as many seek to do) and the whole book collapses. It is, indeed, the unveiling of Jesus Christ.

Christ Continuously Comes to His Saints, And Through Them to the Church

We've already seen that Jesus comes; now let's look at some of the ways He comes in the spirit realm. I believe the letters, seals, trumpets, and bowls (and perhaps other symbols) all represent internal, spirit-realm comings of Jesus to individuals and to the church. They are sets, or cycles, of His countless comings; and they are going on all the time.

Jesus comes in the spirit-dimension to individual Christians to judge their obedience to His Word, and to invite them into intimate fellowship with Him. He knocks on the door and, if we open, He will come in and dwell with us.[36] This involves a whole lot more than we've traditionally talked about as the conversion experience. That's basically talking about Christ being in us. The letters to the churches contain some very specific instructions about what must take place inside us before Jesus can come to *live in us,* and they offer some dire consequences if we ignore His judgments of us.

Once we receive Him in all His spirit-realm reality, we become His messengers to the church—although most of the church rejects His comings. We become the messengers, the trumpets, sounding out God's Word to His church. In effect, the works of Jesus that we do as a result of His coming to us become the vehicles He uses to bring judgment to His church.

The visions, or parables, of the following chapters show us how He continually judges us and the church through us. For example, the worship scene of chapter four shows how we can enter into His presence spiritually through praise and worship and how we submit the various aspects of our lives for His judgment and purification. Chapter five declares His worthiness to open the seals on the scroll of our lives (the shackles that bind us to the fleshly realm) which is a necessary condition to receiving Him in the spirit realm.

"Jesus comes in the spirit-dimension to individual Christians to judge their obedience to His Word, and to invite them into intimate fellowship with Him. He knocks on the door and, if we open, He will come in and dwell with us."

As the Lamb breaks the seven seals within us,[37] we are measured against and cleansed by the sword of His Word. The fleshly nature within us is slain. We become dissatisfied with fleshly living and teachings. God's seal of ownership is placed upon our foreheads, and we are given white robes of righteousness.

These themes keep coming up again and again in the book. They show up in the sounding of the trumpets, in the pouring out of the vials of wrath, and in all the judgment scenes.

Tracing the scores of Scripture references that support this internal fulfillment theme is beyond the scope of this book. Let me urge you to invest the hours it takes to search it out for yourself. But remember to think individually and spiritually, not globally and materially.

The False Church Continuously Rejects the Spirit-Realm Truths and Realities of Christ and Persecutes the Saints Who Proclaim His Message

Just as Jesus was constantly attacked and finally killed by the false church of His day, the saints of every generation who come into His spirit-realm reality and proclaim its truths are persecuted by the false church of their day. It was at hand in the gospel era, it has been at hand in each succeeding generation, and it is at hand for us today.

When we hear God's trumpets (spirit-realm messages)[38] and become His messengers in the church, doing the works of Jesus through the power of His Spirit, we can expect those who hold to fleshly doctrines to resist vehemently. They always have, and they still do.

So abominable is this false church in the sight of God that it is depicted as "the great prostitute (or harlot)."[39] She lures "the kings" and "the inhabitants of the earth" to commit spiritual adultery with her;[40] she grows rich by deceiving the masses into idolizing her and bringing their treasures to her;[41] she becomes intoxicated with the blood of the spiritually martyred saints "who [bear] the testimony of Jesus;"[42] and her power is enhanced by the beastly world system.[43]

How can we identify this great prostitute today? When John saw who she was, he wrote, "I was greatly astonished."[44] Most people are equally shocked today when they receive the revelation of who she represents. Why? Because she is clothed in the garments of respectability and social approval; and she is greatly revered and respected by the kings and peoples of many nations, who endow her with great wealth.

Who is this seductive woman the world both loves and hates? She is the oppressive church system which calls attention to herself rather than to the Christ she claims to represent. Despite her religious appearance, she denies the supernatural reality of Christ and lures people into worshiping the idols of her doctrines, buildings, structures, and institutions. And, if you don't believe this blasphemous church system will have you put to death (at least symbolically by throwing you out), just start doing the same miraculous works that Jesus did during His earthly ministry and see what happens.

The false church is also called Babylon, a parabolic symbol for confusion.[45] But the name implies much more than the chaos of conflicting ideas; it represents idolatrous confusion. The name Babylon has its roots in the Genesis story of the tower of Babel,[46] the rebellious attempt by men to build a structure that would defend them from the judgments of God. It later became the prophetic name of a nation whose rulers defiantly enslaved God's people, enshrined idols in the temple of God, and used the temple vessels for sensuous feasts in celebration of false gods.[47]

Today religious Babylon seeks to defend itself against God's judgments by denying the supernatural reality of Christ. It binds up God's people by reducing the works of Jesus to humanistic doctrines and organizational structures; it usurps the throne of God in the hearts of men by receiving (even demanding) their worship; and it turns the vessels of God (Christians) into self-seeking idolaters by elevating men to the status of gods.

Resisting religious Babylon is one of the recurring themes of the Revelation and of the whole Bible. "Come out of her, my people," Christ said.[48]

The World System Constantly Seeks to Defeat And Reign over the Saints of God

As if persecution by the idolatrous false church were not enough for the saints to endure, they are constantly being attacked by the world system.[49]

The conspirators would like for you to believe that these beasts are physical kingdoms and rulers who will suddenly emerge at some future date, take over a large portion of the world, and fight against God. By focusing attention on a literal, physical beast who inscribes an actual number (such as the much-heralded, literal 666) on helpless victims at some future date, they distract people from the present, unseen demonic forces at work in the spirit realm, causing events to occur in the visible physical/material realm.

And, while Christians are busy looking for some future event, Satan (the great dragon)[50] is wreaking havoc (through his beasts) in the daily lives of millions of people. These scriptural creatures, like all creatures in the Revelation, were at hand in the first century. They are at hand right now and will be at hand in the future.

Who are these beasts, and what are they doing? The answer may shock you. John wrote that "the whole world was *astonished* and followed the beast."[51] All these beastly creatures represent the evil world system that fights against the kingdom of God and its ruler, Jesus Christ. The seven heads symbolize completeness, which means that this oppressive world system pervades every area of human activity. It exercises control through governments, commerce, science, education, the arts, entertainment—everything that exists in the material realm. It even shows up in the church.

Energized and controlled by the "prince of the power of the air,"[52] this world system constantly wars against Christ and His kingdom. It lures people into giving their total allegiance to it, accepting its name and number.[53] Haven't you known people, for example, who were so sold out to their work, to money, or to some pleasure that they had no place in their hearts for God? Such people bear the number and name of the beast instead of the seal of God. They live under the authority of the evil world system, not under the authority of Christ.

Some people are coerced into submitting to the world system. Dictators, like Hitler, kill those who resist their evil systems; communist regimes refuse jobs and life's necessities to people who follow Christ; and even democratic governments demand obedience to their humanistic systems.

Perhaps most astonishing, the beast system also operates through the false church. Many churches defrock or ostracize ministers, teachers, and even laypeople who challenge human doctrines or defy authority structures. This collusion between the idolatrous religious system and the beastly world system is the same conspiracy that crucified Jesus.[54] The false church (first-century religious Israel) and the world system (Rome) conspired to kill Jesus, and their successors have conspired to destroy His true church (the saints who do His works) ever since.

You only need to read Revelation 13 to see how powerful, clever, and destructive these beasts can be. The fact is that the world system, with the idolatrous church as its cohort, deceives the masses of people into worshiping it—even born-again Christians.

God wants us to be aware that the beasts are *within us* in the form of our godless, fleshly nature, and that they constantly seek to infiltrate and seize control of all human institutions. Only when we recognize them and their activities can we overcome them.

The overcoming saints who bear the seal of God can discern in their spirits the ominous presence of spirit-realm evil, and they resist it with patience and endurance.[55] They know that they are fighting a spiritual battle, and they protect themselves with the full armor of God.[56]

> **"By focusing attention on a literal, physical beast who inscribes an actual number (such as the much-heralded, literal 666) on helpless victims at some future date, [the conspirators] distract people from the present, unseen demonic forces at work in the spirit realm, causing events to occur in the visible physical/material realm."**

The Antichrist Spirit Constantly Deceives Most People Into Rebelling Against Christ

As with the beasts, the conspirators portray the Antichrist* as an actual human being who will show up someday and deceive the nations into worshiping him. Again, they plan to cover up the ongoing presence of the spirit of antichrist—a spirit who leads the continuous rebellion against Christ.[57]

The deception of the nations by the antichrist is not some future event—it is going on right now. Of course, the term *anti* not only means against, but also an alternative to or substitute for. You can see the antichrist offering alternatives and substitutes through thousands of humanistic endeavors which seek to disprove man's need for the blood of Christ. It shows up when modern science puts its faith in a big bang theory that supposedly explains the origin of the universe, and in a theory of biological evolution that ostensibly disproves the biblical creation story. It appears in the new age movement, with its metaphysical manifestations and miracles. It parades as humanistic movements and political treaties which outlaw wars, and as international organizations that promise to cure world hunger and oppression.

I don't mean to imply that all human efforts to solve mankind's problems are evil. But I do wish to state emphatically that any human

---

* Many believe that one of the beasts is the Antichrist.

endeavor which opposes, or attempts to substitute for, the reality of Christ is inspired by the spirit of antichrist.

According to the Revelation, this spirit of antichrist constantly arises within us on an individual level. It seeks to deceive us into self-sufficiency and pursuit of personal interests, and away from moment-by-moment worship of Christ and dependence upon His power.

In the church, the spirit of antichrist seizes every opportunity to substitute activities and programs for the supernatural reality of Christ, to channel worship to the church itself and away from Christ, and to discredit the Scriptures and works of Jesus in any way possible.

This evil spirit is so deceptive that most Christians mistake him for the true Christ and gladly worship him.[58] So widespread and complete is the deception of the antichrist spirit that he sets himself up as the head of the church, while the true Christ stands outside the church and knocks on the door to gain entrance.[59]

But God promises great blessings to His saints who recognize and overcome the antichrist spirit by the blood of the Lamb and the testimony of Jesus.[60]

Christ Constantly Triumphs In And Through His Overcoming Saints

The beasts, the great prostitute, Babylon, and the false prophet all symbolize the idolatrous world and religious system that conspires against Christ and His faithful saints. These creatures arise within individuals and in the church. They become powerful when we worship them or let them rule over us.

The great dragon and his archangel (the spirit of antichrist) empower and direct the constant spirit-realm onslaught against the kingdom of God, as reflected in such symbols as the plague of locusts and the demon spirits that look like frogs. We need to recognize that this is the same spirit-realm reality Jesus encountered when He dealt with the demons and evil spirits in the people of the gospel era.

That's the dark side of the Revelation—evil spirit-realm beings deceiving, controlling, and energizing human beings and their institutions—in order to persecute and kill the blood-washed saints who dare to exhibit the testimony of Jesus. Evil spirit-realm beings are at work in and among us, just as Christ is at work in and among the people of His kingdom.

"Any human endeavor which opposes, or attempts to substitute for, the reality of Christ is inspired by the spirit of antichrist."

But there is a bright side—a very bright side—to this inspiring book. Christ has already won the decisive battle over all evil forces! And we can win with Him in our day-to-day lives!

Obviously, the conspirators would love to lump Christ's triumphs over evil into a single Second Coming and shove it out into the future. That way, they can deceive millions of Christians into waiting and longing and looking for something that is already happening. But the Revelation proclaims that Christ's victories over evil are ongoing, present realities. They are at hand. We don't have to just *hope for* victory over evil, someday. Revelation reality is that we can *have* victory over evil, right now.

The prophetic message of the letters, the seals, the trumpets, and the vials of wrath is ongoing, not predictive. Here is a somewhat over-simplified scenario of how the internal and external drama unfolds:

- Christ continuously comes to us through His Word, encouraging, rebuking, and warning us. In the letters to the seven churches, He knocks at our heart's door and offers to come into us.[61]

- If we open the door by praising and worshiping Him, He (the Lamb) stands up inside us.[62]

- He breaks the seals of the scroll within us, exposes the spirit-realm creatures of the Apocalypse, clothes us in His righteousness, and places His protective seal upon us.[63]

- His trumpets (messages) sound within us and through us to the church, proclaiming His triumph over all evil spirit-realm forces and judgment of those who resist His message.[64]

- If we receive His messages in our innermost beings (symbolized by eating the scroll),[65] He enables us to overcome the evil within us and to ride out with Him to conquer the beastly religious and worldly systems.[66]

- The seven plagues (bowls of wrath) show what happens to those who continuously reject the message of the letters, the seals, and the trumpets. God hands them over to Satan and to their own evil natures and devices.[67]

Individual believers, then, overcome the awesome creatures of the Apocalypse when Christ reveals, and when we recognize and resist, their attempts to lure us into looking for spiritual deity within ourselves, or in earthly systems, or in other humans. The cyclical nature of these symbolic events shows that the conflict goes on continuously within us and in the church. The increasing intensity of the judgments reveals that the conflict of the two kingdoms occurs at deeper and deeper levels within us and, through us, in the church.

God has given His judgments to us for our redemption. As we receive His judgments of our own beastly nature, and of the beastly religious and world system which surrounds us, Christ enables us to overcome them through the blood of the Lamb and by our testimony of doing the works of Jesus.

He has won! And, through Him, we can continuously win!

What Does It All Mean?

If we receive God's judgments and go on to live in the fullness of Christ's kingdom, we need not fear the beastly creatures of the Revelation. That's what the parables of the creatures and plagues are supposed to show us.

God intends for every Christian to understand and apply the spirit-realm/physical-realm truths and realities of the Revelation and to receive its promises and blessings. He did not intend to confuse us.

I believe that understanding this message can usher in a fresh wave of God's Spirit in and among His saints. It can create a sense of freshness, a sense of life, that hasn't been present to such a degree before. It can inspire us to reach out, to hunger for the Word of God.

This spirit-level response to God can establish something real, something wonderful, and something eternal.

The Revelation shows that God wants to move by a fresh wave of His Spirit to bring encouragement, power, and victory to His saints. Oh, the victory will not come easily. Satan and his co-conspirators always fight the battle of Armageddon to try to keep it from happening. Let's examine this greatest of all battles in the next chapter.

8

WHY YOU WON'T FIND THE BATTLE OF ARMAGEDDON IN THE MIDDLE EAST

W hat one word most frequently describes a massive conflict? *Armageddon!*

The Battle of Armageddon, most of us have been taught, is the final war which will someday pit God and all His heavenly forces against Satan and all his evil forces. End Times teachers describe it as the war to end all wars. Some even refer to it as the end of the world.

Oddly enough, this idea of a one-time, future Battle of Armageddon, this universal symbol for a final conflict, is another doctrine of man, not a truth of Scripture.

- The term *Battle of Armageddon* never appears in the Bible. The Scriptures call it the battle on the great day of God Almighty.[1] Armageddon is the location of the battle.

- Scripture never mentions a specific place bearing the name Armageddon. The name does not appear in ancient geographical or historical writings; neither does such a place appear on either ancient or modern maps.

- The Hebrew term *Har Meggidon*, which we translate as *Armageddon*, has no apparent meaning (as names usually did) in

131

ancient Hebrew. It appears in a variety of forms in different, ancient New Testament manuscripts, but it does not show up anywhere else in ancient Hebrew literature or in religious or secular writings of the period.

- *Har,* in ancient Hebrew, means *mountain.* Once we understand that the battle on the great day of God Almighty takes place on a mountain, we can readily see how far afield the end timers really are. They place it in a valley!

- Based on various other Scriptures, one could easily make a case for any of the following locations for Armageddon: (a) *Har Mo'edh,* the mountain of assembly,[2] or (b) *Megiddo,* because a great slaughter took place there,[3] or (c) *Ar himdah,* God's city of desire (Jerusalem), or (d) *Har migdo,* His fruitful mountain (Mount Zion).

The context of the name makes *har migdo,* His fruitful mountain (Mount Zion), the most likely choice of locations. Many passages in the Revelation[4] take their imagery from the book of Joel, in which God's warfare against evil forces always proceeds from Mount Zion.[5] Just look in a concordance at how many times mountains appear as spiritually significant locations in Scripture, and you'll see that the mountaintop is the chosen symbol for the site of spiritual warfare and great victories by the people of God.

What Is Armageddon?

Scripture does not readily tell us Armageddon's location, or even what the term means. It is hard to imagine such an omission as a divine oversight. Clearly, since the locality and meaning of Armageddon are not specifically spelled out, and since it appears in a book which abounds in symbolism, it must be a symbolic name.

Don't look for a one-time Battle of Armageddon to be fought in the Middle East at some future date with horses, tanks, soldiers, missiles, and airplanes. The battle goes on in the church at this very moment.

The battle on the great day of God Almighty, like everything else in the Revelation, was "at hand" when John wrote about it, and it has been at hand ever since. It is at hand now and will be at hand in the future. Armageddon symbolizes the location of the *ongoing* conflict between God's overcomers (the elect) and those within the church who oppose the unveiling of the supernatural Christ.

How do we know that the location of this ongoing conflict is in the church? Again, we must look closely at how all Revelation symbolism ties together and how it ties in with so many other Scriptures. Mount

---

"Don't look for a one-time Battle of Armageddon to be fought in the Middle East at some future date with horses, tanks, soldiers, missiles, and airplanes. The battle goes on in the church at this very moment."

Zion, the accepted Old Testament symbol of Israel, was also referred to as God's "Holy Mountain" and "the mountain of your [God's] inheritance."[6] In the New Testament, it symbolizes the new Israel, the church. The writer of Hebrews, for example, used it to describe the church: "But you have come to Mount Zion, to the heavenly Jerusalem, the city of the living God. . . . the church of the firstborn."[7]

Make no mistake about it; evil spirit-realm forces that constantly seek to thwart God's purposes are waging an ongoing war inside the church. Jesus faced these evil forces in His frequent conflicts with temple rulers, and they show up throughout the book of Acts and the Epistles. This spiritual warfare also constitutes one of the primary themes of the entire book of Revelation.

What's more, we, as believing Christians, are called upon to be the warriors in this great conflict. Certainly, Christ leads the battle, just as He always has, but we are the foot soldiers who carry out His battle plan in the trenches on a day-to-day basis.

All sincere Christians need to make sure they are allied with God's forces within the church and not with His enemies, because the Armageddon symbolism makes it clear that God deals very harshly with the evil forces that constantly seek to seize control of His church.

Why Do the Conspirators Go to Such Great Lengths To Distort This Prophecy?

The conspirators have successfully deceived masses of Christians into believing an elaborate End Time doctrine that fixes a precise physical location—a valley outside Jerusalem, near the town of Megiddo—for this battle; establishes a specific future timetable based on the founding of the new state of Israel in 1948 for its beginning; and lists various countries—Russia, a new Rome, China—that will fight against God in it. All of this stems from a gross distortion of Revelation 16–19 and related prophetic Scriptures.

But why would the conspirators perpetrate such a hoax? What could they possibly hope to gain by misleading people to expect a final judgment and destruction of this evil world by a righteous God? Could they hope to gain support for their rebellion by announcing their own ultimate defeat?

This clever deception takes advantage of one basic flaw of human nature—the tendency to procrastinate on decisions and actions that we perceive to have little or no meaning for the present moment, especially when they don't seem to involve us directly. Thus, by depicting this battle as God's war, not ours, and by shoving it out into the future, the conspirators hope to dupe Christians into believing that the battle on the great day of God Almighty has no direct meaning for their daily lives. Sleeping warriors pose no danger to the enemies of God.

Apparently, their plot is working. Most Christians either ignore Bible prophecy about spirit-realm conflict, or they think of conquering evil as something God will do someday. "Let Jesus come back and clean up this mess," they say.

Christians, it is time to wake up! The Revelation is sounding the alarm!

The Time Is *Now!* The Location Is *Here!* The Battle Is *Ours!*

In context, we can clearly see that the battle on the great day of God Almighty describes the ongoing spiritual/physical conflict between overcomers and non-overcomers *within the church*. It creates a visual parable of God's kingdom in conflict with the kingdoms of this world.

The symbolism of Revelation 1–2 has a definite connection with the pouring out of the sixth and seventh bowls of wrath. End Times teachers identify this as the beginning of the so-called Battle of Armageddon. The awesome picture of the present-day Jesus in the Apocalypse, with a double-edged sword coming out of His mouth,[8]

> **"The conspirators have successfully deceived masses of Christians into believing an elaborate End Time doctrine that fixes a precise physical location . . . establishes a specific future timetable . . . and lists various countries—Russia, a new Rome, China—that will fight against God."**

and Jesus' promise to come and "fight against them [those who don't repent] with the sword of [His] mouth"[9] foretell the terrible judgment that falls on the church in Revelation 16 and 19.

But the judgments don't fall upon organized religion as a whole; they fall upon individuals within the church. In Revelation 1, John says that the prophecy from Jesus Christ is addressed to His servants,[10] the people He has designated as His kingdom and priests.[11] Nowhere in the book does He address anyone else.

And why is this prophecy addressed to His servants? Some teachers say that its only purpose is to comfort the suffering saints by showing them what God will someday do. If so, it is the only book in the Bible written for that purpose. No, John explicitly and repeatedly states that God has given His servants the Revelation because He expects them to do something about its message. John speaks in the imperative; these things "must soon take place."[12] Again and again the Revelation promises blessings to believers who read, hear, and keep or obey its message.[13] The saints are blessed if they wash their robes in His righteousness,[14] keep their white garments with them at all times,[15] and keep themselves spotless.[16] This is no passive book, written to passive Christians who are to sit around in a passive state and wait for God to do something someday. It is an active book, for active Christians, who have a definite mission to achieve.

Further, this mission statement is not addressed to an organized church, in a general way. It is addressed to individuals within the church, in very specific ways.*

God's Battle Plan

The Revelation makes it clear that war rages on, and it outlines a battle plan for fighting and winning it. Christians are not to merely sit by and watch the conflict; they are to engage and overcome the enemy. These are our marching orders.

In order to fight and win the ongoing war, believers will need supernatural, spirit-dimension power. They will have to dress in white robes of righteousness and do "the works of Jesus."[17]

In fact, doing the works of Jesus engages the enemy. Why? Because that's where the battle line is drawn—in the boundary between the material realm and the spirit realm. The battle line was drawn there in the gospel era,[18] during the period of the Acts and the Epistles,[19] and it is drawn there today. It is drawn between those who are lukewarm for God and those who are red hot, between those walking in the flesh and those walking in the spirit.

The Setting of the Battle

Let's look more closely at what the Bible says about the Battle of Armageddon. We are primarily concerned with two passages: Revelation 16:12–21 and 19:11–21. Let me suggest that you read them (preferably in the New International Version) before reading the remainder of this chapter. If you really want to get a grasp of this battle, read Revelation 16–19 in its entirety.

But, remember, we have to think spiritually, not just physically.

---

* Note the frequent use of personal pronouns (he, him, and them) throughout the Revelation.

The Anatomy of a Battle: Revelation 16:12–16

- *Verse 12:* "The sixth angel poured out his bowl. . . ." *Angel* is more correctly translated *messenger*, and probably refers to a human saint. Earlier, these bowls are called *the bowls of God's wrath*,[20] and they represent the judgment of God in all its awesome fury. When His messages are repeatedly ignored, the unrepentant face terrible consequences.[21]

- *Verse 12:* " . . . on the great river *Euphrates*. . . ." In the context, a literal reading of "Euphrates" makes no sense. Obviously, this is a spiritual symbol. It was recognized as the eastern boundary line of the Garden of Eden[22] and of the Promised Land.[23] I believe it represents the boundary line between the kingdom of God and the kingdoms of this world. It also represents the supernatural power source that sustains and energizes the false church, Babylon. It contains false doctrines, religious politics, human ego, demonic forces, and many other unsavory things. And it stands in sharp contrast to the crystal clear "river of the water of life . . . flowing from the throne of God and of the Lamb" through the Holy City, the New Jerusalem.[24]

- *Verse 12:* " . . . and its water was dried up. . . ." With modern technology—tanks, troops, and artillery parachuting from airplanes, and missiles traveling thousands of miles—drying up a physical river would be a totally unnecessary step in preparation for a battle. The statement implies that God has to dry up Babylon's polluted power source before a successful onslaught against His enemies can take place.

- *Verse 12:* " . . . to prepare the way. . . ." The dried-up riverbed represents the boundary line between the material and the supernatural, where the battle rages. Further, this is something God does. Satan cannot launch a successful attack against Christ's true church or against the saints who have overcome and are living inside the boundary. Jesus promised to build His church upon the rock of His lordship, and "the gates of Hades [Hell] will not overcome it."[25]

- *Verse 12:* " . . . for the kings from the East." These are not literal, earthly rulers. They are the overcoming saints who have been purified by the letters, seals, and trumpets, given white robes of righteousness, and stamped with the seal of God. These saints go out to engage the enemy and seize the kingdom of God by force.[26] The fact that the kings come from the East symbolizes that they come from God. In prophetic writings, God always comes from the East—from the direction of the rising sun.

- *Verse 13:* "Then I saw three evil spirits that looked like frogs. . . ." These are demonic, spirit-realm forces stationed by Satan in the boundary line to ward off all attacks against his domain, the beast system and the harlot church.

- Verse 13: ". . . they came out of the mouth of the dragon, out of the mouth of the beast and out of the mouth of the false prophet." The blasphemous words of the unholy trio—Satan, the beast system, and the harlot church—release the evil spirits. Since Satan is a spirit, he has to work through physical beings and material systems.[27] And the human action which most effectively releases demonic power is the spoken word.

- *Verse 14:* "They are spirits of demons performing miraculous signs. . . ." These might be human actions (good works) that are so great they seem miraculous. The term *miraculous signs*, however, implies that they are supernatural feats performed by superhuman forces working through boundary dwellers (people who are close but won't cross on over into the kingdom of God). Make no mistake about it, the Bible contains many indications that evil spirits can perform miracles.[28] It is the way they gain credibility for their agents—the boundary dwellers. Challenge their agents, and these demons become formidable enemies.[29]

- *Verse 14:* ". . . and they go out to the kings of the whole world. . . ." These boundary dwellers, operating in evil spirit-realm power, become Satan's messengers to warn that an invasion is coming (just as the overcomers, symbolized as trumpets and angels, become God's messengers by proclaiming the Word of God and doing the works of Jesus). "The kings of the whole world" symbolizes masses of people, not just rulers.

- *Verse 14:* ". . . to gather them for that battle. . . ." No negotiated peace treaty will result from this war. Any effort by Jesus to invade the beastly world system or the idolatrous false church is sure to meet with strong resistance—both human and demonic.[30] One need only look at the rabid opposition of mainline denominations against miracles of healing, spiritual gifts, and casting out demons to see the church at war (despite all their talk about peace and unity) against anything supernatural.

- *Verse 14:* ". . . on the great day of God Almighty." As we have seen, the day of the Lord is a prophetic symbol for the ongoing comings of Jesus to the individual. The context and wording of this phrase implies that Jesus comes to judge the individuals in the church.

- *Verse 15:* "'Behold I come like a thief!'" He comes suddenly and without warning. He comes to fight against evildoers who accept the mark of ownership (the name or number) of the beast system. He comes to pour out His wrath on those in the church who have refused to heed the warnings of the letters, the seals, and the trumpets (messages).

- *Verse 15:* "'Blessed is he who stays awake and keeps his clothes with him, so that he may not go naked and be shamefully exposed.'" He also comes to bless those who have His seal and are clothed in white garments—the righteous acts of the saints. "Stays awake and keeps his clothes with him" serves as a solemn reminder of two things: 1) that it is very easy to get lulled to sleep spiritually and lose your righteous clothing to the beast system,[31] and 2) that the real danger of slipping into unrighteousness is being caught spiritually naked before God.[32] In Genesis, the consequence of being shamefully exposed was exile from Eden, but in the Revelation the consequence is being cut down by the sword of Jesus.

- *Verse 16:* "Then they [the demon-empowered boundary dwellers] gathered the kings together to the place that in Hebrew is called Armageddon." Again, the term *Armageddon* is a spiritual reference signifying where the ongoing battle takes place—within the individual and in the church.

The verses which follow (17–21) give a vivid, symbolic description of the terrible devastation that Christ and His warriors wreak upon the idolatrous, prostitute church. Using spiritual symbols like history's worst earthquake, fierce thunderstorms, and giant hailstones, John says that God gives Babylon "the cup filled with the wine of the fury of his wrath." This is no slap on the wrist; it is open warfare and total defeat.

So complete is the devastation that the next two full chapters are taken up with the beastly world system's laments over the fall of Babylon.

When Is a Church Not a Church?

Some of the most ominous threats in the Revelation are Jesus' prophetic words to the seven churches.[33] He threatens to deal sternly with churches which cease to act like churches—those which lose their love, fail to do the miraculous works of Jesus, and tolerate evil and idolatry. Now, in chapters 16–18, these promised consequences are fulfilled.

Keep in mind that this is not some future, global event that has not yet taken place. Christ is in the midst of the churches, not off somewhere waiting to come back. He is alive in the spirit realm; He is active; He is involved in the physical realm. This is a timeless, ongoing battle with countless fulfillments.

Consider the church at Ephesus, for example. "I will *come* to you and remove your lampstand from its place," Jesus says.[34] In simple words, "You will cease to be a church." Any church that loses its love and fails to do the supernatural works of Jesus will no longer be the church of Jesus Christ. It, like the church at Sardis,[35] may have a reputation for being alive but will actually be dead to the reality of Christ. It may have a thriving program, strong organization, and many members, but it will be spiritually dead. It will not meet God's standards to be *a church*. Thus, it will become a false (harlot) church that is under the judgment of God.

Even Jesus' promises to overcomers and to those who repent in the seven churches imply terrible fates for the unrepentant and the boundary dwellers. To all those who hear His knock and open the door, He promises: "I will come in and eat with him, and he with me."[36] He promises that overcomers will "eat from the tree of life,"[37] "not be hurt at all by the second death,"[38] be given "some hidden manna," and "a white stone with a new name written on it, known only to him who receives it."[39] They will be given "authority over the nations" and will receive "the morning star."[40] They will be "dressed in white" and not have their names erased from the book of life,[41] and they will receive the "right to sit with [Jesus] on [His] throne."[42] This clearly implies that those who don't hear His knock, repent, and overcome, do not receive any of those promises. Even worse, He fights against them.

Perhaps the most vivid picture of a castaway church is the Laodicean church, which Jesus threatens to spit out of His mouth because its members are lukewarm.[43] The King James Version's "spew you out of my mouth" more correctly captures the revulsion Jesus feels toward rebellious boundary dwellers. It implies a sudden, violent expulsion of something that is sickening to the taste. Jesus said He would rather the boundary dwellers be cold than tepid. Nothing in Scripture seems so repulsive to God as people who have a form of godliness but deny His power.[44] "No man, having put his hand to the plough, and looking back, is fit for the kingdom of God," Jesus said.[45]

Boundary dwellers, like Ananias and Sapphira, want to be identified with the fellowship and miraculous works that go on in the church.[46] They go through all the motions publicly, but they are not willing to pay the price, to yield themselves totally to God. And, like that deceptive couple, they are subject to the wrath of God.

One of Jesus' first actions at the opening of His public ministry was to cleanse the temple.[47] God's judgments always start with the church and, specifically, with individuals within the church.[48] Why? Only a purified and spiritually alive church can establish the kingdom of God among the beastly systems of the world.

What's the bottom line of all this judgment? In chapter sixteen, the boundary-dwelling individuals and churches—those who refuse to go on into the kingdom of God—lose their identity as the people of God and become a part of the beastly world system.

Personal Dimensions of Armageddon

Twentieth-century Christians make a big deal of the church as an organized structure, but Jesus said very little about it. In fact, He mentioned the church only twice in all four Gospels. Both times He was talking to and about individuals.

His first statement about the church came in response to Peter's receiving a personal revelation that Jesus was "the Christ, the Son of the living God."[49] He told Peter that it was upon the "rock" of this truth—personal revelation of Jesus' Lordship—that He would build His church. He went on to give Peter (and all who receive this personal revelation) the "keys of the kingdom of heaven," which is the power to bind and loose spirit-realm forces.

In His only other reference to the church, Jesus talked about one individual sinning against another, and ordered that the offender be taken to the church only as a last resort. "If he refuses to listen even to the church, treat him as you would a pagan or a tax collector," He commanded.[50] In other words, consider him a part of Satan's kingdom (the world), whose mark he bears, not a part of God's kingdom (with the seal of God upon him).

Again, He went on to talk about binding and loosing spirit-realm forces on the earth. Then, He made His famous promise, "Where two or three of you come together in my name, *there I am*" (emphasis added). In ancient Greek, a person's name meant his essence or reality. So Jesus was promising to manifest Himself—to come—whenever and wherever two or more people gathered in His spirit-realm reality.

All this doesn't mean that Jesus feels the church is insignificant. Such a view would be inconsistent with other New Testament Scriptures. But it does mean that Jesus thinks of His church, not as a merely human organization, but as a vital part of Himself—a spiritual organism of which He is the head. This collection of individuals is the earthly manifestation of His heavenly kingdom. His kingdom and His true church are all parts of the same spirit-realm/physical-realm reality, "the body of Christ."[51]

That's why the Revelation is addressed to each person within the church. The battle for the kingdom wages within individuals. Jesus comes to individuals within the church, and His comings bring either blessings and rewards or precipitate "the battle on the great day of God Almighty." Christ Himself comes and fights against false doctrines, unrighteousness, and evil spirit-realm forces within individuals in His church.

Only a remnant of Christians—those who repent and overcome—will cross over the boundary line and enter into the kingdom of God. That remnant of overcomers—the elect—will be protected from and become a part of God's ongoing judgment of the church and the world.

Logic alone cannot explain this spirit-realm/physical-realm reality; rather, understanding comes only through a personal revelation of Jesus as He is today.

"God's judgments always start with the church and, specifically, with individuals within the church. Why? Only a purified and spiritually alive church can establish the kingdom of God among the beastly systems of the world."

The Rider on the White Horse Wages War Against Satan's Kingdom: Revelation 19:11–16

No one else in history has ever been like the rider on the white horse. Let's look closely at Revelation 19:11–16.

The names and descriptions of the rider make it clear that He is Jesus Christ. The rider is called "Faithful and True,"[52] and "his name is the Word of God."[53] He even has a name that "no one but he himself knows," signifying that certain aspects of His spirit-realm reality are beyond human comprehension. "He judges and makes war,"[54] "His eyes are like blazing fire,"[55] "He is dressed in a robe dipped in blood,"[56] "the armies of heaven were following him,"[57] and "Out of his mouth comes a sharp sword with which to strike down the nations."[58] There can be no doubt that this is Jesus Christ in all His spirit-realm reality.

But, in verse 12, a very interesting set of symbols begins to emerge, suggesting that there may be more to this rider's identity. Remember, these are physical symbols of ongoing, spirit-realm/physical-realm realities.

First, John says of the rider on the white horse that "on his head are *many crowns*" (emphasis added). Earlier, we were told that Jesus had only one crown on His head;[59] now He has many. What has happened?

In "the wedding supper of the Lamb,"[60] the bride of Christ (the righteous saints) has lifted her veil and has been united with Him. Christ and His true church have become one.[61] What was represented by one crown is now represented by many crowns.

Second, verse 16 says that "on his robe and on his thigh he has this name written: KING OF KINGS AND LORD OF LORDS." We can understand why He might have a monogram on His robe of righteousness. But why would He engrave the name on His thigh? One possibility is that, in the thick of a battle, foot soldiers might confuse the identity of a rider on a horse. The name on His thigh would be at eye level—easily recognizable by anyone. It may also symbolize that the righteous saints have become bone of His bones and flesh of His flesh.[62] His identity with them is complete. The saints are actually riding with Him in the battle and share in His triumph. In other words, He has "made us to be a kingdom and priests," to reign and rule with Him.[63]

Third, verse 14 says that "the armies of heaven were following him, riding on white horses and dressed in fine linen, white and clean." Note that the armies are *of* heaven, not *from* heaven. Nowhere does it say that this army comes down from heaven. Jesus used this same terminology to describe His disciples as *in* the world but not *of* the world, even as He was not *of* the world.[64] The blood-washed saints belong to the armies of heaven.

A Kingdom of Kings and Priests

Having judged and purified His bride, the true church, and having become one with the saints in white robes at the wedding supper,* Christ now leads His righteous hosts into battle against Satan and his kingdom. This purified and righteous church, even though it may contain only one or two saints in any one of the countless fulfillments, operates in the full power of spirit-realm/physical-realm truths and realities; it proves more than a match for the dragon Satan and his beastly world system. This is an ongoing spirit-realm/physical-realm reality—not a one-time, future event, as the conspirators have led so many to believe. This is the church as God intends it to be.

In prophetic Scripture, a crown symbolizes authority; and we are given crowns. The white horse symbolizes the perfect and irresistible power of God.

---

* The "Wedding Supper of the Lamb" deserves much more treatment than we can give it here and will be dealt with in the next chapter.

All this can only mean that the rider on the white horse is Jesus Christ *and* His Body. We, with Him, are a kingdom of kings and priests God sends into the world to conquer and rule. When we speak His Word, the sharp sword of His mouth becomes a sharp sword in

---

"Face it! Armageddon has always been going on, and it is going on right now! It is within you, it is within the church, and it is wherever the beastly world system seeks to place its mark of ownership on you."

---

our mouths. When we touch the nations (people), our hands become His miraculous hands. When we bind spirit-realm forces on earth, He binds them in heaven. Wherever we are, there He is.

So, who is the rider on the white horse? It is us, with Christ in us.

Armageddon, Now

Face it! Armageddon has always been going on, and it is going on right now! It is within you, it is within the church, and it is wherever the beastly world system seeks to place its mark of ownership on you. It was at hand in the first century; it has been at hand ever since; it is at hand now; it will be at hand in the future. This is no time to hang around on the boundary line between the kingdoms of this world and the kingdom of God. You can get eaten alive by the evil forces stationed there.

So, what should we do? We must bind up the evil spirit-realm forces that seek to control our lives and come into the full realities and truths of Jesus Christ. Then, once we have overcome the evil within ourselves, we must engage and overcome Christ's enemies within the church and throughout the world.

That means:

- We are to hear His knock and open the door to our hearts so the unveiled Christ can come into us and eat with us.

- We are to enter into His supernatural reality through praise, worship, and righteous acts.

- We are to allow the Lamb to break all the seals and open every aspect of our lives to the judgment of God, conquering all the unrighteousness within us so that we can overcome.

- We are to hear and respond to His messages (trumpets) calling us into the battle which rages within the church and in the world.

- We are to act as messengers of His kingdom, sounding the trumpets and pouring out bowls of His wrath (by proclaiming His Word and doing the works of Jesus) upon those boundary-dwelling believers who refuse to hear, repent, and come into the kingdom.

- We are to bind up and rule over evil spirits that are fighting against God's Kingdom.

In short, you and I are the Body of Christ, and we are to fight and win "the battle of the great day of Almighty God" within us, in the church, and in the world. If we do all that, we have His promise that He will place His name and seal upon us, so that we cannot be touched by the second death. We will receive crowns of authority, so that we can rule and reign with Him forever.

How can we do all that? We can do it only as we ride the white horse with Him and live daily in the supernatural power of the unveiled Christ. That becomes possible only when we eat "the wedding supper of the Lamb."

In the next chapter, we'll discover how we can eat that wedding supper.

HOW YOU CAN EAT "THE WEDDING SUPPER"—NOW

Those who conspire against the Apocalypse definitely do not want you to read this chapter. Why? Because it gets right to the heart of the unveiled Christ in all His spirit-realm reality—what the conspirators have worked so feverishly to conceal.

Once you discover the glorious mystery the wedding supper of the Lamb reveals, you'll readily see why the conspirators will do anything to keep masses of Christians from understanding it.

Believe me, covering up this truth has not been an easy chore for the conspirators. They've had to twist, distort, and cover up the reality of literally scores of Scriptures to pull it off. But, because so many Christians don't know what the Bible actually says, and because a future only, up-in-the-sky, one-time, special event called the wedding supper fits so nicely into End Times doctrines, they've been able to trap many people into believing myths and fairy tales about it.

In this chapter, we'll examine how the conspirators have robbed most Christians of this vital reality by surrounding it with fantasies. We'll also see scripturally what the wedding supper of the Lamb really represents. We'll even check out what's on the menu. And finally, we'll discover how you can sit down to the Lord's banquet table and eat a sumptuous feast right now, wherever you are. As we've done throughout this book, we'll stick strictly to the Scriptures and let the Bible interpret itself.

How Myths and Fairy Tales About the Wedding Supper Keep Millions Of Christians Spiritually Starved

Traditional End Times teachers paint a scenario something like this. First, the church, whom they call the Bride of Christ, is whisked away into the sky, where millions of Christians sit down at a physical table that stretches to infinity and eat their fill of heavenly hash.

Many say this feast lasts for seven years, while the great tribulation is wreaking havoc on the earth. Then, these stuffed saints come back and watch while God destroys the world in the Battle of Armageddon. After that, Satan is bound up in chains and thrown into hell, and all the saints reign with Christ for precisely one thousand years. (Just what they will reign over is not exactly clear, since all the troublemakers will be gone, and even lions will be lying down with lambs.) When the one thousand years are over, for some inexplicable reason, Satan will be let loose again to deceive masses of people all over the earth. Eventually, he'll be thrown back into the bottomless pit, however, and the saints will rule and reign with Christ forever—somewhere.

Don't be surprised if that scenario doesn't exactly fit the sequence of events you have been taught. Controversy abounds over the details of when, where, and how the wedding supper and all these other events will supposedly take place. Churches—even whole denominations—have split over whether these events happen before or after the Tribulation, or the Millennium; or whether they take place in heaven or back on earth in the New Jerusalem.

The only two points all End Times teachers seem to agree on are 1) that a literal, physical wedding supper is going to happen someday, somewhere; and 2) that its main significance for now is to warn us to be ready.

Why is the idea of the wedding supper of the Lamb as a future-only, up-in-the-sky, one-time, grand event so filled with inconsistencies and doctrinal controversies? It's because making this feast a once-only event and pushing it out into the future is a doctrine of man, not a revelation of God. It is based on the reasonings and imagination of human beings, not on the Word of God.

This devastating approach contributes to spiritual famine among the very people with whom Jesus longs to eat the wedding supper

---

"Making [the wedding supper of the Lamb] a once-only event and pushing it out into the future is a doctrine of man, not a revelation of God. It is based on the reasonings and imagination of human beings, not on the Word of God."

---

here and now. Of course, the conspirators love it, because Christians who are suffering from spiritual malnutrition offer little or no resistance to all the evil spirit-realm forces or to the beast systems they operate.

What Does the Bible Actually Say About the Wedding Supper of the Lamb?

An amazing number of doctrines have built up around the wedding supper of the Lamb, especially considering that the expression appears only once in the whole Bible—in Revelation 19:9. John simply says that the angel told him, "Write: 'Blessed are those who are invited to the wedding supper of the Lamb!'" And he adds, "These are the true words of God." That's it!* All other references are implied.

This does not mean that all the talk about the wedding supper is much ado about nothing. This spiritual reality signifies the culmination

---

* Note: In Revelation 19:7 there is a reference to the "wedding (or marriage) of the Lamb," but the word "supper" is not used. These obviously refer to the same thing.

of Old Testament prophecies, expresses the fulfillment of the gospel story, and ushers in the full reality of the new heaven and new earth. It is, therefore, vital that those who are serious about receiving Christ's kingdom[1] both understand and participate fully in it.

So what is the wedding supper, and what does it mean? It is a Revelation symbol describing the kingdom of God as an ongoing spirit-realm/physical-realm reality—not a one-time, future event. This physical symbol of a spiritual/physical reality is the same type of metaphor Jesus used in describing Himself as the bread of life, which could take away our hunger for anything else,[2] and as the water which could forever quench our spiritual thirst.[3]

Like everything else in the Revelation, it was at hand for first century Christians, it has been at hand ever since, it is at hand for us now and will be at hand in the future. Its fulfillments are countless.

I don't understand how Christians who readily accept Jesus' statements about the bread and wine (at the Last Supper) as spiritual symbols of His body and blood[4] insist on interpreting the wedding supper of the Lamb literally—especially when the latter term is surrounded by symbolic language.

Jesus' Teachings Conflict with the One-Time, Future Event Theory

You have to distort Jesus' teachings considerably to make the wedding supper into a one-time, future event. Let me illustrate. In the parable of the wedding feast[5] (which is often used to support the doctrine of a future event in heaven), Jesus included these statements:

> But when the king came in to see the guests, he noticed a man there who was not wearing wedding clothes. "Friend," he asked, "how did you get in here without wedding clothes?" The man was speechless.
>
> Then the king told the attendants, "Tie him hand and foot, and throw him outside, into the darkness, where there will be weeping and gnashing of teeth." For many are invited, but few are chosen.[6]

How did that guy get in there? Think about it. If this is a one-time, future event that is to take place in heaven *after the Rapture,* how did the man get there? Was he raptured by mistake? Was he the original Rapture-buster? Did he grab hold of some saint's heel and hitch a ride? Was he a stowaway on the good old gospel ship?

Also, think about this: was he thrown back to earth?

No, the wedding feast symbolizes the ongoing reality of God's kingdom on the earth. It is not a one-shot, physical happening up in the sky.

Consider another descriptive kingdom teaching of Jesus which many connect with the wedding supper. Jesus had gathered His disciples into a private room to celebrate His final Passover with them the night before He was crucified.

> And he said to them, "I have eagerly desired to eat this Passover with you before I suffer. For I tell you, I will not eat it again until it finds fulfillment in the kingdom of God." After taking the cup, he gave thanks and said, "Take this and divide it among you. For I tell you I will not drink again of the fruit of the vine until the kingdom of God comes." And he took bread, gave thanks and broke it, and gave it to them, saying "This is my body given for you; do this in remembrance of me."[7]

"Aha!" say the End Times teachers, "that's a prediction of a one-time, future event in the sky." Holy Communion, they contend, is

---

> ## "The wedding feast symbolizes the ongoing reality of God's kingdom on the earth. It is not a one-shot, physical happening up in the sky."

---

merely an earthly and physical act we do in remembrance of Jesus' crucifixion—an expression of our hope for the wedding supper. Where and when will such an event take place? According to the end-timers, it will occur in the sky, after the Rapture, when the kingdom of God (or the later Kingdom) comes.

But notice what Jesus said a few verses later in this same discourse. The disciples were arguing among themselves about who would be considered greatest in the kingdom.

> You are those who have stood by me in my trials. And I confer on you a kingdom, just as my father conferred one on me, so that you may eat and drink at my table in my kingdom and sit on thrones, judging the twelve tribes of Israel.[8]

Jesus says, "I *confer* [not will confer] on you a kingdom" (emphasis added). Does that sound like something yet to come? No, it was there, it was then; and it's here, it's now. "Just as my father conferred [past tense] one on me."

Note, too, that Jesus, after promising not to eat and drink until His kingdom had come, ate and drank with His disciples on several occasions after His resurrection.

This idea of dividing the coming of God's kingdom into two stages—a limited kingdom now and a full kingdom later—is a doctrine of man, not a truth of God's Word. Nowhere did Jesus teach a two-stage kingdom, and it is not taught anywhere else in the Bible. Yet, our understanding of the kingdom of God determines our concept of the wedding supper.

So let's take a closer look at what the Scriptures tell us about this vital, spirit-realm/physical-realm reality.

When, Where, and What
Is the Wedding Supper of the Lamb?

The idea of a wedding supper does not originate in the New Testament. Old Testament writers make many references to God's preparing a banquet table for His servants.[9]

If we had space, we could examine each of those references in detail and show how they are connected to the kingdom parables of Jesus and the message of the Revelation. I urge you to study them for yourself. You'll be amazed at how strikingly the Old Testament references resemble the New Testament references to feasts and eating.

Let me illustrate the similarity by citing one of the most vivid descriptions, found in Proverbs 9:1–6.

Wisdom has built her house. She has hewed out its seven pillars. She has prepared her meat and mixed her wine; she has also set her table. She has sent out her maids, and she calls from the highest point of the city, "Let all who are simple come in here!" She says to those who lack judgment, "Come, eat my food, drink the wine I have mixed. Leave your simple ways, and you will live; walk in the way of understanding."

This passage also describes the kingdom of God—eating and drinking. Remember how in Jesus' parables the servants were always calling people to come in and eat the banquet that had been prepared?

"Wisdom has built her house," the writer says, using a symbol that crops up repeatedly throughout the Bible. It is the house established by the Lord,[10] the "house of the Lord,"[11] a "house of prayer for all nations,"[12] a house built on a rock,[13] and the "Father's house" of many rooms (dwelling places) where Jesus went to prepare a place for His disciples[14]—to mention only a few of the many references to God's house, the house of wisdom.

The Apostle Peter adds a new dimension to the concept of God's house. He speaks of Jesus as the living stone, and says that "you also, like living stones, are being built into a spiritual house."[15]

Also, notice the Proverbs reference to the seven pillars. That's not there by accident. That language connects it to the Revelation message, where John speaks of seven churches, seven messages, seven seals, and seven bowls of wrath. Seven is the prophetic number for completion.

And what is this wisdom which has set her table? "The fear of the Lord is the beginning of wisdom, and knowledge of the Holy One is understanding," the writer of Proverbs explains a few verses after the above passage.[16]

The wisdom and knowledge referred to here are not human wisdom and knowledge, because they only come from fearing the Lord. This is supernatural understanding—divine revelation. When we recognize the absolute sovereignty of God, He begins to reveal to us His spirit-realm reality.

What we're talking about is the great "mystery" of God which Paul describes so eloquently in his letter to the Ephesians.[17] He says emphatically that this "mystery," which is revealed to us by the Holy

Spirit is none other than Jesus Christ.[18] Wisdom and knowledge, then, are the revelation to believers of the mystery of Christ.

So the feast table is set in the house of God, which is made up of the lively stones of Jesus Christ and His saints. Yet, we are invited to partake of the feast. The feast takes place spiritually within us—it is in us and among us. It is within the kingdom of heaven.[19]

All this means that the wedding supper of the Lamb is not a meal that God will someday serve in outer space; it is an ongoing spirit-realm/physical-realm reality that continuously takes place within the church and in the individual. Jesus invites "anyone [who] hears my voice and opens the door."[20] It was at hand in the first century, it has been at hand ever since, it is at hand now, and it will be at hand in the future.

One of the best descriptions of the wedding supper of the Lamb occurs in the parable of the wedding feast.

> Jesus spoke to them again in parables, saying: "The kingdom of heaven is like a king who prepared a wedding banquet for his son. He sent his servants to those who had been invited to the banquet to tell them to come, but they refused to come.
>
> "Then he sent some more servants and said, 'Tell those who have been invited that I have prepared my dinner: my oxen and fattened cattle have been butchered, and everything is ready. Come to the wedding banquet.'
>
> "But they paid no attention and went off—one to his field, another to his business. The rest seized his servants, mistreated them and killed them. The king was enraged. He sent his army and destroyed those murderers and burned their city.
>
> "Then he said to his servants, 'The wedding banquet is ready, but those I invited did not deserve to come. Go to the street corners and invite to the banquet anyone you find.' So the servants went out into the streets and gathered all the people they could find, both good and bad, and the wedding hall was filled with guests."[21]

This parable is deeply rooted in the ancient wedding traditions of the Israelites. They held a banquet after each wedding, much like we hold a reception today. Those wedding banquets, however, were not short, cake-cutting ceremonies, with light refreshments served. They typically lasted for days—often a week or more—and featured giant smorgasbords on which people gorged themselves almost around the clock. The people sang, danced, and played games.

Jesus likened the kingdom of God in the spirit realm to the Israelite wedding celebration. The writer of the Revelation had the same image in mind when he spoke of the wedding supper of the Lamb.

"The wedding supper of the Lamb is not a meal that God will someday serve in outer space; it is an ongoing spirit-realm/physical-realm reality that continuously takes place within the church and in the individual."

The Host of the Wedding Feast

The gala wedding feasts stood in sharp contrast to the somber ceremonial fasts, concocted from the Mosaic Law which the religious leaders required the people to observe rigorously. Public fasts were characterized by stark silence, ceremonial cleansings, public offerings, sober reflection, and religious rites. Thus, the fasts of the Pharisees represented all that was superficial and empty in their religiosity, while the wedding feasts represented all that was alive, fresh, and new about the kingdom of God.

Early in His ministry, Jesus made His preference quite clear. He performed His first public miracle—turning water into wine—at a wedding banquet.[22] Yet, although Jesus apparently fasted personally and privately, He seemed to have little enthusiasm for the ritualistic fasts of the Pharisees. In fact, He often soundly criticized the Scribes and Pharisees for their fasting habits.

His zest for feasting was so pronounced that He was accused of being "a glutton and a drunkard." Even loyal John the Baptist questioned Him about His disdain for public fasts. "How is it that we and the Pharisees fast," John's disciples asked, "but your disciples do not fast?" To that, Jesus responded with a question and a statement: "How can the guests of the bridegroom mourn while he is with them? The time will come when the bridegroom is taken from them; then they will fast."[23]

Jesus is obviously implying that the bridegroom's presence makes the difference in fasting and feasting. The bridegroom's presence also makes the difference in dead religious ritual and life-giving reality.

In the next few verses, Jesus used the parables of the new patch on an old garment and the new wine in old skins to indicate that the coming kingdom of God represented something new and radically different from what had gone before.

What is so different about the new order of the kingdom of God? It is the abiding presence of the Bridegroom. And who is the Bridegroom? There can be no doubt that He is none other than Jesus Christ. Jesus is the central figure of all the kingdom parables. He is the Good Shepherd who goes out looking for the lost sheep, He is the Good Samaritan who rescues the man who had been beaten and robbed, and He is the Bridegroom who goes out to meet the five wise virgins. He was indeed taken away from His disciples at the crucifixion, and He is still far removed from many people who are caught up in dead religion today.

Therefore, it is not surprising that the writer of the Revelation characterizes the great banquet as the wedding supper of the Lamb. Jesus Christ invites all people to "come and eat."[24] The spirit-realm presence of the Bridegroom in our life determines whether we are fasting or feasting spiritually.

The Nature of the Wedding Feast

Does all this mean that Jesus really was a glutton and drunkard, and that He advocated overeating and drunkenness? Certainly not! This is another good reason not to make the wedding supper a one-time, physical event and shove it out into the future. Is God's objective to turn us all into gluttons and drunkards? Even if you go through the linguistic exercise of saying we'll have glorified bodies, the idea of saints gorging themselves on physical food seems more like pagan revelry than righteous worship and celebration. The very idea opposes everything the Bible teaches and stands for.

Jesus often used the symbols of physical food and drink to describe the spirit-realm/physical-realm reality of God's kingdom. Notice how many of His parables and figures of speech had to do with food and water or wine. On several occasions He miraculously provided food for His followers. He even promised that His Father would provide food for all who put their trust in Him.[25]

Yet Jesus made it abundantly clear that the kingdom does not come through eating and drinking in the physical sense.[26] Obviously, He intends these physical symbols to refer to the spiritual kingdom of God. Why, then, is it so hard for most people to accept the idea that the wedding supper is a physical symbol of a spiritual/physical reality? Much of the answer lies in the fact that most of us have been taught all our lives to expect a literal table, spread with all kinds of goodies, someday, somewhere. But it runs much deeper than doctrinal conditioning.

The Problem Is the Veil

The highlight of the ancient Jewish wedding ceremony was the thrilling moment when the bride removed her veil so she could see and be seen by the bridegroom, face to face, and could eat the wedding banquet. And yes, she and the bridegroom could unite in the ceremonial kiss that publicly sealed their marriage.

Once she removed the veil, she was never to put it back over her face. Never again would it interfere with her union with the bridegroom or with her partaking of all his sumptuous feasts. This act symbolized that the two of them had become one flesh.

John chose the term "the wedding supper of the Lamb" to describe the full, spirit-realm union of Christ and His bride because this ceremony was so significant. At the moment we remove the veil, we receive the full revelation of Jesus Christ; and we can begin to eat the wedding supper of the Lamb. What's more, we don't have to wait until we're raptured out of this world to do it. Now, if you think that is exciting, just wait until you discover later in this chapter what's on the menu!

But first, we have to remove the veil.

What is this veil that keeps us from seeing and knowing and being fully, spiritually united with Christ? It is quite simply our *mental image of Jesus.*[27] As long as we insist on seeing Jesus in just His earthly ministry, we cannot receive and experience Him in all His present, glorious reality—we cannot see Him face to face and eat the wedding supper with Him.

Why? Because He is more than Jesus of Nazareth; He is the risen, unveiled Jesus of the Apocalypse. Many people are like the women who went to the cemetery looking for Jesus on the morning of His resurrection. The angels asked them, "Why do you look for the living among the dead?"[28] They were looking for Jesus as just a man, but He was in the spirit realm.

Oddly enough, many would argue with that analogy. "Oh, no!" they'd protest, "We believe in the risen Christ." Yet, if you ask them to tell you where this risen and ascended Christ is, they'll tell you He's off somewhere in space, but they are expecting Him to come back at any time and set up a material kingdom in a temple in Jerusalem. All that sounds pretty fleshly to me. It's pushing us back in history to the old covenant, or the old law. It's keeping Jesus veiled.

Most Christians are caught up mentally and emotionally in the pre-glorified Christ. After all, that's what most of us have read, heard, and studied. We picture Him as the little baby born in a manger, or as the poor guy in Jerusalem who got hung on the cross. Now all that's important, but it is history. *He's not like that anymore.*

In order to eat the wedding supper of the Lamb, however, we have to remove that veil. We have to move beyond just thinking of Jesus in terms of His earthly ministry, as important as that is. We have to worship Him in spirit and truth, as He now is and will always be. We have to take the veil off our faces so we won't worship Him after the flesh, and that can happen only when we see Him as He is now.

Why must we remove the veil? Because it affects the way we think of Jesus, the way we study Him, and the way we worship Him. When, for example, we study the Revelation to grasp the full reality of its message and receive the blessings it promises, we can't limit ourselves by thinking of Jesus solely in terms of His earthly ministry. Jesus is now fully unveiled.

If you want the latest, most recent description of Jesus, read Revelation 1:12–18. This passage depicts Him with a sword coming out of his mouth, with fiery eyes, with feet of bronze, and with a voice that sounds like rushing water. Now if you're trying to visualize that literally, or if you're thinking about most art which depicts Jesus, you're just not going to be able to grasp that revelation. If you are just focusing on the earthly ministry of Jesus, the veil will prevent you from eating the wedding supper with Him in the spirit realm, right now.

Of course, you can be saved and bound for heaven. You can go to church, teach Sunday school, sing in the choir, and go through all the religious motions, but still not have the glorious intimacy with Christ

---

"What is this veil that keeps us from seeing and knowing and being fully, spiritually united with Christ? It is quite simply our mental image of Jesus."

---

that He desires. Why? You can't see Him face to face, because you're still looking for a face that doesn't exist anymore. That veil, again, is your mental and emotional attachment to His earthly form. He's not like that anymore.

It's important to remember that the word *Apocalypse* means to lift a veil, or to remove a shroud or curtain, in order to resolve a mystery. And right here, in the symbolism of the wedding supper of the Lamb, that Apocalypse of Jesus Christ reaches its peak. It's as if everything that precedes Revelation 19:9 is prelude, and everything that follows it is explanation. If you miss the full reality of this glorious truth, you'll miss the deepest intimacy that Christ longs to share with you right here, right now. But to grasp that reality, you must lift the veil.

Lifting the Veil

The symbolism of the veil runs much deeper than Jewish wedding tradition. Its roots are anchored in the worship symbols of God's old covenant with the nation Israel. The tabernacle, the symbol of God's presence with His people during their wilderness wanderings,[29] was divided into two parts: the Holy Place and the Holy of Holies (or Most

Holy Place).* This was where God promised to visit the people and
receive their acts of worship. Only the high priest could go into the
Holy of Holies to offer the sacrifices of the people and to commune
with God. He was the intermediary between man and God.

A curtain (the King James Version calls it a veil), reaching from
the ceiling to the floor, sealed off the Holy of Holies. It was this curtain, or veil, which was torn asunder at the crucifixion of Jesus, signifying that He had become the eternal High Priest and that, through
Him, every human being now had free access to God.[30]

The external regulations about food and drink and the various ceremonial rites and sacrifices gave way to the new order when Christ
came and made a sacrifice for all people of all times. The writer of
Hebrews explains how.

> When Christ came as High Priest of the good things that are already
> here, he went through the greater and more perfect tabernacle that
> is not man-made, that is to say, not a part of this creation. He did not
> enter by means of the blood of goats and calves; but he entered the
> Most Holy Place once for all by his own blood, having obtained eter-
> nal redemption.[31]

So Jesus' crucifixion replaced the ritualistic, physical sacrifices offered each year by the high priest under the old law, with the constant, abiding, spirit-realm presence of God, through Christ.

This explains why we don't have to keep going back through those
physical sacrifices year after year. We don't have to keep crucifying
Jesus. He is alive in the spirit realm forever. We have free and open
access to God all day, every day—now! Notice the way Hebrews expresses it:

> But now he has appeared for all at the end of the ages to do away
> with sin by the sacrifice of himself.[32]

Observe that it does not say he *will appear* . . . at the end of the
ages, but that "he *has appeared* once for all at the end of the ages"
(emphasis added). It has already happened; He is here, now, in the
spirit realm.

---

* The same configuration was used in the later, more permanent structures
called temples and synagogues.

God has torn away the veil that enshrouded Him in mystery. In Christ, the mystery is revealed. All that remains is for us to remove the veil from our own faces so we can see Him as clearly as He longs for us to see Him.

Once we remove the veil, we are free to eat the wedding supper of the Lamb with Him, to be married to Him, and to bear offspring (new Christians) as a result of our marital union with Him.

But *we* have to remove that veil; God cannot do that for us. We have to give up our fleshly ideas of Jesus and lay aside our fleshly worship in order to see Him face to face in the spirit realm—in order to eat the wedding supper with Him.

How do we remove that veil? We'll see shortly. But first, let's look at what's on the menu for the wedding banquet. I believe that, once you see what we're going to be eating, your appetite will be so great that you won't want to wait for some future event in the sky. You'll long to dive right in—here and now.

What's on the Menu
For the Wedding Supper of the Lamb?

What do we eat at the wedding supper of the Lamb? Again, don't take my word for it. Read the menu yourself from God's Word. The Bible proclaims that we *eat the Lamb!* We actually eat of Christ.

Eating of the Lamb

Exodus 16:14–36 describes how flakes of manna appeared on the desert floor for Israel during their forty years in the desert and how the people had enough to eat each day. They couldn't hold it over or it would spoil, except on the seventh day. The Israelites ate manna—physical food that God provided—until they reached the border of Canaan.

Later, Numbers 11:7–9 tells about some more manna coming down from heaven. This manna, however, was like a coriander seed and looked like resin. The people gathered it, ground it in a hand mill, and cooked it into cakes. It tasted like something made with olive oil. So the manna was getting better. And it gets even better as you move through Scripture.

Psalm 78:23–25 says, "He gave a command to the skies above and opened the doors of the heavens; he rained down manna for the people to eat, he gave them the grain of heaven. Men ate the bread of the angels; he sent them all the food they could eat."

Keep in mind that everything in the Old Testament is a type of the spiritual truth in the new covenant. This is important because it helps explain what we eat at the wedding supper of the Lamb.

Jesus once spoke about the Old Testament manna we've been describing. The crowd which thronged around Him asked,

> "What immaculate sign then will you give that we may see it and believe you? What will you do? Our forefathers ate manna in the desert; as it is written; 'He gave them bread from the heavens to eat.'"[33]

What did Jesus say? He switched from natural, or physical, food to spiritual food. "I tell you the truth, it is not Moses who has given you the bread from heaven, but it is my Father who gives you the true bread of heaven. For the bread of God is he who comes down from heaven and gives life to the world."[34]

But He doesn't stop there. He gets very precise, declaring in the strongest terms exactly what He's talking about: "I am the bread of life."[35] Three verses later, He explains, "I am the living bread that came down from Heaven. If a man eats of this bread, he will live forever. This bread is my flesh, which I will give for the life of the world."[36]

So Jesus is the manna, the "angel food." How can we eat of Him if we are still thinking of Him as an earthly man? We can't. We've got to get through the veil and into the spirit, because we eat Him as a spiritual/physical reality.

More than Showbread

We are talking about much more than the physical ritual of taking communion. Communion is a physical-realm act of obedience and that can be part of this, but what's really vital is the spiritual reality behind it.

If you went back and read Hebrews 9, you discovered that there was consecrated bread in the holy place, the outer chamber of the tabernacle. Everything had a two-fold exhibition. Tablets of stone were given twice, for example. One set forth the flesh covenant, the other the spiritual covenant. There were two different kinds of bread. The consecrated bread (the showbread) was in the outer chamber and the hidden manna was in the inner chamber. These things don't just happen by chance.

There are two great works: one of salvation and one of the kingdom. One is saving truth; the other is a purifying reality. The manna that fell on the ground would last only for a day, typifying the transi-

---

"Great masses of nominal churches teach that you cannot have this fullness in Christ until you get to heaven. They say you are not able to eat the wedding supper here and now. Thus, millions of Christians are starving."

---

tory blessings and nourishment of just a salvation state. Now, spiritually, anyone can eat that bread. That bread is Jesus, and eating of it will get you saved.

But the term *hidden manna* indicates a permanent blessedness, a richness in our spiritual lives while we dwell in the Holy of Holies in Him, under the direct operation of the Holy Spirit. We eat this hidden manna at the wedding supper of the Lamb. It is available only for those who come through the veil and see Him face to face, who eat of Him and live in a marriage relationship with the glorified Christ. This requires spiritual revelation.

Great masses of nominal churches teach that you cannot have this fullness in Christ until you get to heaven. They say you are not able to eat the wedding supper here and now. Thus, millions of Christians are starving. Yet, eating this hidden manna is what being in Christ (not just having Christ in us) means—we eat of Him, here and now.

How do we know this? It's not some idea I've concocted. Revelation 2:17 says, "To him who overcomes, I will give some of the hidden manna." Keep in mind that, as we have seen, every message to the churches is to the individuals in that church, and all the messages are for individuals in all the churches. Hidden manna is one of the promises of the kingdom. This is what we eat at "the wedding supper of the Lamb." It is spiritual manna that won't melt when the sun comes out and the heat gets turned on. It won't rot, because it's the everlasting manna.

We Become What We Eat

An event from the life of Jesus gives some indication of how wonderful and powerful this spiritual manna is. Jesus' disciples, disturbed that He had not eaten in some time, urged Him to eat something. "I have food to eat that you know nothing about," He told them.[37]

Of course, like all today who still hang onto the veil of an earthly Jesus, the disciples thought He was talking about physical food. "Could someone have brought him food?" they asked.[38]

"My food," Jesus said, "is to do the will of him who sent me."[39] And, now that the veil has been removed, those who eat of His hidden manna at the wedding supper find that it gives them the power to do the works of Jesus.

Science has proven that what we take in through our mouths greatly impacts our bodies and even affects our minds and emotions. We actually become a product of what we eat. Likewise, what goes in through our eyes and ears greatly impacts our spirits. If we eat religious junk food, we become spiritually anemic and unfit. But, if we keep eating the hidden manna, we become spiritually healthy and robust. If we eat what Jesus ate, we become as Jesus is.

What is this hidden manna? It is the fullness of the Word of God, because Jesus is the Word. We eat of Him; we digest Him; we bring Him inside.

As we continue to eat of Him, we come more into His likeness. We eat of His life, His truth, His attributes, His perfection, His overcoming power, His mind, His self-control, His health, His perfection, His compassion, His long-suffering, His love, His peace, His joy. We eat platters and platters of all these things at the wedding supper. It's not glorified turkey. It's not heavenly hash. It's Lamb. And we can

> **"What is this hidden manna? It is the fullness of the Word of God, because Jesus is the Word. We eat of Him; we digest Him; we bring Him inside."**

partake of Him because He comes. It's a spiritual truth. We eat His fullness through His Word, now.

That's why Jesus said, "I have food to eat that you know nothing about." He was talking about hidden manna. Jesus gives us this hidden manna when He comes to dine with us inside our spirits.

How Can You Share in the Wedding Supper Of the Lamb Right Now?

By now, I hope you are hungry to eat the fullness of Christ at the wedding supper of the Lamb, because we're going to see how you can do just that.

As with everything else in this book, I don't want to make a doctrine out of eating the wedding supper. It is not a mental/emotional experience—it is an ongoing, spiritual/physical reality.

All Is Now Ready

Spiritually hungry? Why not sit down to the Lord's banquet table and take in a sumptuous, spiritual feast? When? Right now! Where? Right where you are! How? Let's search the Scriptures to find out.

Jesus gave two parables—the parable of the wedding banquet and the parable of the ten virgins[40]—which offer insights into how we can open ourselves to receive the wedding supper. Let's look at three key issues in these parables.

(1) We have to prepare ourselves to receive the Bridegroom. The key issue in the parable of the wedding banquet has two dimensions: being clean and having on wedding clothes. We have to be prepared to receive the Bridegroom.

Our preparation begins with purifying our hearts. "Blessed are the pure in heart, for they shall *see God*," Jesus said.[41] That simply means we've got to get Babylon out of us before we can operate in the spirit realm. We all have corrupted flesh. Jude alludes to this cleansing process as turning away from all the self-sufficiency and evil of the flesh, as "hating even the clothing stained by corrupted flesh."[42] As we constantly repent and open our heart, soul, mind, and body to Christ, His blood cleanses us.

When we are pure in heart, we are ready to put on the wedding clothes. And what are the wedding clothes? According to the great multitude of Revelation 19, they are "fine linen, bright and clean."[43] So that there could be no doubt as to what this means, John explains in parentheses: "(Fine linen stands for the righteous acts of the saints.)"

Jesus listed some of the righteous acts of the saints. "Then the righteous will ask Him: 'Lord, when did we see you hungry and feed you, or thirsty and give you something to drink? When did we see you a stranger and invite you in, or needing clothes and clothe you? When did we see you sick or in prison and go to visit you?' And the king will reply: 'I tell you the truth, whatever you did for one of the least of these brothers of mine, you did for me.'"[44] Now those are righteous acts. You'll find others throughout the Bible.

So, preparing ourselves to meet the Bridegroom involves becoming pure in heart (getting our sins forgiven and motives and morals right) and doing the works that Jesus did.

(2) We have to open ourselves to spirit-realm reality. One of the key issues in the parable of the ten virgins is being filled with and energized by the Holy Spirit, as symbolized by the oil.

The wedding supper of the Lamb takes place in the spirit realm. Why? Because that's where the Bridegroom dwells. And, to eat with the Bridegroom, you have to go where He has spread the table.

How do you do that? Again, there are two dimensions: giving up the dominance of worldly, fleshly thinking and operating in the spirit realm.

In 1 Corinthians 10, Paul says that we're not to eat and drink food that is sacrificed to idols. "Demon food," he calls it. What makes it demon food? It is idolatry—elevating the flesh to dominance over the spirit. It includes religious words and actions rooted in the flesh, sacrificed to fleshly religion.

How deeply should we shun the works of the flesh? "So, from now on we regard no one from a worldly point of view [or after the flesh]. Though we once regarded Christ in this way, we do so no longer."[45] We aren't to look at anyone through the eyes of the flesh, including Jesus—especially Jesus. How do we want to know Him? Through the spirit. Why? Paul explains it this way: "Therefore, if anyone is in Christ, he is a new creation; the old has gone, the new has come!"[46] It's the difference between Christ being *in you* and you being *in Christ*. You can be in the Holy Place with Christ in you. But you can't

---

"Preparing ourselves to meet the Bridegroom involves becoming pure in heart (getting our sins forgiven and motives and morals right) and doing the works that Jesus did."

---

be in the Most Holy Place without you being in Christ. You have to go through the veil of Jesus' flesh[47] to go into the Most Holy Place, where the wedding supper takes place.

We need to focus beyond the earthly ministry of Jesus and onto His present-day, glorified reality. This is a supernatural phenomenon. God can only work with us and share full intimacy with us to the degree that we are willing to behold the glorified Christ. The bride must remove her veil in order to eat at the banquet.

Once we have given up the dominance of worldly, fleshly thinking, we can go on to the second dimension of operating in the spirit. We can worship Christ in spirit and in truth, in the reality in which He now exists.

John was carried away in the spirit to see these revelations, as we must be. The Holy Spirit will then energize us, sustain us, and bring us face to face with Jesus. As we yield our spirits to the Holy Spirit— through praise and worship, prayer, reading, meditation, dwelling, and obeying the Word—He presents us to the Bridegroom for the wedding feast.

(3) We have to stay spiritually alert for the comings of Jesus. The other key issue in the parable of the ten virgins is that we must be spiritually alert to the comings of Jesus.

As we have seen in previous chapters, the kingdom of God *has come*. There's no reason to wait for some future event. The waiting is finished. It was finished at Pentecost. The door is open in Christ, now and forever. We can sit at His table and eat now, as the bride, as the Holy City, as the true church of Christ. But we must be alert and ready, not looking into the sky for some mansion.

Christ can come to us in countless ways—through some person (or people), through circumstances, through the words of Scripture, through direct revelation, through an appearance. Christ is God, and He can come any way He chooses. Our task is not to try to figure out how or when He will come to us, but to keep the eyes and ears of our spirits attuned for His comings at all times. "My sheep listen to my voice; I know them, and they follow me."[48]

And what happens when we listen to His voice? "If anyone hears my voice and opens the door, I will come in and eat with him."[49]

But don't forget, Christ is flesh and spirit. He can speak with a physical voice if He so chooses, but He longs for us to stay alert to hear His spiritual voice. He can appear in the physical realm, but we are also to watch for His appearances in the spiritual realm.

What Does It All Mean?

The glorious reality of the Revelation is that we don't have to wait for some future, pie-in-the-sky event to occur. We can be married to Jesus right now, and we can eat His wedding supper on a day-to-day basis.

As we open the door, He will come in and eat with us. We don't need to be raptured away. He comes to us, inside us. First we become betrothed, or engaged to Him, by accepting Jesus as our Savior. Then, we prepare ourselves by purifying our hearts and doing the righteous acts of the saints, by putting on the wedding garment. As we prepare to become equally yoked, to be joined in marriage to Him, we can lift our veil so we can see Him face to face and eat of Him. Then we can have an intimate relationship with Jesus (because we are married to Him), and we can reign and rule with Him as His bride. From this union with Him, we're impregnated with the incorruptible seed of God. We reproduce spiritually.

Now the harlot church and the beast system teach that we aren't married to Christ yet. If what they say is true, we must be carrying on an adulterous affair and having illegitimate children. When we're married, we're the bride, and the marriage bed is undefiled.

But it's kind of hard to eat the wedding supper of the Lamb if you still have the veil of Jesus' earthly ministry over your face. Take off the veil so you can see Him face to face as He is today. Start eating, start making love to Him, and start bearing children by Him.

These spiritual metaphors constitute the profound mystery Paul spoke about in Ephesians 5. This is where a Christian moves into the fullness of Christ—not just being saved but learning how to operate in the spirit realm. And we can have that kind of relationship with Him only in the spirit.

Within the veil is the place of communion with God, total authority, full life, infinite power—perfect everything. And, it's all contained in Him.

We don't have to hope for a Rapture to eat the wedding supper of the Lamb. It is available now. God has brought heaven down to us. It's in the church. It's in you and among you. It's been going on for centuries. It's going on today. It will go on tomorrow.

Are you fasting or feasting?

WHY SEVEN YEARS DON'T MAKE A WEEK NOR A THOUSAND YEARS A MILLENNIUM

What do the Scriptures actually say about a seven-year period called the Great Tribulation? Nothing!

That's right! A one-time, future-only, seven-year tribulation period is another fabrication of man; nowhere does the Bible contain such a prophecy.

Yet who of us has not heard dire predictions of a literal, seven-year period of unimaginable horrors called the Great Tribulation? It will occur, many of the conspirators say, immediately after Christians have been raptured out of the earth and are off in space eating the wedding supper of the Lamb.

During this seven-year period, they say, God's judgments on the earth will be so terrible that men will literally gnaw their tongues in anguish and cry for the rocks and mountains to fall on them. When that's over, according to the theory, the saints will come back to the earth, watch God wipe out all His enemies in the Battle of Armageddon, and then will reign with Christ for exactly one thousand years.

But there's one major problem these time-line theorists haven't been able to work out: their theory simply doesn't fit with the Scriptures. They either ignore or twist out of proportion a number of prophetic passages to make this time-line doctrine work. As a result, they have to keep changing their predictions of when the so-called events will occur.

As we'll see in this chapter, all we need to do to make all the pieces of this great mystery fit is to recognize that these prophecies are figurative and timeless—not literal, physical, and chronological.

We'll begin by exploring what the Scriptures actually say about the Great Tribulation. Later in the chapter, we'll look more closely at the Millennium. As we go along, we'll let Scriptures interpret Scriptures to clarify that they are talking about ongoing spiritual truths and realities, not one-time, future events. Finally, we'll discover what the Great Tribulation, the Millennium, and related symbols mean to us today in light of the Apocalypse.

What Do the Scriptures Actually Teach About the Great Tribulation?

First, let's examine the Great Tribulation doctrine. The term appears only once in the Bible—in Revelation 7:14. It was at hand in the first century and still is at hand for us. Of course, the word *tribulation* appears many times throughout the Bible. It is often translated *affliction, persecution, trouble,* or *suffering.*[1] Various translators use those words interchangeably.

So how have the end-timers developed this concept of the Great Tribulation into such an elaborate doctrine with a specific seven-year* limitation? They have collected and interpreted various Scriptures literally.

Daniel and the Revelation

Their idea of a definite seven-year period comes primarily from combining Daniel's seventy-week prophecy[2] with numbers used in the

---

* Some millennialists place the length of "the great tribulation" at three-and-a-half years, instead of seven.

"A one-time, future-only, seven-year tribulation period is another fabrication of man; nowhere does the Bible contain such a prophecy."

Revelation.[3] To make it a future event, many have connected a statement Jesus made about the budding of the fig tree[4] with Israel's rebirth as a nation in 1948.

Let's look at what the Bible actually says about the schedule of coming events and at the way time-line teachers have interpreted these Scriptures.

> While I was still in prayer, Gabriel, the man I had seen in the earlier vision, came to me in swift flight about the time of the evening sacrifice. He instructed me and said to me, "Daniel, I have now come to give you insight and understanding. As soon as you began to pray, an answer was given, which I have come to tell you, for you are highly esteemed. Therefore, consider the message and understand the vision.
>
> "Seventy 'sevens' are decreed for your people and your holy city to finish transgression, to put an end to sin, to atone for wickedness, to bring in everlasting righteousness, to seal up vision and prophecy and to anoint the most holy.
>
> "Know and understand this; From the issuing of the decree to restore and rebuild Jerusalem until the Anointed One, the ruler, comes, there will be seven 'sevens' and sixty-two 'sevens.' It will be rebuilt with streets and a trench, but in times of trouble. After sixty-two 'sevens,' the Anointed One will be cut off and will have nothing. The people of the ruler who will come will destroy the city and the sanctuary. The end will come like a flood: War will continue until the end, and desolations have been decreed. He will confirm a covenant with many for one 'seven,' but in the middle of that 'seven,' he will put an end to sacrifice and offerings. And on a wing of the temple he will set up an abomination that causes desolation, until the end that is decreed is poured out on him."[5]

The time-liners teach that the last set of seven years comprise a definite time period called the Great Tribulation. To make all the pieces fit, they break this seven-year period down into two three-and-a-half-year periods. In the middle of the Great Tribulation, they say, the Antichrist (who they claim is a world dictator) desecrates the temple, goes back on his covenant, and stops the practices of sacrifices and offerings.

Since the Daniel passage makes no reference to the Great Tribulation mentioned in Revelation, they have to arbitrarily connect the two Scriptures to form a whole picture.

The Big Gap Theory

Of course, history records precisely sixty-nine weeks of years* between the time of Daniel and the coming of Christ. This is predictive and powerful. Then, however, it breaks down; you have to jump over nearly two thousand years to make the Great Tribulation a future event for our, or a future, generation.

Not to worry, say the time-liners, there is a gap, a postponement, an interruption of time between the sixty-ninth and seventieth weeks of years. Where do they get that hiatus? Certainly not from the Scriptures. Nowhere do any of the prophetic verses mention a gap that could even loosely be construed as a reference to the prophecy of Daniel—or of a seven-year Tribulation period, for that matter. The closest thing they can find is Jesus' parable of the budding of the fig tree, so they connect it to the rebirth of Israel as a nation in 1948. That, they claim, is the sign that the hiatus is over and that the Great Tribulation will begin.

Now that poses another huge problem. Why didn't the Great Tribulation start in 1948? Well, say the time-line teachers, Jesus predicted that this generation would not pass away until they saw all the great calamities He was predicting.[6] This generation, according to their circular-logic interpretation, means the generation that sees the budding of the fig tree.

A generation, by most standards, is the average number of years from the birth of one set of parents to the birth of their first grand-

---

* In the Hebrew, "sevens" means "a unit of sevens," as a week represents seven days. Virtually everyone agrees that the "sevens," or "weeks" referred to here symbolize years, not literal seven-day weeks.

child—which averages about forty years. That means, according to the time-liners, the Great Tribulation should begin about forty years after Israel's reestablishment as a nation in 1948.

But wait a minute! That would have happened in 1988! For awhile after that historic milestone came and went, some time-liners tried to hedge by saying that the forty years was not a precise figure and could fluctuate a year or two.

Having missed on that one, many of the scriptural futurists started claiming that the timeframe must really refer to a lifetime, and they placed the figure at seventy (the biblical three-score and ten) years. Thus, the new date to watch became A.D. 2018. But, they cautioned, since Jesus didn't say it would occur at the end of the generation but would happen before this generation passed away, it could happen at any time between now and A.D. 2018.

As we saw earlier, the *this* in *this generation* (in Matthew 24:34) has no antecedent, so it can only mean those who were with Jesus right then—not some unmentioned future generation. It really doesn't matter whether we are talking about forty years or seventy years or even 470 years. This Scripture has to be grossly distorted to get any semblance of a time schedule out of it. Even worse, what if (as I believe) the parable of the budding of the fig tree has nothing to do with the rebirth of Israel as a nation?

The implications are much greater than some future event. On a practical level, they tend to place political Israel on a pedestal and keep millions of Christians confused about their stance on issues affecting the Middle East.

The real problem, however, is that making the Great Tribulation a one-time, future event (to which raptured Christians are immune) has lulled millions of people into complacency and closed their eyes to critical, present spirit-realm/physical-realm realities.

Later in this chapter, we'll look more closely at what tribulation means to Christians today, but first let's examine how the Scriptures interpret Daniel's vital prophecies.

How Do the Scriptures Interpret These Scriptures?

Few Scriptures have received more study and produced more opinions than Daniel's seventy weeks. This is understandable, because the way

you interpret the Daniel passage influences how you view God's entire
Bible and how you view your role in this present world.

Three things are helpful to remember as we seek to grasp the
meaning of Daniel's seventy weeks—or any prophetic Scripture.

1. Does it reflect the spirit of prophecy, which is the testimony of
   Jesus? In other words, what kinds of fruit does it produce?

2. Is it consistent with the teachings of Jesus about the kingdom
   of God? Does it fit the principles and patterns of Jesus' kingdom teachings?

3. Is it consistent with all other Scriptures—whether from the Old
   or New Testament? Does it stand in harmony with the themes
   and types of the entire Bible?

The time-line theory of a seven-year tribulation period and a precise future Millennium do not measure up to those criteria.

First, instead of producing good fruit, like doing the works of
Jesus, they produce the bad fruit of anxiety, escapism, and confusion.

Second, as we will soon see, they stand in open conflict with the
principles and patterns of Jesus' kingdom teachings.

Third, the time-line theories don't fit the harmony criteria, because one has to twist and distort many other Scriptures to make them
work out.

The Time-Line Theory Comes Apart
At the Crucifixion of Jesus

The biggest problem with the time-line theory is that it fails to take
into account the most crucial element of biblical prophecy: the crucifixion of Jesus.

Why is that so important? Because the Scriptures make it abundantly
clear that, at the crucifixion of Jesus, the essential nature of every element of worship and every prophetic symbol changed from physical to
spiritual/physical reality. If we don't understand this vital truth, then
we're going to misinterpret all the rest of prophetic Scripture.

Let's look at how the Apostle Paul confirms this shift from the
physical to the spiritual/physical.

For this reason, since the day we heard about you, we have not stopped praying for you and asking God to fill you with the knowledge of his will through all spiritual wisdom and understanding.[7]

My purpose is that they may be encouraged in heart and united in love, so that they may have the full riches of complete understanding, in order that they may know the mystery of God, namely, Christ, in whom are hidden all treasures of wisdom and knowledge.[8]

That spiritual wisdom, understanding, and knowledge comes to us through the testimony of Jesus, which is the spirit of prophecy. It is a profound mystery.

The writer of Hebrews explains this mystery in more specific terms:

They [the ceremonial gifts and sacrifices of the old order] are only a matter of food and drink at various ceremonial washings—external regulations applying until the time of the new order.

When Christ came as high priest of the good things that are already here, he went through the greater and more perfect tabernacle that is not man-made, that is to say, not a part of this creation. He did not enter by the means of the blood of goats and calves; but he entered the Most Holy Place once for all by his own blood, having obtained eternal redemption. The blood of goats and bulls and ashes of a heifer sprinkled on those who are ceremonially unclean sanctify them so that they are outwardly clean. How much more, then, will the blood of Christ, who through the eternal Spirit offered himself unblemished to God, cleanse our consciences from acts that lead to death, so that we may serve the living God!

For this reason Christ is the mediator of a new covenant, that those who are called may receive the promised eternal inheritance— now that he has died as a ransom to set them free from the sins committed under the first covenant.[9]

This passage starts out talking about the earthly tabernacle and ceremonies that are only physical representations of the new order. Then, the description shifts to spiritual/physical realities. This is God's pattern for Daniel's seventy weeks and for all prophecy. All symbols change from physical fulfillment to spiritual fulfillment.

Jesus Himself expressed the same principle and pattern in chapter two of the gospel of John. Jesus had just finished clearing the temple, and the Jews came to Him demanding a sign:

"What miraculous sign can you show us to prove your authority to do all this?" [The authority to clean out the temple.]

Jesus answered them, "Destroy this temple, and I will raise it in three days."

The Jews replied, "It has taken forty-six years to build this temple, and you are going to raise it in three days?" But the temple he had spoken of was his body. After he was raised from the dead, his disciples recalled what he had said.[10]

Notice how He turned the emphasis from the temple in which He was standing to the spiritual/physical reality of Himself. At this point prophetic Scripture turns from physical fulfillment to spiritual/physical fulfillment—when the Jews destroyed Jesus' physical body at his crucifixion.

In the new order, the temple is Jesus—and it is the saints in blood-washed robes. We are being built into a spiritual house.[11] God has taken the physical things and events of the Old and New Testaments and turned them into spiritual/physical realities. We have examined some of the other examples that illustrate this critical shift: the tabernacle, the ark of the covenant, the sacrificial lamb, and the manna, to name a few. We now represent God's temple. That's why we're now called the New Jerusalem, which we'll discover in a later chapter of this book.

Does all this mean that Daniel's seventy weeks, the Tribulation, and Millennium have no significance? Indeed not! On the contrary, it means that the time-line theories that interpret those symbols physically and chronologically rob them of their deepest realities. The spirit realm is just as real as the physical realm. Don't ever think it isn't.

Daniel's Seventieth Week Is at Hand

In simple terms, the seventieth week symbolizes the timeless kingdom of God. It is at hand—an ongoing spiritual kingdom.

Daniel's seventy weeks do indeed represent the remainder of time. But the time-liners, by failing to look at this prophecy through the testimony of Jesus, miss the main reality of Daniel's message: the spiritual nature of the last week. They think sixty-nine weeks have been completed and that thousands of years now interrupt the sixty-ninth and seventieth weeks. But Scripture contains absolutely no foundation for such an interruption.

"In simple terms, the seventieth week symbolizes the timeless kingdom of God. It is at hand—an ongoing spiritual kingdom."

The first segment (seven times seven, or forty-nine years) covers the period from the Cyrus' decree to rebuild Jerusalem until the rebuilding was complete. And that's exactly what happened.

Then, Daniel cites a second segment (sixty-two times seven, or 434 years)—the 434 years until the coming of the Messiah, Jesus Christ. Mathematically, it all works out. That's a total of 483 years, represented by sixty-nine weeks of years, leaving one week of years.

Those first sixty-nine weeks dealt exclusively with the destiny of physical Israel. Under the Old Testament covenant, it was a literal, chronological fulfillment of history. I don't disagree with that at all. I find it impressive, powerful, and convincing.

But in the final week of the prophecy, a sharp difference arises. The time-liners tell us there is one week yet to come and that the timetable has been interrupted for a period of thousands of years. But Scripture neither predicts nor even hints at such an interruption. According to the Bible, the seventieth week started immediately after the sixty-ninth week ended.

Why is this true? Because Jesus ministered publicly for three-and-a-half years (which is the first half of Daniel's seventieth week) and then was cut off. So Jesus' ministry fulfills the first half of the seventieth week. The old covenant ended at Jesus' death; He (not Satan or the Antichrist) put an end to sacrifices and ceremonial offerings by becoming our eternal High Priest; the "people of the ruler who will come" (the Jews) destroyed the city and the sanctuary (by crucifying Jesus) to make way for the New Jerusalem and the new temple.

Just as Daniel had prophesied, the Messiah was cut off in the middle of the seventieth week. The death, burial, and resurrection of Christ completed the first three-and-a-half days, or years, of the seventieth week.

That means we're in a new day now—an eternal day. The physical fulfillment has become spiritual/physical fulfillment. Time no longer applies. Time is ongoing. We're living in the age of the Spirit, in the middle of seventieth week, right now. We are the completion, the sealing up, of the vision.

Now what are the remaining three-and-a-half years? We're in the spirit-realm time frame now, as is the book of Genesis, when the first four days had no sun and moon. That was a spiritual, not chronological, timeframe.

The remaining three-and-a-half years are in a spiritual time frame. It's a period of continuous unfolding throughout all the ages. It can never be confined to a literal three-and-a-half-year period—any more than the seven churches can be confined to just seven actual churches, or the Millennium can be confined to an actual one thousand years.

What Does the Second Half
Of the Seventieth Week Represent?

What happens in this second half of the seventieth week, which represents the timeless reality of the kingdom of God?

Revelation 11 gives some interesting insights into how it all unfolds. Let's look at the first few verses, with some parenthetical comments:

> I [John] was given a reed like a measuring rod and was told, "Go out and measure the temple of God [us] and the altar, and count the worshipers there. But exclude the outer court; do not measure it, because it has been given to the Gentiles. They will trample on the holy city [Jesus said, "You are a city."[12]] for forty-two months. [Divide that by twelve and you get three-and-a-half years.] And I will give power to my two witnesses, and they will prophesy for 1,260 days [Divide that by thirty and you get forty-two months—three-and-a-half years], clothed in sackcloth." These are the two olive trees and the two lampstands [the Jews and the Gentiles] that stand before the

Lord of the earth. If anyone tries to harm them, fire comes from their mouths and devours their enemies. This is how anyone who wants to harm them must die. These men have power to shut up the sky so that it will not rain during the time they are prophesying [Who prophesies? We do.]; and they have power to turn waters into blood and to strike the earth with every kind of plague as often as they want.[13]

Those verses describe the second half of the seventieth week. You and I are the ones who do the works of Jesus, just as He did them. Three-and-a-half years is a symbol for the Bride of Christ in operation. Those blood-washed believers who do the works of Jesus—who follow the Spirit, who are led by Him—are His bride. The two witnesses are

---

"We're living in the age of the Spirit, in the middle of seventieth week, right now. We are the completion, the sealing up, of the vision."

---

those who stand up in the church system and prophesy and are slain in the street of Babylon—not necessarily physically, but in a spiritual sense. We are God's temple; we know that from Scripture. As His bride we become equally yoked with Jesus. Thus the bride's three-and-a-half-year symbol is connected with Jesus' three-and-a-half years to complete, to seal up the vision of Daniel's seventieth week.

Let me emphasize that we're talking about both spirit-realm and physical-realm reality. The testimony of Jesus is the *spirit* of prophecy. Spirit is the testimony—not flesh. The fully unveiled Jesus in all His spirit-realm glory is the testimony—not just the Jesus of the Gospels.

The fire that comes out of the mouths of the two witnesses is prophesying by the Word of God in the power of the Spirit that burns and consumes those who fight against it. It burns and consumes that which opposes it. That's the fire—not atomic bombs, as the end-timers claim. Likewise, the rain is not physical rain, but streams of living water—a symbol of the power of the Spirit.[14]

These witnesses also have the power to turn the water of the nations into blood and to bring plagues on the earth by doing the works of Jesus. All this may sound terribly un-Christian—at least, until you remember that Jesus said, "I did not come to bring peace, but a sword."[15] He went on to talk about how His coming would even turn members of the same family against each other. Just as His coming as the Son of Man exposed the evil in men and turned them against each other, His comings as the Alpha and Omega, and through His Bride throw evil religious people into fits of rage.

Spewing out fire can get you killed. Notice that the two witnesses' power to spew fire, lock up the rains, and turn water into blood lasts only a limited time—three-and-a-half years—until they have finished their testimony.

Then what happens? They are slain, and their bodies lie in the streets while their enemies mock them. The slaying is not necessarily physical, although Paul, Stephen, and at least ten of the eleven original disciples of Jesus found out that sometimes it is. Now, that's tribulation!

The beast system in the apostate church rears its ugly head and goes into a rage against any saint who threatens its stranglehold—just as it did when Jesus challenged the religious leaders of His day.

Bear in mind that the religious leaders demanded Jesus' crucifixion. And religion still crucifies Jesus today through his two witnesses, through those who hold the testimony of Jesus.

If someone walks into a church today and goes against its customs and traditions, the people say, "Away with him! We don't want anyone doing that stuff in here!" When people become the witnesses God needs—holding to the testimony of Jesus by doing His works—Satan comes against them in the church. And he often succeeds in destroying their witness by character assassination, innuendoes, and suspicious thoughts planted in people's minds. The struggles erupt within the church. This, as we have seen, is all part of the Battle of Armageddon.

That is why Jesus warned His disciples, "In the world ye shall have tribulation."[16] Earlier in that same discourse, He had predicted that they would suffer severe persecution and be thrown out of the church. "If the world hates you, keep in mind that it hated me first."[17] Then He reminded them, "No servant is greater than his master."[18]

It all sounds pretty ominous, doesn't it? Well, yes, it does—at least, if you're expecting everybody in the world, and especially in the church, to rejoice when they see you do the same works that Jesus did and even greater works.

In fact, one good clue as to how effectively you are doing the works of Jesus is the amount of opposition from the beast system and the false church you are encountering. If the world loves you and thinks you are wonderful, look again at what Jesus said: "If you belonged to the world, it would love you as its own."[19]

Now this is not to imply that anybody who is catching a lot of flack from the church is living as a blood-washed saint. Some people are so ornery that nobody can get along with them, and little beasts are always attacking each other. The real test is this: Are you being persecuted because you are doing the supernatural works of Jesus?

Remember that the word *testimony*, as in the testimony of Jesus, comes from the Greek *marturia*, from which we get our word *martyr*. It is not the death but the spirit of prophecy being manifested through the person that makes the martyr. So, who wants to volunteer to be slain for doing the works of Jesus? Well, as the old saying goes, "It's not over 'til it's over."

Getting killed for Jesus can get you resurrected! True prophets, blood-washed saints, don't stay dead. Look at how the two witnesses' account continues:

> But after the three and a half days a breath of life from God entered them, and they stood on their feet, and terror struck those who saw them. Then they heard a loud voice from heaven saying to them, "Come up here." And they went up to heaven in a cloud, while their enemies looked on.
>
> At that very hour there was a severe earthquake and a tenth of the city collapsed. Seven thousand people were killed in the earthquake, and the survivors were terrified and gave glory to the God of Heaven.[20]

Does this describe a cataclysmic future event? No, it describes ongoing judgment. This is the kingdom of God in motion. It is individual, it is spiritual, it is physical, it is ongoing, it is timeless. It is in the world, but not of the world.

The world can, and always does, bring tribulation on the bride for doing the works of Jesus—it can even slay her. But God always has the last word.

This process has been repeated countless times since Jesus was dragged out of Jerusalem and crucified by Babylon. It's happening around the world now. And it will continue to happen.

What Is the Meaning
Of the One-Thousand-Year Reign?

The binding of Satan and the reign of the saints for one thousand years are also physical symbols of a spirit-realm/physical-realm reality. Let's look at what the Bible actually says:

> And I saw an angel coming down out of heaven, having the key to the abyss and holding in his hand a great chain. He seized the dragon, that ancient serpent, who is the devil, or Satan, and bound him for a thousand years. He threw him into the Abyss, and locked and sealed it over him, to keep him from deceiving the nations any more until the thousand years were ended. After that, he must be set free for a short time.
>
> I saw thrones on which were seated those who had been given authority to judge. And I saw the souls of those who had been beheaded because of their testimony for Jesus and because of the Word of God. They had not worshiped the beast or his image and had not received his mark on their foreheads or their hands. They came to life and reigned with Christ for a thousand years. [The rest of the dead did not come to life until the thousand years were ended.] This is the first resurrection. Blessed and holy are those who have part in the first resurrection. The second death has no power over them, but they will be priests of God and of Christ and will reign with him for a thousand years.
>
> When the thousand years are over, Satan will be released from his prison and will go out to deceive the nations in the four corners of the earth—Gog and Magog—to gather them for battle. In number they are like the sand on the seashore.[21]

Two closely related symbols emerge in this passage: the binding of Satan and the resurrection and reign of the saints. The time given for both is a thousand years.

"The world can, and always does, bring tribulation on the bride for doing the works of Jesus—it can even slay her. But God always has the last word."

Why One Thousand Years?

A casual glance at an English translation of this passage would lead one to believe that John's figure of one thousand years means literally a thousand years. A closer look at the context and at other biblical uses of this expression, however, reveals that it symbolized a very long time, or thousands of years—perhaps even forever.[22]

First, this is one of the prophecies (like all the others in the Revelation) that was at hand for first-century Christians and is still at hand for us. If, as the time-liners say, it is an actual period of one thousand years, and if we agree that it was at hand for the people the book was originally written to, then the only possible conclusion is that it's over!

Second, the expression occurs several times elsewhere in the Bible, and it is allegorical in every other instance.[23] It was an idiom in Bible times comparable to our expression, "Never in a million years!" Just as we don't mean literally a million years, John did not mean precisely one thousand years.

The psalmist spoke of God owning the cattle "on a thousand hills."[24] Certainly, he did not mean that someone else owns the cattle on all but those one thousand hills![25] Likewise, the references to a thousand in Revelation 20 don't mean literally one thousand years. They simply refer to a vast, unspecified period of time.

Third, to translate a thousand years literally contradicts many other Scriptures that refer to the reign of Christ. Daniel characterizes Christ's reign as "an everlasting kingdom."[26] John tells us that the bride of Christ will "reign for ever and ever."[27] In Deuteronomy, we read that God keeps His "covenant of love to a thousand generations. . . ."[28] Does that mean He breaks the covenant after the one thousandth generation? Of course not! It simply means that God always keeps His covenants.

So which is the reign of Christ and His bride? Is it a Millennium, as the end-timers claim? Or is it for ever and ever, which the Bible proclaims? And when does it begin? Somewhere out in the future, after the Battle of Armageddon? Or did it begin with the death, burial, and resurrection of Christ (or maybe even before then)?

Finally, the thousand years idiom occurs in a book that abounds in symbolic idioms. If we take this one literally, why not take literally 144,000 as the number of Israelites who will be sealed (saved) by God?[29] But if we do that, we have a problem with those people being from Israel because they are later said to be those who had been "purchased from among men"—people who had been redeemed by the blood of Christ.[30] Do you see how confusing it can get?

A Description of the Eternal Kingdom of God

The bottom line is that there is no literal Millennium, as the end-timers claim. A thousand years is a temporal symbol of the ongoing, timeless, eternal kingdom of God. Blood-washed saints have been living in its reality for nearly two thousand years and will continue to reign and rule in it for eternity. It is something that God has created and, like God, it stands outside of time.

Most end-timers insist that the Millennium is still futuristic because they just can't conceive of the kingdom of God being here, at hand, now. They keep looking for an earthly utopia—wolves literally eating with lambs and children playing on top of snake holes. Worse yet, they are making the same mistake as the Jews in the days of Jesus' earthly ministry. They are looking for a political Messiah to come back and rule the world from a temple over in Jerusalem.

What a comedown it would be for Jesus to leave His present, glorified, and omnipresent position to confine Himself for one thousand years inside a temple built by hands. On the contrary, Jesus emphatically stated that His kingdom is not visible[31] and is not of this world.[32] A future millennial kingdom would be both. Jesus further stated that His kingdom is not a matter of food or drink.[33] What do you suppose the two most universal political problems in the world are? That's right—food and water.

Here's the point: is Jesus ruling His kingdom now or not? Timeliners say no. Some admit to a partial kingdom now but make little of it, opting for a full one later. But Scripture answers resoundingly, *yes, He is!*

That Jesus is indeed ruling His kingdom now is consistent with every prophetic Scripture and represents the highest spirit of Jesus'

"The bottom line is that there is no literal Millennium, as the end-timers claim. A thousand years is a temporal symbol of the ongoing, timeless, eternal kingdom of God."

---

teachings about the kingdom of God. The kingdom was at hand when Revelation 20 was written, it has been at hand ever since, it is at hand now, and it will continue to be at hand.

The Binding of Satan

The symbolism of Satan being bound and thrown into the abyss does not predict a single future event either. Rather, it is a parabolic description of Jesus' promise to His disciples, "I will give you the keys of the kingdom of heaven; whatever you bind on earth will be bound in heaven, and whatever you loose on earth will be loosed in heaven."[34]

When we live in this timeless kingdom of God, we have authority to bind up Satan and all his evil spirit-realm forces in our spheres of influence. But when we either step out of this kingdom or refuse to exercise the authority we have been given, Satan is loosed to wreak his havoc. The only limitation to the total control of Satan in the world is the willingness (or unwillingness) of Christ's blood-washed saints to accept and exercise the authority we have been given.

When we don't execute the authority of the kingdom, Satan keeps jumping out of the pit and stirring up people (nations) to rebel against God. But, as blood-washed saints keep proclaiming the Word of God and doing the works of Jesus, Satan keeps being bound and thrown back into the pit.

So many Christians want God to blow up this earth and defeat
Satan. They seem to have a deep desire for the whole thing to end.
Why should it end? Who says it will end?

God desires His kingdom to come, His will to be done on the
earth, and His saints to continue to defeat Satan through Christ's lim-
itless power. That has been and is the most relevant, pertinent application of this prophecy.

Who Are the Two Witnesses?

Who are the two witnesses who demonstrate the mighty power of God
by doing the works of Jesus?[35] They are the bride of Christ—the blood-
washed Jews and Gentiles—who operate in the spirit of prophecy.

But don't forget, Jesus cannot be yoked with just anybody. Being
equally yoked with Jesus ties into the marriage supper and the bride.
This is a great, profound mystery—one that the mind alone cannot
understand. It must also be revealed.

Paul, however, gives us a strong scriptural base for this spirit-
realm/physical-realm reality:

> Do not be yoked together with unbelievers. For what do righteousness
> and wickedness have in common? Or what fellowship can light have
> with darkness? What harmony is there between Christ and Belial? What
> does a believer have in common with an unbeliever? What agreement is
> there between the temple of God and idols? For we are the temple of
> the living God. As God has said: "I will live with them and walk among
> them, and I will be their God, and they will be my people.
>
> "Therefore come out from them and be separate," says the Lord.[36]

What did God tell us in Revelation 18:4? "Come out of her, my
people." Come out of Babylon. You can't rule and reign in Christ's
kingdom, do the works of Jesus, and prophesy in the power of God's
Spirit as long as you are unequally yoked with religious Babylon.

The Inner Kingdom

The most pertinent and relevant application of all biblical prophecy
can be fulfilled in each individual. Daniel's second three-and-a-half
years, the Tribulation, and the Millennial reign are ongoing, individual

realities. Each saint who is part of the bride does the works that Jesus did (and even greater works) and holds to the testimony.

We have seen all through the book of Revelation, in references to the testimony of Jesus, that individual saints are the martyrs who are slain—some spiritually, some physically, some mentally. Slain by whom? By people in the false church who don't want anything to do with spirit-realm/physical-realm truths and realities or with God's supernatural ways.

Says the Lord, "Touch no unclean thing, and I will receive you. I will be a Father to you and you will be my sons and daughters."[37]

That's the three-and-a-half years of God's new temple. The first temple was material (a building built by Solomon and rebuilt by Herod). The second temple was physical (the human body of Jesus). We're the third temple of God—a spiritual temple. Destroy this temple, our temple, and God will rebuild it. This fulfills the last half of Daniel's seventieth week. It's ongoing. You can't confine it to three-and-a-half, or seven, literal years.

The Millennial reign describes how Jesus rules in the world, through His bride. He rules through people who allow Him to rule through them, who hold to the testimony of Jesus, who do the supernatural works of Jesus, and who continuously bind up Satan and his evil spirit-realm forces.

Jesus said the kingdom is both within you and among you. His Kingdom comes within and among us. That's why He taught us to pray, "Thy kingdom come. Thy will be done on earth as it is in heaven."[38]

Let's turn back to Daniel and look briefly at how this individual fulfillment takes place.

> Seventy "sevens" are decreed for your people and your holy city [us]
> to finish transgression, to put an end to sin, to atone for wickedness,
> to bring in everlasting righteousness, to seal up vision and prophecy
> and to anoint the most holy."

It takes all this to do all that in each individual person. Why? Because that's where the fulfillment of prophecy is—in us. And, it doesn't happen overnight.

Know and understand this: From the issuing of the decree to restore and rebuild Jerusalem until the Anointed One, the ruler, comes, there will be seven "sevens" and sixty-two "sevens." It will be rebuilt with streets and a trench, but in times of trouble. After sixty-two "sevens," the Anointed One will be cut off and will have nothing. [That is, Jesus will be crucified.] The people of the ruler who will come will destroy the city and the sanctuary. The end will come like a flood: War will continue until the end and desolations have been decreed. He [Jesus] will confirm a covenant with many for one "seven," but in the middle of that "seven," he will put an end to sacrifice. And one who causes desolation [Satan. Through whom? The Pharisees.] will place abominations on a wing of the temple until the end that is decreed is poured out on him.[39]

We see that Jesus confirms the covenant. Jesus' death put the end to sacrifice. God's ultimate plan was finished with the death, burial, and resurrection of Jesus. That's why He said, "It is finished."[40] It was a plan to end sin, to end sacrifice, to make a way to God, for God to continually manifest Himself to His people, to complete the fulfillment of the first half of the seventieth week.

The second half of that week is our response to the work that Jesus did, as we execute the kingdom of God through our lives. We do that by worshiping Him, by doing the works of Jesus, and by seeking His righteousness. As we do those things, the prophecy of the seventy weeks is fulfilled inside us.

Doesn't this interpretation make more sense than the time-liners' saying, "Well, there must have been an interruption"?

Tying It All Together

Nowhere does the Bible talk about seven years of tribulation. Just like the thousand-year reign, it is a parabolic description of the timeless kingdom of God.

Will we have tribulation in this world? Yes, we will all have tribulation (trouble). Proclaiming God's Word through His bride will continuously bring judgment on all who refuse to repent and obey His Word. And Satan will continue to do everything he can to keep us from doing the works of Jesus. Those things cause the Great Tribulation. But nowhere does the Bible say that it will last for only seven years.

Will we reign and rule with Christ for a thousand years? Yes—not just for a thousand years, but forever and ever. "His dominion is an eternal dominion; his kingdom endures from generation to generation," said Daniel.[41] And Christ wants us to reign and rule with Him in that kingdom.

When does it all start? Actually, it started long before Daniel's prophecy. God's plan for it was laid before the foundation of the earth. But it

---

"Nowhere does the Bible talk about seven years of tribulation. Just like the thousand-year reign, it is a parabolic description of the timeless kingdom of God."

---

starts in us the moment we come out of Babylon, take God's seal upon us, eat the wedding supper of the Lamb, yield ourselves to the spirit of prophecy, and begin to manifest the supernatural works of Jesus.

So when is seven years not a week and a Millennium not a thousand years? It's when we quit looking off into the future for the Great Tribulation and start allowing God's kingdom to come within us—right now! It's when we start reigning and ruling with Him forever.

Now, let's look more closely at how Christ equips us to reign and rule with Him.

WHY IT WON'T TAKE A NUCLEAR HOLOCAUST TO MAKE WAY FOR "A NEW HEAVEN AND A NEW EARTH"

T he end is near!" proclaim the signs of the self-styled prophets who parade up and down the streets of America's major cities.

"This world is going to burn!" and "We are living in the last days!" shout preachers along the sawdust trail. Some even claim that God will destroy this present world with nuclear weapons to make way for a new heaven and new earth.

Why do so many people find the idea of the end of the world so fascinating? Why are masses of people so preoccupied with the notion that either God or man will destroy civilization?

It's all an effort by the conspirators° to cover up the spirit-realm/physical-realm truths and realities that have been revealed in

---

° In chapter 2, we identified the conspirators as Satan and his evil cohorts who maliciously distort the truths of God's Word. We also explained that many sincere Christians and teachers participate tacitly, though not intentionally, in the conspiracy by echoing the themes of the active conspirators.

the Apocalypse. As fascinating as it may be, this doctrine of the end of the world has drawn the attention of far too many Christians away from the most pertinent and relevant application of prophetic Scripture—God's ongoing, timeless judgment and restoration of individuals and Christ's true church.

The final destruction doctrine calls for a literal, physical, universal, and chronological interpretation of all so-called End Times biblical prophecies. The theory is that, at the great white throne judgment, God will destroy this present material world and its atmosphere, then create a whole new material heaven and a new earth.

In this chapter, we'll look first at what the Bible actually says about the great white throne judgment and the new heaven and new earth. Next, we'll see how other Scriptures interpret the various symbols of judgment and restoration. Then, as we've done in each of the preceding chapters, we'll examine what these biblical truths mean for Christians in their daily lives.

What the Bible Actually Says
About God's Judgment and a New Creation

What does the Revelation actually say about the great white throne judgment and the new heaven and new earth?

When you begin searching this passage, you need to disregard the breaks between chapters 20, 21, and 22. This prophecy has a continuous flow and logic; it is all one continuous vision.

> Then I saw a great white throne and him who was seated on it. Earth and sky fled from his presence, and there was no place for them. And I saw the dead, great and small, standing before the throne, and books were opened. Another book was opened, which is the book of life. The dead were judged according to what they had done as recorded in the books. The sea gave up the dead that were in it, and death and Hades gave up the dead that were in them, and each person was judged according to what he had done. Then death and Hades were thrown into the lake of fire. The lake of fire is the second death. If anyone's name was not found written in the book of life, he was thrown into the lake of fire.
>
> Then I saw a new heaven and a new earth, for the first heaven and the first earth had passed away, and there was no longer any sea.

I saw the Holy City, the New Jerusalem, coming down out of heaven from God, prepared as a bride beautifully dressed for her husband. And I heard a loud voice from the throne saying, "Now the dwelling of God is with men, and he will live with them . . . and be their God. He will wipe every tear from their eyes. There will be no more death or mourning or crying or pain, for the old order of things has passed away."

He who was seated on the throne said, "I am making everything new!" Then he said, "Write this down, for these words are trustworthy and true."

He said to me: "It is done. I am the Alpha and the Omega, the Beginning and the End. To him who is thirsty I will give to drink without cost from the spring of the water of life. He who overcomes will inherit all this, and I will be his God and he will be my son. But the cowardly, the unbelieving, the vile, the murderers, the sexually immoral, those who practice magic arts, the idolaters and all liars—their place will be in the fiery lake of burning sulphur. This is the second death."[1]

"Scripture contains many indications that the great white throne judgment and the new creation are not merely one-time, future events. Rather, they symbolize God's ongoing judgment and restoration in individual believers."

Although many other passages in the Bible reflect various elements of this vision, this is the most complete, explicit description of judgment and restoration.

These Spirit-Realm/Physical-Realm Truths And Realities Are At Hand

Scripture contains many indications that the great white throne judgment and the new creation are not merely one-time, future events.

Rather, they symbolize God's ongoing judgment and restoration in individual believers. They describe a continuous process of personal cleansing and the creation of new spirits and rejuvenated minds and bodies (earthen vessels) in overcoming believers. The language describing this process is figurative, spiritual/physical, individual, and ongoing—not literal, physical, global, and chronological.

Does this mean that there will not be a final, ultimate judgment and destruction of the world? No! As I've said before, God is sovereign and omnipotent. If He spoke the world into existence with a word, certainly He can destroy it—and He has every right to judge the human race He created. I do believe, however, that viewing this passage as a description of the kingdom of God at work within individuals and among God's people is the most pertinent and relevant application.

And what of the last days we hear so much about, as if they are yet to come or have just begun? When Peter stood up on the day of Pentecost, he said, "No, this is what was spoken by the prophet Joel: 'In the last days, God says . . .'"[2] Unless Peter and the Holy Spirit were mistaken, we have been living in the last days for nearly two thousand years. There's nothing new about that.

I believe the great white throne judgment and new creation prophecy are applied individually because the Revelation repeatedly addresses individuals within the churches. And it continually reminds us, "Let *him* who hears," and "let *him* come," and "*whoever* wishes, let *him* take of the free gift" (emphasis added). There's a constant emphasis on the individual.

But it's also important to pull away from the individual nature of these prophecies and look at their corporate aspects. God delivers the messages (trumpets) to the church and to the world through individuals who hold to the testimony of Jesus (do His works) and proclaim the Word of God.

This is another one of the prophecies (like all others in the Revelation) that was at hand for first-century Christians and is at hand for us now. We should read it as a parable of the kingdom (like those in the Gospels), not as a prediction of future events.

The truths of this prophecy touch our lives today in very tangible ways. They are graspable, heedable, and obeyable, not veiled in secrecy, and everything we need to know is told. But we can grasp these full spirit-realm/physical-realm truths and realities only as God reveals them to us.

Does this application of prophecy make judgment any less awesome or restoration any less glorious? Indeed not! It makes judgment a far more pressing concern and restoration an exciting, present reality. Spiritual reality is just as real as physical reality, if not more so. What's more, while the judgment and restoration themes are mostly spiritual in character, they have strong implications for the physical/material realm.

Coming to Grips with the Symbols
Of the Great White Throne Judgment

The physical symbols John uses to describe the great white throne judgment are among the most controversial in the entire Bible. Let's look briefly at some of the major questions these symbols raise.

Why a Throne?

Throughout the Bible, a throne symbolizes a seat of authority. This is one of the recurring themes of the Revelation. The stated purpose of the Apocalypse (the unveiling) is to show that Christ is no longer the suffering servant, the Jesus of the Gospels who was rejected and abused by the authorities (thrones) of this earth. It pulls away the curtain of His earthly ministry and shows Him as the triumphant, sovereign Lord of the universe. Thus, it is fitting and proper that He should sit on a throne of authority and exercise judgment.

Notice that the great white throne is different from the throne of God mentioned earlier,[3] located in what Paul called the third heaven and characterized by awe-inspired worship and unreserved obedience. The throne described in the final chapters of the Revelation is on the earth and is characterized by judgment and accountability. They are related but not identical; they are positionally and functionally distinct.

Why a White Throne?

White is the primary biblical symbol of purity and righteousness. Matthew said that in the Transfiguration, Jesus' clothes became "as white as the light."[4] When John saw Jesus in the opening chapter of the

Revelation, he observed that "His head and hair were white like wool, as white as snow."[5]

But Jesus is not the only one associated with white. Jesus promises to give overcomers a white stone with a new name written on it.[6] He says that the faithful saints will "walk with me, dressed in white, for they are worthy."[7] He promises that those who overcome will be given "white raiment."[8] He counsels the lukewarm, "buy from me . . . white raiment."[9] John says that the overcoming saints are dressed in white robes,[10] clothed with white linen,[11] and ride on white horses.[12]

The clear implication, then, is that this throne is not only one of judgment but of righteousness and purity. And, it also implies a great deal about the subjects and nature of this judgment.

Who Is Being Judged?

Most End Times teachers say that the great white throne judgment is for unbelievers only. Others say it's for both believers and unbelievers. But the "white" context suggests that it is only for believers. Plus, it is contained in a book written to believers (not to unbelievers) for them to read, hear, and obey.

Unbelievers face a different judgment from God's throne in heaven.[13] They are judged only on the basis of whether or not they have been washed in the blood of Christ.

Out of the center of God's throne comes the Lamb of God, Jesus Christ, who is given a great white throne in the earth.[14] Yet, Jesus chooses not to sit alone on that throne. "To him who overcomes, I will give the right to sit with me on my throne, just as I overcame and sat down with my Father on his throne."[15] When we are born again, Jesus gives us authority to sit on the throne with Him. (Remember, this is not something off out in the future. It was at hand in the first century, and it is at hand now.)

The judge in the great white throne judgment is clearly Jesus, and He is judging the subjects of His kingdom.[16]

Where Does the White Throne Judgment Occur?

Now, where is this throne of Jesus' kingdom? It is inside those who have been born again.[17] Inside us and among the churches the King sits on His throne, judging and reigning over His kingdom. The great white throne judgment is fulfilled within believers, one way or the other, depending on their obedience to God's Word.

The whole Revelation, including this judgment, is to be internalized. That's why John was instructed to eat the scroll. As we've seen, the Lamb stands up inside us, opens the seals, and pours out the vials. At the new birth, Christ's throne is established inside us through righteousness.[18] That is a positional reality.

"The great white throne judgment is fulfilled within believers, one way or the other, depending on their obedience to God's Word."

When we are born again, Jesus takes up His throne inside us and gives us the right to sit on that throne with Him.[19] Unbelievers do not have that right.[20]

But, although we have the authority to sit with Christ on the throne inside us, the choice is up to us. We can either sit on the throne to reign and rule with Christ, or we can stand before that throne and be judged by Him. If we are sitting on the throne inside us, we are alive in Christ; if not, we are dead in Christ. It is always our choice.

Thus, the great white throne judgment applies to believers who have the throne of Christ within them but are not sitting on it to reign and rule with Christ. They are the ones receiving this judgment.

What Happens at this Judgment?

The whole purpose of the great white throne judgment is to clear away the old heaven and earth to make way for a new heaven and earth—to establish within individual believers the full authority and power of the kingdom of God.

This is the ongoing process by which Christ is "making everything new."[21] By it, He transforms us into a new creation in which the unveiled Jesus can reign fully, and through which He can advance the kingdom of God among the churches and in the world.

This judgment constantly calls all Christians to cross over and span the boundary between the physical realm and the spirit realm—to become kings and priests in the kingdom of God. Each person's response produces within him either transformation or spiritual death.

If our old earth and sky flee from the Lord's presence, and if we allow no room for them in our lives, God's judging and refining process destroys all our sinfulness and reliance on the flesh. But, if our old earth and old sky refuse to flee from God's presence (if we hang onto sin and the flesh), we continue to live under judgment and are considered dead to God (condemned to live in Babylon).

What brings all this judgment to the individual and among the churches? It's the messages (seals, trumpets, and vials)—the proclamation of God's Word by the power of His Spirit—that bring the judgment. Just as Jesus comes to the individual, judgment comes—not out in the future, but now—to each of us. This is pertinent and relevant to our lives at this very moment.

Does this mean that we will never face a final judgment? No! The Bible clearly says, "man is destined to die once, and after that to face judgment."[22] The great white throne judgment provides us an opportunity to face up to that while we can still do something about it. Through it, we can come into Christ, continually overcome the flesh, and live by the Spirit. As we do that, we can live here and now in authority as kings and priests. Then, after death, we can face the judgment with "no condemnation."[23] When do you want to face up to the judgment? Now, or later?

What are the New Heaven and New Earth?

These material-realm symbols of heaven and earth are also parabolic, not literal. *They are individual and internal,* not cosmic and global as the end-timers have taught. In this passage, Jesus said, "To *him* who is thirsty I will give to drink . . ."[24] He also said *"He* who overcomes will inherit all this [new heaven and earth, the New Jerusalem, etc.], and I will be *his* God and *he* will be my son" [not just a child in a general sense, but God's son in a special sense].[25]

"The whole purpose of the great white throne judgment is to clear away the old heaven and earth to make way for a new heaven and earth—to establish within individual believers the full authority and power of the kingdom of God."

Thus, the first (or former) heaven represents the born-again believer's old natural spirit, which was dead to and at enmity with God. The new heaven represents the new spirit God gives a person at salvation.[26] It is made new by God's Spirit and becomes the dwelling place (tabernacle) of God inside the believer. This event occurs at conversion.

Our old (or former) earth consists of our unregenerated physical bodies, minds, and emotions—our flesh.[27] When Paul uses the word *flesh* (the Greek word is *sarx*) in his letters, he means a great deal more than just the physical body. He uses the term to describe human nature with all its passions, lusts, self-reliance, and carnal nature. It often includes conformity to the values and morals of this world. When used collectively about all humanity, it represents the realms of sin, of religious tradition, and of death. Our new earth is an ongoing process by which God, with our consent and cooperation, breaks the power of our bodies, minds, and emotions (our flesh). Our lives are no longer dominated by them but controlled by the power of God through our renewed spirits.[28] Paul summed it up in his letter to the Romans: "Do not be conformed to this world, but be transformed by the renewing of your mind, that you may prove what the will of God is, that which is good and acceptable and perfect."[29]

Remember that the Revelation is called the Apocalypse—the unveiling of the mystery of Christ. And what is that mystery? "And he [God] made known to us the mystery of his will . . . to bring all things *in heaven and on earth* together under one head, even Christ."[30] That is a description of the kingdom of God. And where is all that brought together? Inside believers. There is also a corporate dimension to all this, as we'll see later.

How do we know that heaven and earth are material-realm symbols of spirit-realm/physical-realm realities? Because they occur in a book that abounds in such symbols; and they occur allegorically in other Scriptures.

Earlier, God had promised through the prophet Isaiah, "I will create new heavens and a new earth. The former things will not be remembered."[31] Also note, ". . . with fire [His Spirit] and with his sword [His Word] the Lord will execute judgment upon all men."[32] These verses clearly represent the prophecies of Revelation 20 and 21. Remember that Isaiah is the same prophet who said, "Hear, O heavens! Listen, O earth!"[33] Physical heavens don't hear, and the earth doesn't listen. Obviously he's talking to people. Heavens (spirits) is plural because there are many spirits and they are all different. But earth (flesh) is singular because we are all made of the same stuff—dust, dirt, earth.

Now, in the Revelation passage, Jesus says, "I *am making* everything new."[34] At first, that statement may appear to contradict an earlier statement, "*Now* the dwelling [tabernacle, or temple] of God *is with men* . . . ," and the next verse, "It *is done.*"[35] There is, however, no conflict. As we've already seen, we are His tabernacle and His temple. Conditionally and spiritually, it is done when we are born again and become new heavens. But it is still being worked out in us through the ongoing great white throne judgment of our flesh and the creation of a new earth within us.

As I've often said throughout this book, I don't know what God will or won't do in the future (nor does anyone else, for that matter). I do believe, however, that what I've just outlined is the most pertinent, relevant, and life-giving understanding to the new heaven and new earth prophecy.

What About the Judgment Day?

This vision has been stripped of much of its deeper, timeless significance because the final destruction teachers have made it a one-time event called the Judgment Day and pushed it out into the future.

Thus, millions of people have grown up believing that God is going to get them some day if they don't watch out, and that's the only relevance God's judgment has for their lives.

Many even believe that judgment is only for unbelievers—people who have not been washed by the blood of Christ. But let's look more closely at what the Scriptures say and don't say.

First, God's judgment clearly involves Christians. A number of other Scriptures support this stance. Consider, for example:

- "Woe to you who are complacent in Zion."[36] Zion is God's holy mountain—believers.

- "A curse on him who is lax in doing the Lord's work. A curse on him who keeps his sword from bloodshed."[37] That doesn't sound like unbelievers to me, does it to you?

- "Let no one deceive you with empty words, for because of such things God's wrath comes on those who are disobedient. Therefore, do not be partners with them. For you were once darkness, but now you are light in the Lord. Live as children of light. For the fruit of light consists in all goodness, righteousness, and truth, and find out what pleases the Lord. Have nothing to do with the fruitless deeds of darkness, but rather expose them. For it is shameful even to mention what the disobedient do in secret. . . . This is why it said, 'Wake up, O sleeper, rise from the dead, and Christ will shine on you!'"[38]

Paul is talking to believers here, isn't he? He's writing to people who are physically alive, yet telling them to rise up from the dead. Why? Because being dead has to do with one's relationship to God. In fact, if anyone is not reigning and ruling with Christ, God considers him or her dead—and it is for the purpose of destroying the spiritual death within them that Christ brings them to the great white throne judgment.

Second, nowhere in Revelation 20 or 21 is the term "the judgment day" ever used. In fact, the latter part of the passage indicates that the concept of temporal days has lost all its significance.[39] Why? Because Jesus is the day.[40]

A similar description of this judgment process appears in Peter's second letter to the church. End Times teachers often cite it to support their doctrine that God is going to destroy this globe. Let's look briefly at this message, or trumpet.

> But the day of the Lord will come like a thief. The heavens will disappear with a roar; the elements will be destroyed by fire, and the earth and everything in it will be laid bare.
>
> Since everything will be destroyed in this way, what kind of people ought you to be? You ought to live holy and godly lives as you look forward to the day of God and speed its coming. That day will bring about the destruction of the heavens by fire, and the elements will melt in the heat. But in keeping with his promise we are looking forward to a new heaven and a new earth, the home of righteousness.[41]

Again, notice the individual emphasis here. This is just as heed-able, just as much at hand, as the prophecy in the Revelation.

As we discovered in the previous chapter, the people to whom Peter was writing were living in the day of the Lord, just as we are. The day of the Lord is ongoing, and it comes suddenly, like a thief. Jesus comes to individuals, each in their own turn, and His comings always bring judgment on those who are not reigning and ruling with Him.

"The heavens will disappear with a roar; the elements will be destroyed by fire, and the earth and everything in it will be laid bare." What elements will be destroyed? Most teachers believe this refers to land, air, water, and fire. Those are the four elements, aren't they? But it's not talking about that kind of element at all. The Greek word *stoicheion*, translated *elements*, means something orderly in arrangement, a principle, a rudiment. It is a derivative of *stoicheo*, which means to confirm to virtue and piety, to walk orderly. So, he is talking about religious tradition. These are the elements.[42]

Remember, this is prophetic language. The elements are the form and works of religion. Paul warned Timothy to beware of people "having a form of godliness but denying its power."[43] And Jesus had much to say about having the form of religion but denying the power of God. It is the practice of empty, godless religion—adherence to the law by doing good works—that comes under judgment and is cast into the lake of fire, or into God (as we shall soon see). Our works—not physical earth and sky—get burned up here and now—not out in the future.

Now, what does Peter mean by a new heaven and new earth? These are physical symbols of spiritual/physical reality. It's the same symbolism used in the Revelation passage. It's the same reality Paul explained this way: "The first man [Adam] was of the dust of the earth, the second man [Jesus] from heaven. As was the earthly man, so also are those who are of the earth; and as is the man from heaven, so are those who are of heaven. And just as we have borne the likeness of the

---

"Being dead has to do with one's relationship to God. In fact, if anyone is not reigning and ruling with Christ, God considers him or her dead—and it is for the purpose of destroying the spiritual death within them that Christ brings them to the great white throne judgment."

---

earthly man, so shall we bear the likeness of the man from heaven."[44]

Paul goes on to explain that "flesh and blood cannot inherit the kingdom of God, nor does the perishable inherit the imperishable."[45] Death is a process of physical change for believers who cannot, or will not, change themselves into new earth. Many won't let the flesh, the old earth, pass away while they're still walking on this physical planet. And they've got to go through death to get rid of their old earth.

On the other hand, you can become the new earth by faith. It is this beautiful spiritual reality that Paul has in mind when he says, "We have this treasure in earthen vessels."[46] The judgment and destruction of the old heaven and earth, to make way for the new, is a timeless process that occurs continuously as Jesus comes to us, not a cataclysmic end to the physical/material world.

What Is the Criterion Against Which Believers Are Judged?

You've probably heard, seen, and read countless stories about some individual dying, going up to the pearly gates and meeting Saint Peter.

In the most common scenario, Saint Peter looks in a huge book to see if the person has done more good than bad in order to get into heaven. If not, the person either goes to hell or gets a second chance to come back to earth and do more good deeds. The mere existence and widespread popularity of that plot indicates just how far off and confused most people are about the basis of God's judgment.

Certainly, in the great white throne judgment, the dead are judged by what they have done! But who are the dead? And against what criterion are they judged?

We can answer those questions only when we grasp the symbolic meanings of the books that are mentioned. "And the books were opened. Another book was opened, which is the book of life. The dead were judged according to what they had done as recorded in the books."[47] "If anyone's name was not found written in the book of life, he was thrown into the lake of fire."[48]

Although John tells us that these books are opened, he doesn't tell us precisely what they represent. That is not a divine oversight. Many symbols in Revelation are not defined, because they represent spirit-realm/physical-realm truths and realities which are based on other Scriptures.

John says there are books, and there is another book "which is the book of life." I believe that *we* are what's described as the books, and that the gospel of the kingdom is written on our hearts.[49] "The book of life" is Jesus.[50] In my opinion, the book of life contains all the names of believers who are spiritually alive in Christ, whether they are physically alive or dead. Life is a relationship with God. Only sin and unbelief will get our name blotted out of that book, because sin and unbelief make us dead to Christ. So, we are the books, and Jesus is the book of life. Our names are written on Him and His on us.

The dead in Christ, then, are those believers who are not reigning and ruling with Christ, and they are judged by the fruits they bring forth in relation to the messages (the trumpets) that have been given.

The criterion used in the great white throne judgment is the gospel of the kingdom which is written on their hearts. As in all the kingdom teachings and parables, we are all judged by our response to the kingdom of God.[51]

What Happens to the Sea and to Death and Hades?

John tells us, "The sea gave up the dead that were in it, and death and Hades gave up the dead that were in them."[52] In the next verse, he says, "Then death and Hades were thrown into the lake of fire."

Doesn't it seem strange that death and Hades were thrown into hell, as most end-timers teach? Doesn't it tell you that the lake of fire is not hell?

Let's take a closer look.

First, the sea is used throughout the Revelation as a symbol for masses of people.[53] This is not a literal sea, giving up physical dead—it is a spirit-realm sea giving up real people who are dead to the spirit realm.

Interestingly, this sea had vanished in the next chapter; when John saw the new heaven and new earth ". . . there was no longer any sea."[54] Only the blood-washed, overcoming saints have a place in this new order. The sea of unbelief does not exist inside the kingdom of God.

Second, Hades, or hell, is the Greek equivalent of the Hebrew Sheol, which is used to designate the realm of the dead. As a Revelation symbol, Hades doesn't refer to the physically dead but to the spiritually dead. You can be walking around and still be considered dead, or separated, from God, whether you're a nonbeliever or a believer who continues in transgressions and sins.[55] This is the clear implication of Jesus' statement "Follow me, and let the dead bury their own dead."[56] He further emphasized the theme when He quoted the father of the returned prodigal, "For this son of mine was dead and is alive. . . ."[57] and when He characterized the Pharisees as "whitewashed tombs . . . full of dead men's bones and everything unclean."[58]

The great emphasis of Paul's writings is that believers can be either dead to sin and alive in Christ, or alive to sin and dead to Christ.[59] And, according to him, the most vital sign that tells whether a believer is alive or dead to Christ is if they are offering the parts of their bodies to Him as instruments of righteousness. That's new earth!

Thus, Hades refers here to the realm of spiritually dead believers. This spiritual Hades is cast into the lake of fire.

Third, remember that the beast and the false prophet have been cast into the lake of fire,[60] and Satan has been cast into the lake of fire.[61] Also note that Babylon and the great prostitute (harlot) have been destroyed by God's judgment of fire.[62]

John's statement that death and Hades are thrown into the lake of fire symbolizes the spirit-realm reality that the lake of fire is part of God. "Our God is a consuming fire"[63] which either destroys or purifies and empowers.[64] And, when spiritual death and Hades (its domain) are cast into this consuming fire (God), He destroys them.

Fourth, Jesus has already destroyed spiritual death universally,[65] yet the power of death reigns in individual lives through our flesh (body, mind, emotions). How do we destroy death in our individual lives? We throw our flesh into God.

Not all who are dead are in the graveyard, for those who are not in Christ are spiritually dead, even though they may have Christ in them. But, when we go into Christ, we are in God, and we throw death back into the lake of fire, which is God.

Fifth, individual believers always have a choice. As often as Jesus comes to us in a great white throne judgment, we can throw the spiritual death and its domain (our flesh) that is under judgment into God (the lake of fire) and have our names written in the book with those who are spiritually alive. Or, we can refuse and not have our names written there.

Of course, there are benefits and consequences. If we give up our fleshly death, we go on to become new earth. But, if we continue to live in spiritual death, we are cast along with it into the lake of fire to be consumed by God. "If anyone's name was not found written in the book of life, he was thrown into the lake of fire."[66]

The first death is the one we die to the world and our flesh so we can reign and rule with Jesus in the kingdom of God, in this present life. If we refuse to die to the world and the flesh, then we face the second death.

Sixth, the second death involves physical death. If we die the optional first death, then we don't have to go through the mandatory second death before we can reign and rule with Him. Many believers must be purified by the second (physical) death because they refuse to purify themselves voluntarily. Reigning and ruling, however, are for those who are alive.

If we are born again, we can crucify our flesh now so we can reign and rule with Christ; or we can wait and let our flesh (which holds us in the bondage of spiritual death) be destroyed by physical death so we can reign and rule with Him. But that's our choice. We can do it voluntarily now or let God do it at death.

By doing it now, we are rejuvenated—we become new earths, dwelling places for God. This is the first resurrection. This, incidentally, is the fulfillment of Jesus' statement, "I tell you the truth, the time is coming and *has now come* when the dead will hear the voice of the Son of God and those who hear [heed] will live."[67]

Our flesh—and by this I mean our old man or fallen nature, not our physical bodies—holds many of us in bondage. Paul characterized our flesh as our biggest problem. Why? Our flesh is what keeps us from believing and receiving the message of the kingdom in this present life.

We need to get our minds off the cemetery and a future physical resurrection (both of which are coming) so we can receive the spiritual reality of the great white throne of judgment now.

What's It Like to Live in the New Heaven and New Earth?

As we've already seen, the goal of the great white throne judgment is to wipe away the old to make way for the new, to destroy reliance on the flesh so that we can be fully alive in both the spirit and physical realms. Once our old nature and our flesh have either fled from the presence of God or been burned up by the judgment, we can inherit the kingdom of God—a new heaven and new earth.

"Then I saw a new heaven and a new earth, for the first heaven and the first earth had passed away."[68] That which had fled from the presence of Jesus has now been restored and made new. The corrupted flesh has been replaced by the incorruptible spirit.

"I saw the Holy City, the New Jerusalem coming down out of heaven from God, prepared as a bride beautifully dressed for her husband."[69] You don't have to die or be raptured to go up to the New Jerusalem; it comes to you. In the next chapter, we'll see what the symbolism of this magnificent Holy City coming down is all about.

"And I heard a loud voice from the throne saying, 'Now the dwelling [the tabernacle] of God is with men and he will live with them. They will be His people, and God Himself will be with them and be their God.'"[70] God didn't always dwell inside people. Once He dwelt on Mount Sinai and gave Moses the Ten Commandments. Then He had the Hebrew people build a tabernacle, or a tent, for Him to dwell in. Later He had Solomon build Him a more permanent temple for His dwelling place. Now He dwells inside Christians, in new heavens, and He wants to make them new earth. That's what overcomers are called to do—to be God's tabernacle, His dwelling place, lively stones in His temple. The kingdom of God is now within and among the overcomers.

"He will wipe every tear from their eyes. There will be no more death or mourning or crying or pain, for the old order of things has passed away."[71] What old order? It's the old order described by the writer of Hebrews:

> They are only a matter of food and drink and the various ceremonial washings—external regulations applying until the time of the new order. When Christ came as high priest of the good things that are already here, he went through the greater and more perfect tabernacle that is not man-made, that is to say, not a part of this creation.[72]

That's the new order. It is the new covenant, based on the blood of Christ, which replaces ceremonies and works of the flesh with spiritual realities and the power of God. And it's already in place.

"He who was seated on the throne said, 'I am making everything new!'"[73] When Christ comes into us, our spirit is renewed, but we still have an old mind and body. And they only become new when we are in Christ. "Therefore, if anyone is in Christ, he is a new creation, the old has gone, the new has come."[74] The key is being *in Christ*. Christ being in you brings your flesh before the throne of judgment; but you being in Christ means complete restoration. God is saying here, "I am making *everything* new" (emphasis added). That's not just renewal of the spirit (although it begins there) but also the renewal of the mind and body. This is the physical aspect of the first resurrection—all things new, not just the spirit.

"He said to me, 'It is done. I am the Alpha and the Omega, the Beginning and the End. To him who is thirsty I will give to drink without cost from the spring of the water of life.'"[75] What do you think *it is done* means? It's written in the past tense—"It is done!" I believe that what Jesus referred to on the cross as being finished universally is

---

"Once our old nature and our flesh have either fled from the presence of God or been burned up by the judgment, we can inherit the kingdom of God—a new heaven and new earth."

---

done within the individual when we come into Christ. It is the difference between the announcement of a universal, timeless fact and individuals coming into the reality of that fact.

How Christians Experience God's Judgment And Become New Heavens and New Earth

So, how do individual believers experience the great white throne judgment on an ongoing basis, and how can we become a new heaven and a new earth and inherit all that God promises us?

We can reign and rule with Jesus only as our old earth (our flesh) and our sky (our old natural spirit) flee from His presence. Many Christians are not seated on the throne with Him. They are standing in front of it. They are not reigning and ruling with Jesus; they are under judgment from this throne.

It is my sincere hope that Christians reading this will open their hearts to let God give them His "spirit of wisdom and revelation"[76] about the ongoing, present-tense truths and realities of this vital Scripture. Let me offer three suggestions that can help you receive the glorious spirit-realm/physical-realm realities of the destruction and restoration vision.

1. Quit Putting This Out into the Future

The first step is to quit putting all the significance of the Revelation message out into the future. Over the last three or four decades Christianity has emphasized coping with life in the physical and material world and getting ready for future events. Jesus has been depicted as a cosmic buddy who looks out for us, gives us whatever we want, and will someday zap all our enemies and wipe out this evil planet. Heaven has often been presented as little more than an ethereal place Christians go to when they die.

Yet that's not the message of the Revelation. It's time for a renewed sense of judgment and fear of the Lord in the body of Christ. Christians are deceived if they think they are not being judged for their cowardly, unbelieving approach to serving God. Many are being judged right now. That's why so many Christians are leading troubled, defeated lives—because they are standing before the great white throne of judgment. Many churches are being judged right now and are caught up in great turmoil and confusion because of their disobedience to the Word of God.

The great white throne judgment always produces one of two results within the individual: it either purifies or it destroys. When it purifies, it makes new heaven and new earth. It's not for unbelievers; it's for believers. We suffer destruction if we continue in unbelief and in unholy living and if we are cowardly about facing up to the Word of God.

It's time to abandon our preoccupation with the end of the world; the end of the world is God's business. Our business is hearing, heeding, and acting upon what is at hand. Our task is to overcome—here and now—and inherit all that God has provided for us.

This is the end the Bible predicts. It is God's goal—to destroy all the sin and self-reliance of our flesh so that He can share intimate, personal relationships with purified, reigning, and ruling saints. This end was at hand then, and it is at hand now. That is the great message of the Revelation: we are to overcome the beast, the dragon, the great prostitute, the flesh—everything that keeps us from reigning and ruling with Christ. And it is always individual.

So quit pushing all this out into the future and thinking it does not presently apply to you. It applies to me, it applies to you, it applies to all believers whether we seek to grasp it, heed it, and obey it—or not.

2. Let God Make All Things New in You

What's wrong with this world is not the physical earth or its atmosphere. It's not this material planet that needs to be wiped out and replaced with a new one. Certainly, it's polluted, but that's not really the problem.

The problem with this earth is the people who live on it. They need to be made new. The Greek word for *new* means to be rejuvenated, a perfecting experience. When God remakes people, they become new heavens and new earth.

As believers, our biggest problem is our own flesh. That's where we need to get the victory. That's why we need to have new heavens and new earth. We need to quit being terrified and start being transformed.

This flesh comes under the judgment of the great white throne. When we are sitting on that throne with Jesus, we are reigning and ruling over spirit-realm forces. Our own fleshly nature has fled from Christ's, and we reign together. When we are in Christ, like that, His messages go out from us to bring others in the churches to stand before the great white throne for judgment.

But, if we are standing before the great white throne ourselves, our own flesh is not under the control of our spirit; we are under judgment. We will either voluntarily throw our flesh back into God (the lake of fire) to be burned up, or we will be thrown (along with our fleshly nature) into the lake of fire.

Certainly, this is the work of God, and He says, "It is done!" But we have a vital role in it, too. We have to make this earth (flesh) and sky (including dominance by evil spirits) flee from God's presence so He can make us into new heavens (new spirits) and new earth (rejuvenated body, mind, and emotions). How do we do that?

Paul explained the process this way:

> Therefore, I urge you, brothers, in view of God's mercy, to offer your bodies as living sacrifices, holy and pleasing to God—which is your spiritual act of worship. Do not conform any longer to the pattern of this world, but be transformed by the renewing of your mind. Then you will be able to test and approve what God's will is—his good, pleasing and perfect will.[77]

Since the body is controlled by the mind, this transformation process starts with changing our mental focus from the flesh realm to the spirit realm. John spoke of it as being "carried away in the spirit."[78]

That's why I say that the first step is to quit thinking of judgment and the coming of the kingdom of God only as something that's going to happen someday out in the future. Accept the fact that it's happening inside you right now. If you're always thinking about God coming back and jerking you off this planet and melting planet Earth, you aren't really going to be motivated to change and become Christlike, are you? This future-oriented stargazing has been the devil's stumbling block for many in the church. It keeps us from tapping into the spiritual power and supernatural authority that we have now to reign and rule. It keeps us from experiencing the fullness of God.

3. Come Alive!

God's Word often refers to us as new heavens and new earth.[79] And God wants to make us come alive as new heavens and earth. The new earth symbolizes your flesh (body, mind, and emotions) that is redeemed, crucified, and transfigured with Christ. You walk in newness of life. And when your mind, emotions, and body are transformed, you are a new earth, a new creation.

The new heaven contains God's new throne inside you. It's a spiritual dimension, and it includes your spirit. It's a throne which can direct all your actions. It can create total liberty, love, and forgiveness. As a new heaven, you are no longer caught up in sin or in old religious forms and practices. You are living in a vital, glorious relationship with the Father. Heaven is a spirit realm, and it's inside us.

"Your kingdom come [in us], your will be done on earth [in us] as it is in heaven."[80] The kingdom of God comes inside you. It's not a location out in the sky. We are a tabernacle, a tent, a dwelling place for God—now. We either believe it or we don't believe it. If we don't, we can go ahead and struggle and hope for something out in the future.

What Does It All Mean?

"He who overcomes will inherit all this."[81] Now, that's the key—he who *overcomes*. The book of Revelation is full of admonitions to overcome. That was the primary message to individuals within the churches. If we want to be new heavens and new earth and reign and rule with Him, we have to overcome.

"And he will be my son."[82] The most glorious benefit of living in the kingdom is being a full-fledged son of the King—God Himself. This sonship not only gives entry to the New Jerusalem; it entitles the overcomer to reign and rule jointly with the King over everything in the kingdom.

"But the cowardly, the unbelieving, the vile, the murderers, the sexually immoral, those who practice magic arts, the idolaters and all liars—their place will be in the fiery lake of burning sulphur. This is the second death."[83] Notice what heads that list—the cowardly, the unbelieving. If you're ashamed of the Son of Man in front of people, isn't that cowardly? If you're knuckling under to the flesh, isn't that cowardly? Unbelief includes not obeying any portion of God's Word, any of the messages of the Revelation, or any of the trumpet messages. When someone rejects the message, there's judgment, the great white throne judgment. It's going on inside you—right now.

This is what the great white throne of judgment and new heavens and new earth are all about—the present reality of the kingdom of God in us and among us. It is not some calamitous event that's going to happen some time out in the future. It is at hand. Judgment is here now—inside us and among us as believers.

With all the End Times teachings that have bombarded us over the years, changing our thinking about God's judgment and looking at it in the light of God's Word is, for some people, almost like trying to shovel water uphill. And trying to get this message across to the churches is like trying to move the ocean with a thimble.

Why is it so hard to get people to accept this at-hand message? It's because *having* seems to have fallen into disfavor lately; most Christians are more into *hoping*. But hoping is not God's best. Hoping is God's second best. Christ in you is *the hope* of glory. You in Christ is glory. Having is seizing what is at hand. Having is believing and acting upon what is at hand. Having is believing and acting upon what is graspable, heedable, and obeyable.

If we are not reigning and ruling, God sees us as dead in Christ. And dead folks do not have access to the Holy City. I know you want to go there! Just read the next chapter, and you'll discover what a wonderful place it is.

12

WHY YOU WON'T FIND THE NEW JERUSALEM IN THE MIDDLE EAST

H eaven on earth! Reigning in the Holy City—the New Jerusalem! Entering through pearly gates! Walking on gold! Eating fruit from the tree of life! Drinking from the river of life! Perfect everything! What could possibly be wrong with such dreams?

Absolutely nothing! Revelation 21 and 22 promise all those things and a whole lot more! The City of God is the grand finale of the Revelation. It is also the natural extension of the obvious fact that there is a New Jerusalem in the *new* heavens and earth.

But there is something dreadfully wrong with what the conspirators keep telling us about those glorious realities.

First, they tell us that, as wonderful as all those glorious realities are, we can't have them now. They want us to believe that God's most exciting promises are all out in the future somewhere.

Second, they tell us that these are all literal, physical, and material objects. They want us to believe that God's highest ideal for man is a physical, material paradise—a space city.

But the Bible does not make those claims. Satan used a serpent in the Garden of Eden to deceive Adam and Eve by twisting God's

words, and he uses religious Babylon and the beast system to deceive
Christians today by distorting God's Word.

Why Such Deceptions?

Why would Satan and his cohorts go to such elaborate lengths to get
us to believe a bunch of half-truths and fantasies about God's ultimate
plan for mankind? I can think of three very good reasons.

1. He knows that human beings don't feel nearly the sense of ur-
   gency about future hopes and fantasies that they feel about the
   pressing concerns of their day-to-day lives.

2. He knows that once we grasp and tap into the full reality of
   what God has promised, he can never again use the weaknesses
   of our flesh to intimidate us and keep us from reaching our full
   potential in Christ in the here and now.

3. He knows that once people enter the present reality of the
   Holy City, he loses all control over them; and that they pose a
   major threat to his strongholds in the world.

Think about it. Satan is smart enough to know that he cannot get
Christians to abandon the idea of the kingdom of God. Jesus had too
much to say about it. And, he knows that Christians long for a better
day, in a better world.

So what does he do? He takes God's truths and twists them just
enough to make his distortions sound plausible. With Eve, he said in
effect, "You can beat this death rap God is holding over your head. Besides, God knows that knowing good and evil will make you your own
god, and you'll no longer need Him or be subject to His commands."
What did Eve do? She said, "That sounds good to me. . . . Give me a
bite. . . . Adam, you've gotta' taste this forbidden fruit!" And, sure
enough, she and Adam did not immediately drop dead physically. It took
awhile before they began to realize just how much they'd lost, both physically and spiritually. Many people still don't understand.

Now, in the promise of the Holy City, God has announced the
restoration of everything that was lost in the Garden of Eden. So, what
does Satan do? He says, "Sure, there's going to be a New Jerusalem,
and you can live with God in it if that's what you want . . . but that's

"Masses of Christians are squabbling with each other over when it will all take place and whether a literal city— where they will live in perfect harmony with everybody—will come down out of the sky some day, or whether they'll be caught up to it."

all out in the future. . . . Right now, you have more important things to think about."

Does this deception work? Just look around at the fruit it is producing. Masses of Christians are squabbling with each other over when it will all take place and whether a literal city—where they will live in perfect harmony with everybody—will come down out of the sky some day, or whether they'll be caught up to it. Millions of Christians, who talk endlessly about the future dawning of a better day, drag out of bed each morning and go out to lead defeated lives in the day that faces them. People who can't even control their own lives talk about reigning and ruling over the whole universe someday.

In this final chapter, let's see what the Scriptures actually say about the reality and nature of the New Jerusalem, what we'll be doing there, and why you don't have to die to go and live there.

The Scriptures Proclaim That the New Jerusalem Is a Present Spirit-Realm/Physical-Realm Reality

Christianity, in general, has become a pale shadow of the kingdom its founder announced and intended. Nowhere is this disparity more obvious than in Revelation 21 and 22, where Jesus described the normal state of those who live in the kingdom of God, and the pathetic doctrines that are being taught and experienced in most churches today. Let me explain.

In His Gospel teachings, Jesus spoke of the kingdom of God as a present, ongoing, spirit-realm reality that impacts powerfully on the physical and material realm. In Revelation 21 and 22, He presents His bride as a Holy City, the New Jerusalem, which is made up of overcomers—people who are being refined through great tribulation, people who are standing firm against the beast system and holding to His testimony by doing His works, and people who continuously clothe themselves in the robes of His righteousness.

Yet religious Babylon (the antithesis of the New Jerusalem) falsely announces herself to be the future bride of Christ. She proclaims the judgment of God and the New Jerusalem to be literal, future events and holds them like a sword to the throats of all who dare to live in their reality in this present world. She uses the symbols of judgment and rewards to make idols of the law and of her rituals and programs, and she extracts great sacrifices and material wealth from all who get caught up in her bondage of self-fulfillment and faithless works. For every promise of life in the Apocalypse of Jesus Christ, Babylon offers a deadly counterfeit that can only be discerned by the eyes and ears of the spirit.

The Jews of Jesus' day were so busy looking for a political messiah to come and liberate physical Israel that they crucified the real Messiah when He appeared. Likewise, the religious Babylon of our day is so busy looking for an earthly Jesus to come back and set up a material kingdom on this earth that they are crucifying the unveiled, spirit-realm Jesus who lives in and among us now.

This isn't something I've dreamed up. The Apostle Paul used the term *the present city of Jerusalem* to represent what John called Babylon: ". . . the present city of Jerusalem" represents slavery (bondage). "But the Jerusalem that is above is free."[1]

What Is the New Jerusalem?

According to the Revelation, the New Jerusalem is not a literal, physical city with golden streets and jeweled walls. Those are man's ideas, not God's.

In the Revelation, the language is parabolic and figurative, not literal and physical. It uses physical symbols we understand to convey spiritual/physical truths and realities that we don't understand. Also, numbers have spiritual significance, not mathematical meanings.

John, the revelator, states clearly and succinctly that the Holy City *is* the bride of Christ:

> One of the seven angels who had the seven bowls full of the seven last plagues came and said to me, "Come, I will show you *the bride*, the wife of the lamb." And he carried me away in the spirit to a mountain great and high, and showed me the *Holy City, Jerusalem*, coming down out of Heaven from God.[2]

And who is the bride? We've met her before in the Revelation. She is the bride who has made herself ready for the wedding supper of the Lamb, who is dressed in "fine linen, bright and clean [which stands for the righteous acts of the saints]," and who lifts her veil [the mental image of Jesus' earthly ministry] in order to eat the marriage

---

"The religious Babylon of our day is so busy looking for an earthly Jesus to come back and set up a material kingdom on this earth that they are crucifying the unveiled, spirit-realm Jesus who lives in and among us now."

---

supper and become one with the Bridegroom.[3] Before that, John had described her as the 144,000 (symbolizing a very large number) who bore the name of the Father on their foreheads (a symbol of ownership, in sharp contrast with those who have the mark or number of the beast),[4] and as a multitude who were singing a new song that only they knew, who did not defile themselves but kept themselves pure, who follow the Lamb wherever He goes, who were purchased by the Lamb and offered to God and the Lamb as first-fruits, and in whose mouths no lie was found.[5]

Now we meet the bride as the Holy City, the New Jerusalem. Notice that most of the same symbols characterize her in this description. She looks like a bride beautifully dressed for her husband, the glory of God shines on her like the brilliance of a fine jewel, she is built on twelve foundations (the teachings of the apostles), she has intimate relations with the Lamb, and nothing impure is ever to enter into her.[6]

Is that clear enough? If you need more, contrast the people who make up the Holy City (the bride) with those of who are left outside. "Outside are the dogs, those who practice magic arts, the sexually immoral, the murderers, the idolaters and everyone who loves and practices falsehood."[7] Who are those people? They are the great prostitute (Babylon, the false church) and the great sea of people on whom she sits.[8]

The bride is definitely not the great prostitute who calls herself the church. The bride consists of the overcomers, "those who [continuously] wash their robes, that they may have the right to the tree of life and may go through the gates into the city."[9]

Notice, however, that the Lord God and the Lamb are also a part of the city. They are its temple, its light source, its throne, and its river of living water. It is the City of God, and it is also a city of people. This symbolizes just what Jesus declared the night before He was crucified: "On that day you will realize that I am in my Father, and you are in me, and I am in you."[10] This kind of perfect union comes only from lifting the veil to behold the unveiled Christ and dining at His wedding supper in our spirits.

The Holy City, the New Jerusalem, is not a physical city that's going to drop down out of the sky into the Middle East someday or be suspended in space. It is the present, ongoing reality of Jesus Christ and His blood-washed saints living in perfect union in God the Father.

The Perfect City for Perfected People

The Holy City describes a state of perfection, or completion, in Christ. It symbolizes spiritual/physical truths and realities and describes what is ideal, perfect, or complete in each overcomer's life. It is here, and it is now.

The Revelation description follows the pattern given to Moses for building the tabernacle, especially the Holy of Holies.[11] Now, many religious people will say that perfection is a heresy. No, the heresy is the doctrine that considers imperfection the normal state for the

Christians. God calls people to perfection, not imperfection. "Be perfect, therefore, as your heavenly Father is perfect."[12] I don't believe Jesus would call us to something that is unattainable.

God gave each of us a single purpose in life, and that's to reach our maximum potential—to be everything God created us to be in Him. That's what the Holy City represents. It's our goal—to be perfected in

---

"This Holy City exists now, and it has never been empty. Its residents include heavenly hosts, spirits of righteous men made perfect, and blood-washed saints who are living in it today."

Him and to reign and rule with Him as the New Jerusalem. This city is what Abraham was looking for; a city not made by hands but built on faith in God.[13] It is what Hebrews called a new covenant.[14]

Now, I want to warn you that the new age people have taken God's dream for perfected humanity and twisted it to say something He never intended. Their doctrine, a thoroughly humanistic philosophy, exalts man as God and says that we are gods. They tell us to release the god-power that is within us. That sounds very similar to what I'm saying. Believe me, the counterfeit is always close to the truth. But a half-truth parading as the whole truth is a lie. In the description of the Holy City, we never become little gods; rather, Christ manifests Himself more and more through us as we strive for perfection in Him.

Unfortunately, the new age doctrine is a lot closer to the truth than what most churches teach today about perfection in Christ. Many churches belittle, deny, refute, and distance themselves from this glorious truth. Yet that doesn't make it any less true.

This Holy City exists now, and it has never been empty. Its residents include heavenly hosts, spirits of righteous men made perfect, and blood-washed saints who are living in it today. God has prepared this city for His people—those who overcome and who don't shrink back into sins and unbelief.

No, it is not easy to get into it, as we will see later in this chapter. Jesus said, "Small is the gate and narrow the road that leads to life, and only a few find it."[15]

What Is It Like to Live in the Holy City?

John's parabolic description gives us a glimpse into the Holy City and what it's like to live there. But he is not describing a physical city of the future but a spiritual city of the present. It was at hand when John wrote about it, it has been at hand ever since, and it will always be at hand. It is ongoing. Revelation 21 and 22 tell us what it's like to be full-fledged citizens in the kingdom of God.

One need only look at the symbols and their previous uses in Scripture to see quickly that John used these elegant, material-realm symbols to describe beautiful, spirit-realm/physical-realm truths and realities—just as Jesus used grains of wheat, lost coins, and a pearl of great value to describe the realities of the kingdom.

We're going to look at some of these symbols and the truths they reveal. It is beyond the scope of this book, however, to explain in detail all the symbols. But I want you to open your spiritual eyes and see the great mystery revealed here. Once you capture this vision, you can dig out all the deeper meanings from your own Bible.

Also, I'm not prepared to make a doctrine or defend to the death any of my interpretations of these symbols. I'll tell you what I believe they represent, based on God's Word. But that's not the point. The point is that we need to stop putting this all out into the future and awaken to the glorious, present realities these symbols contain.

With that in mind, let's look at these descriptions.

What is the shape of the city? John says its length, breadth, and height are equal. Of course, a pyramid fits that description. I believe, however, that it's a cube, because the only other cube described in the Bible is the Holy of Holies in the Old Testament tabernacle. There is an obvious parallel between these two. First Kings 6:20 describes the Holy of Holies as a cube where God once dwelt and communed with man. But now He tabernacles inside us. A cube describes completion, perfection, and fullness. Overcomers can be perfected, filled, and completed in the kingdom of God.

So the shape of the city symbolizes the perfection and completion of overcomers in Christ and the fullness of God that dwells within them.

What is its size? If this were a physical city, it would stretch from Texas to Florida, up to New York, over to Illinois, and back down to Texas. John says the angel measured the city and "found it to be 12,000 stadia in length, and as wide and high as it is long."[16] A footnote in the New International Bible says that 12,000 stadia is about 1,400 miles, or 2,200 kilometers.

But this is not a physical city. It's a spiritual city, and it's big enough for all the overcomers who have ever lived, are alive now, and ever will live.[17]

Notice the symbolism of the numbers: three represents the fullness of God (the Trinity); four describes the totality of a work in the world (like four winds or the four corners of the earth); and twelve stands for sonship in Christ. Put them together, and you arrive at a symbol for God working out His total purpose in a human being ($3 \times 4 = 12$) and in the world. Also, in chapter 10, we saw that 1,000 represents a vast number, or a large amount, or a long time.

Remember, numbers in the Revelation do not deal with arithmetic—they deal with spiritual truths and realities. Let's examine this more closely.

A cube has 12 edges: 12 edges x 12,000 stadia for each side = 144,000: the number of saints sealed. The 144,000 is not the literal population or a symbol of historical and political Israel, as many have taught. It is a symbol of the multitudes of overcomers and of the new Israel, a spiritual Israel.

We can only find this city by the Spirit of God, because it is a spiritual city, a dwelling in God. We are not to wait for a physical/material city to come down and satisfy our Star Wars fantasies.

What are its gates? You don't go up to this city—it comes down to you! It came down in John's day, and it keeps on coming down.

But notice, you can only enter through its gates. Gates are mentioned throughout the Bible and have much spiritual meaning. Jesus said, "upon this rock [the revelation of Christ's deity] I will build my church; and *the gates* of hell shall not prevail against it."[18] These are not physical gates; they are spiritual gates.

There are twelve gates to the New Jerusalem, and each gate was named after one of the tribes of Israel. If you look back at Genesis 49, you'll discover that each tribe was given the name of a son of Jacob, each name has a spiritual meaning, and each was given a specific blessing.

The gates are spiritual entrances and exits; we go *in* and *out* of the city through them. For example, the name Judah means praise, so praise is one of the gates. Now some have taken this passage so literally that they say to their loved ones, "When you get to heaven, wait for me by XXX gate." That misses the whole point. These are spiritual gates!

Not everyone enters the city through the same gate, and we don't enter through the same gate each time. In other words, nobody is going to force you to enter or even stay in the kingdom of God. If you're living outside, you have opportunities to enter; if you are inside, you can choose to exit. But notice that those who have the name of the harlot can never enter the city.

We learn from other Scriptures that obstacles block the gates. For example, self-centeredness blocks the gates through pride, fear, ignorance, and sin. Religious people often stand by the gates and keep people from entering: "Woe to you teachers of the Law and Pharisees, you hypocrites, you shut the kingdom of Heaven in men's faces." How do they shut the gates? By either denying that they exist or attacking those who try to enter. "You yourselves do not enter, nor will you let those enter who are trying to enter."[19]

But great blessings come to those who press through and enter the gates. Wisdom takes her stand "beside the gates leading into the city."[20] And wisdom is "more precious than rubies," because it comes from divine revelation.

What are the famous gates of pearl? These are repeated references in the Revelation to speaking. For example, "The Spirit and the bride *say* come."[21] The mouth, with its pearly calcium teeth, opens up the gates to the kingdom.

We enter it ourselves through our mouths. The psalmist says, "Enter his gates with thanksgiving and his courts with praise."[22]

We inherit the right to enter the kingdom, and we stay in it by overcoming the evil one. How do we overcome him? "They overcame him by the blood of the Lamb and *by the word of their testimony.*"[23]

We also reproduce the kingdom in other people by speaking the message of the kingdom. "The house of God is the gate of Heaven."[24] We are the house of God. Thus, our mouths are the gates through which people come into the city. Our very own mouths—our teeth through which the message passes—are symbolized by the pearly gates.

Note that every one of the gates is a pearl, yet they are all of one pearl. Does that remind you of anything? What about Jesus' parabolic description of the kingdom of God: "Again, the kingdom of Heaven is like a merchant looking for fine pearls. When he found one of great value, he went away and sold everything he had and bought it."[25] We are the pearl of great value, and Jesus is the merchant; He bought us with His blood. Now, we are all of one pearl (gate)—Jesus. "I am the gate,"[26] He said. We all enter the city through Him.

Why the Pearl? God uses what humans value in the physical realm to illustrate what exists in the spirit realm.

According to *Encyclopaedia Britannica*, the pearl is "one of the most valuable gems. Large, perfectly shaped pearls rank in value with the most precious stones.

"Pearls differ from other gems. Most gems are minerals that are mined from beneath the earth, but pearls are formed inside the shells of oysters. Mineral gems are hard and usually reflect light, but pearls are rather soft and absorb as well as reflect light."

Sound familiar? Jesus said, "I am the light of the world. . . . You are the light of the world."[27]

Continuing from *Britannica*, "Cultured pearls are grown by placing a grain of sand or a chip inside an oyster. This inflames the oyster and it begins to coat the irritant substance repeatedly, producing a pearl."

Does that sound like redemption? A pearl symbolizes something that was ugly and undesirable, an irritant. When it is covered with something beautiful and pure (the blood of Christ), it produces something precious. This depicts perfectly what Christ did for us. God couldn't have picked a more perfect material for the gates—the only way we can enter the city.

It is interesting to note that the substance oysters secrete to turn irritants into pearls is calcium—the same substance our teeth are made of.

What, then, are the gates of pearl through which we and other people can enter the kingdom? They are our pearly white teeth, in our mouths, through which we repent and utter praises to God and thereby gain entrance ourselves, and through which we proclaim the gospel message that opens the kingdom to other people, and through which we bind and loose.

What are the foundations of the city? The city sits on top of twelve foundations—the teachings of the twelve apostles. This symbolizes the full Word of God. If your walls are not built on the full Word of God, they're going to crumble.

We build on that foundation. Jesus talked about a wise man building his house upon a rock,[28] and Paul said, "You are no longer foreigners and aliens, but fellow citizens with God's people and members of God's household, built on the foundation of the apostles and prophets, with Christ Jesus himself as the chief cornerstone. In Him the whole building is joined together and rises to become a holy temple in the Lord."[29]

There are many, many more references which support this spirit-realm/physical-realm reality,[30] but I hope you are getting the idea. The whole Word of God is the bedrock of the foundation and, since everything in the Word points to Him, Jesus Christ is the cornerstone upon which the city is built.

What are the walls of the city? The walls are the people—the lively stones—of the city.[31] The walls are made up of twelve kinds of precious stones—us. These are the same precious stones that were in the breastplate of the high priest.[32] We are precious to God. We are His treasure, His glory.[33]

Walls provide protection. And, since the kingdom (the city) is inside us, there is a sense in which the walls of the whole city provide protection for us individually. We build these walls in our minds by learning and renewing the Word of God in our memories and by drawing on the supernatural power of God. "Like a city whose walls are broken down, is a man who lacks self-control."[34] The devil and his cohorts cannot get inside if you have high walls.

The devil and his cohorts get into a church when it doesn't have high walls, or when the walls have crumbled. And when they do, they declare war on those who hold to the testimony of Jesus. Note that "the woman [the great prostitute] was dressed in purple and scarlet and was glittering with gold, precious stones and pearls."[35] Babylon has taken many precious stones and put them on a string, wearing them like trophies. We have to overcome Babylon, the beast, and the dragon. These walls give us the protection we need.

What is the street? Note that *street* is singular, not plural (*streets of gold*, as so many gospel songs proclaim). This street is the highway to holiness—the unrestricted opportunity and ability to communicate with God—that runs through each of us. We have direct access to the King of the city.

We don't have to go through a temple; besides, the temple of the Old Covenant has disappeared. We are now the temple, and the temple is in Christ. The physical temple has given way to a spiritual one.

John was able to see man as God sees him, in the fullness of Christ. God can only delight in His own glory, as reflected in us.

The street of gold signifies the divine nature of holiness. Nothing unclean can travel on this street. It is transparent because it is spiritual reality, and you can only walk on it by entering the spirit dimension.

What is the River of Life? Again, this is not a physical river; the river is the Spirit of God. It is eternal life. Jesus said that eternal life is to know the Father and the Son.[36]

This river runs inside us. It is the same river Jesus promised when He said, "Whoever believes in me, as the Scripture has said, streams of living water will flow from within him."[37]

Get rid of all the fantasies of a big river flowing by mansions and condos in some future physical city, and start realizing that He's speaking of the Spirit of God welling up within us—here and now!

This river flows on forever, and its fountain never dries up. There is even enough water to baptize new converts into the kingdom.

What is the tree of life? It is, of course, Jesus Christ. He is in the midst of the city, and when we eat of the tree of life (just as when we eat of the Lamb), we eat of Christ in the spirit realm.

Note that the city has a garden in it. As we saw earlier in this chapter, the Bible begins with a garden and ends with a garden. Both of these gardens contain the tree of life. In Genesis, God takes away man's access to the tree of life. In Revelation, He restores it. Why? Because, in Christ, we eat of and actually become part of the tree of life.

"I am the vine, you are the branches," Jesus said.[38] Branches produce leaves, and the leaves are on us—they are our hands. Leaves enable us to praise God, they open up the Kingdom to the nations, and they are for the healing of the nations.

Jesus also described us as fruit-bearing trees: "Every tree that does not produce good fruit will be cut down."[39] And notice that John speaks of this tree producing twelve fruits. That means it is bearing fruit continuously. People should be able to eat fruit from us at all times.

Ezekiel, in his vision of the kingdom, saw many trees, all waving their branches and leaves to bring healing to the nations. God's plan is for the people who live in His Holy City to become a forest of trees of life, walking in this truth, and bringing healing to all the nations of the earth.°

The New Inner City

Reading John's description of the Holy City is a little like reading a travel brochure. It is not designed to satisfy your intellectual curiosity—only to whet your appetite and to make you hungry to go there.

But, unlike the people who produce those travel brochures, John could not convey the splendor of his city with pictures. Why? This city is inside you. It is a spiritual city and can only be entered by the spirit.

Thus, the Revelation gives us a verbal description, using earthly metaphors and symbols, of the present reality of living in the kingdom of God. Now, maybe you're like I am. Some of those symbols don't really get me excited. For instance, the idea of walking on gold does nothing for me. But that's not the point. If we are ever going to capture the mystery of The Revelation, we have to quit looking at the symbols themselves and look to the realities behind them. How do you do that? I'm glad you asked, because that's the next major point of this chapter.

° Later in this chapter, we'll describe what the "sickness of the nations" is and explain how residents of the Holy City bring healing.

Why You Don't Have to Die Or Be Raptured
To Live in the New Jerusalem

You don't have to die or be raptured to go to the New Jerusalem! Jesus came, died, and rose from the dead to bring His Holy City to you! And He comes to bring the full reality of His kingdom to you and within you!

"You don't have to die or be raptured to go to the New Jerusalem! Jesus came, died, and rose from the dead to bring His Holy City to you!"

Quit stargazing and begin Star grazing! The star the wise men followed at Jesus' birth is the Bright and Morning Star; He's the Light of the World; He's the Lamp of the Holy City; He's the Tree of Life. And, He invites you to come and eat of Him—*here and now!*

It is time for a Revelation revival. The Holy City is not a material land that is fairer than day in the sweet by and by; it is a visual symbol of a present reality—a symbol of the ongoing, timeless kingdom of God. If this book accomplishes anything, it should illustrate that the End Times categorization of Scriptures is a flawed system.

Just as Jesus comes quickly (suddenly) in power and glory to individuals, the New Jerusalem comes quickly to those who have the spiritual eyes and ears to perceive it. All who will wash their robes in the blood of Christ, and are willing to do what it takes to overcome, can open their pearly gates and enter in. We can drink from the river of living water, eat from the tree of life, walk on the highway of holiness, and become precious stones in the walls of God's Holy City.

You might be surprised by whom you'll meet when you enter this city. I've had the strangest feeling throughout the writing of this book that many who will read it are already experiencing the glorious realities I've been talking about. If asked, they may not express it in the same terms, but they're already living in the fullness of the kingdom and are reigning and ruling with Jesus. Hopefully, if you are one of them, this book has enabled you to better define and express to others what you've been experiencing on your own. At least, maybe you won't feel so alone in the future.

If you are not one of them, I hope this book has awakened within you a hunger for the deeper things of God. Maybe it has made you aware that the deep mysteries of God are fathomable, and that His promises and commands are both applicable and attainable to us individually, now.

What Will We Be Doing in the Holy City?

One thing you won't spend your time doing in the New Jerusalem is flitting around the clouds on angel wings, playing cherubic melodies on a golden harp—as depicted in most celestial art. Citizens of God's kingdom are far too busy reigning and ruling over their own lives and in the sphere of the world they are occupying for their King.

You see, the Great Commission[40] is far greater than most of us have been led to believe. Jesus speaks of being given and conferring upon us *all* authority in *heaven and earth.* He commands us to go into *all* the world" and to *all creation,* to "make disciples of *all nations,*" and to "teach them to obey *everything I have commanded you*" (emphasis added).

And the Great Commission has been magnified by the unveiling of Jesus Christ in His Alpha and Omega form. The bottom line of the Great Commission, as amplified by the Revelation, is that we are to reign and rule over everything in the spirit realm and the material realm—the whole creation. In fact, the Bible begins with, is filled with, and ends with instructions for God's people to reign and rule over His creation.

For too long now the church has been in retreat. We've given up too much of God's territory to the beast system and to the great dragon from whom they derive their natural and supernatural powers. God is calling His saints to take it all back.

Too many churches have been seduced by false prophets into idolatrous self-fulfillment and godless worship, and have been taken over by the great prostitute. Atheistic humanism has seized control of our nation's political, governmental, judicial, educational, communicative, commercial, and ecclesiastical systems and institutions. Christ is raising up His bride with the mandate to take them all back.

"It's time for us Christians to quit resting and retreating and start reigning and ruling."

It's time for us Christians to quit resting and retreating and start reigning and ruling. The pessimistic outlook of gloom and destruction of God's world, brought on by catastrophic End Times doctrines, has led far too many to take a short-term view of their tasks in this present world. After all, they reason, why bother with trying to make disciples of all nations when they're all going to be burned up some day anyway? How can you view the world with a long-term perspective or invest in future generations when you think you are part of the terminal generation?

The Revelation proclaims that God has not given up on the human race, and He has not given us permission to give up on it either. Isaiah said of Jesus, "The government will be on his shoulders. . . . Of the increase of his government and peace there will be no end. He will reign on David's throne and over his kingdom, establishing and upholding it with justice and righteousness from that time on and forever."[41] Does that sound as if God has given up on the world? No!

It is almost beyond human comprehension that God has entrusted the task of reigning and ruling over His Kingdom to the likes of us. He who said, "*I am* the light of the world"[42] also said, "*You are* the light of the world, *a city* on a hill cannot be hidden."[43] How and why did we get to be God's light? "*I have made you a light* for the Gentiles, that you may bring salvation to the ends of the earth," God says.[44]

Certainly He is the King, but He has placed us in charge of His kingdom and has given us specific instructions on how we are to reign and rule over it.

How Are We to Reign and Rule?

The Great Commission is recorded in all four Gospels, but Matthew's account of it seems most explicit and all-inclusive: "Therefore, go and make disciples of all nations, baptizing them in the name of the Father and of the Son and of the Holy Spirit, and teaching them to obey everything I have commanded you."[45]

What does the word *therefore* mean in this context? Look at the verse before it: "All authority in heaven and on earth has been given to me."[46] Jesus has given us His all-inclusive authority to carry on the work of His kingdom. And He has given us the keys to His kingdom so that we can bind and loose anything or any force that hinders our reigning and ruling over.[47] He has made everything in heaven and earth available to us.

Now that we've been given this Great Commission and the full authority to execute it, how do we carry it out? Here are a few things I believe we must do.

We have to press our way into and become the Holy City. We don't just visit or take up residence there; we actually become the walls, the trees, and everything that makes up the city.

How do we enter and become the city? We do it the same way John did it—by the spirit, and through our own pearly gates. John was not literally taken away into outer space; his feet stayed on the earth. He was caught up in the spirit realm—taken in the spirit to a mountain of faith by the Spirit so that he was able to see the perfection of the saints, the church as God sees it.

I don't know all that being in the spirit implies, but I do know that it goes against our natural instincts. I believe it involves a real transformation. Pray for the Holy Spirit to lead you into a full revelation of what this means for you.

We have to measure up to God's standards. "The angel who talked with me had a measuring rod of gold to measure the city, its gates and its walls."[48] First, we have to see ourselves as in Christ, then we have to see if we measure up.

In Solomon's temple, every stone was chiseled, honed, shaped, and polished in the quarry. Then, it was measured against a precise standard. When it measured up perfectly, it could then be fitted into place without sound. Tribulation shapes us up and prepares us to fit smoothly into the walls of the city.

Note that the angel was measuring overcomers; the Gentiles (all who are not overcomers) were outside and could not be measured.

To measure is to ascertain size or stature by a fixed standard. We must measure up in our fullness in Christ,[49] our spiritual maturity,[50] our faith,[51] our obedience to God's Word,[52] and the degree to which we have the Holy Spirit[53] within us.

How are we measured? The passage does not specifically say, but one obvious way is by the fruits we produce. And that leads us to the next thing we have to do to reign and rule.

We are to do the works of Jesus. The launching pad for all effective ministry is doing the works that Jesus did and commands us to do. People must see evidence of God's presence in you before they will listen to anything you have to say about what it can do for them. In fact, Jesus said that is the way you can tell true prophets from false ones—by the fruits they produce.[54]

Certainly, doing the works of Jesus means exhibiting the fruit of the Spirit: love, joy, peace, patience, meekness, and so forth.[55] Those are the basics. But the works of Jesus also include all the natural and miraculous works He did in His earthly ministry. "I tell you the truth," Jesus said, "anyone who has faith in me will do what I have been doing."[56] And what did He do? He proclaimed the gospel, healed the sick, cast out evil spirits, fed the multitudes, raised the dead, and performed many other miracles.

Am I saying that we are to be doing those things? I'm just reporting what God's Word says about it: that "the testimony of Jesus" is the very "spirit of prophecy."[57] That word *testimony* means *evidence given*.

The prophets did miracles, Jesus did miracles, His disciples did miracles, first-century Christians did miracles. Why shouldn't we? Oh, I know, many have distorted Paul's statement that love is most important and outlasts everything[58] to prove that anything supernatural has ceased. Hogwash! The Bible—from the first verse of Genesis through the last verses of Revelation—is a supernatural book. Why should everything since then change so radically that nothing is supernatural?

While Christians and churches are downplaying the existence of the spirit realm, evil spiritual forces are wreaking havoc in individual lives. It's time for Christians to wake up to the power of the spirit realm and get on with doing the supernatural works of Jesus, as well as all the other things we're supposed to be doing.

We are to do the greater works. Jesus promised, "He [who has faith in me] will do even greater things than these, because I am going to the Father."[59]

What did He mean by that statement? It's not so hard to figure out. It's all spelled out in Scripture: in prophecies about Him, in Jesus' life and kingdom teachings, in the Great Commission. Isaiah said of Jesus, "The government shall be on his shoulders. . . . Of the increase of his government and peace there will be no end."[60] Jesus gave the keys of the kingdom to us,[61] and appointed us to reign and rule over that kingdom as kings and to serve it as priests.[62] In His kingdom parables and teachings, and by His examples, He showed us exactly how to do it, and He demonstrated the spirit in which it should be done.

In short, we are first to do all the things He did (including the supernatural), then to do all the things He didn't do but that we are instructed in Scripture to do. For example, He didn't make disciples of all nations; He commands us to do that. He didn't take back all the territory Satan had seized, but He instructs us to do it. He didn't reign and rule over governments, peoples, and nations; but He says we are to do it.[63]

So, if you want to figure out what the greater works are, just look at all the things Jesus didn't do that need to be done for us to take all-inclusive dominion over all the spiritual and material world.

But we can't do the greater works we're commanded to do until we first do the supernatural works of Jesus. He coupled them together in the same way James connected faith and works.[64] You simply can't do one without the other.

Of course, reigning and ruling starts with us as individuals. We have to be able to reign and rule over our own lives before we can reign and rule in the world. That means having our flesh and our minds under the control of the spirit, reaching our full potential in Christ, and being the best we can be, whatever our chosen vocation.[65]

Next, we're to reign and rule in our families. That includes leading our families into the Holy City, overcoming evil spirit-realm forces that seek to destroy our loved ones, and doing the works of Jesus in our own homes.

The greater works also include demonstrating the testimony of Jesus in our churches, communities, schools, nations—every aspect of our earthly existence. That doesn't just mean talking the talk; it means walking the walk. And it means exercising authority in all our areas of responsibility.

Does this include being involved in politics and social action? It can, and often does, when that's necessary to reign and rule. But the beginning point of the greater works is doing the works of Jesus in the spirit of love. Trying to start with social actions, and jumping over the supernatural works of Jesus, is like trying to build a second story on a vacant lot. It just won't stand up.

Remember that "the leaves of the trees [us] are for the healing of the nations."[66] And what is the sickness or deception of the nations that needs to be healed? It is the delusion that the nations can come together and solve all the world's problems—without God. Healing sometimes involves pouring in the balm of kindness; but, in cases of serious illness (deception), it often means radical surgery.

The bottom line of the Revelation, of the whole Bible, is that we are to take dominion over God's creation—to reign and rule over everything. If something has been lost, we are to take it back; and whatever has not been brought under God's authority is to be conquered for Him.

We are to defeat the enemies of God and to expand His kingdom. The battle for control of this world starts in the spirit realm, where evil powers run rampant. Paul said, "Our struggle is not against flesh and blood, but against the rulers, against the authorities, against the powers of this dark world and against the spiritual forces of evil in the heavenly realms."[67]

I believe the biggest reason the church has given up so much ground in our generation is that it has failed to take into account (and in many cases has even denied the existence of) the supernatural enemies of God. Jesus recognized them and did battle with them. So did the first-century church. How can we expect to conquer and rule the world for Christ when we don't even acknowledge or know how to deal with the powers and beings that control it now?

By the way, you don't have to worry about finding these spirit-realm enemies to engage them. If you start doing the works of Jesus, they'll find you.

Can we conquer them? Again, Paul explains the weapons we have at our disposal. "The weapons we fight with are not the weapons of the world. On the contrary, they have divine power to demolish strongholds."[68] In the Word of God, as revealed to us by the Spirit of God, we have all we need for complete victory in every sphere of our lives and ministry.

Why Is This Message So Controversial?

Why is the idea that the Holy City exists as a present reality, and that it is inside us and among us, so hard for most Christians today to swallow?

Think about it. This message means that we are to reign and rule. All this is available now. All this is the final outworking of God's new covenant with man.[69] We are to enter into and become the New Jerusalem now, and we are to bring the nations into it, because Jesus says, "Behold I am making *everything* new."[70]

Yet, most Christians won't have anything to do with what they call this radical new idea, even though it's been around for over nineteen hundred years. They'd rather hang onto a short-term, pessimistic view of the end of the world. They'd rather sit around and hope that Jesus is going to come back and straighten everything out. Why? Why can't they accept the biblical truth that He is already back and that He wants us to help Him reign and rule in this present world?

I believe it is because most Christians are too tired of struggling, that subduing the power of the flesh is too painful and inconvenient, that fighting against the beast system, the dragon, and the harlot church is too bloody for them. Besides, their identity is so wrapped up in their religious systems and practices that forging a new identity in Christ is too emotionally threatening.

That's why I believe it is so vital to invest this message in the next generation. Maybe we can catch them before they are too tired, too anesthetized by doctrines, too comfortable, and too timid to force their way into the kingdom and start reigning and ruling.[71]

What Does It All Mean?

The prophecy of the Holy City is calling God's people out of mediocrity into fullness, completion, and perfection.[72] It gives us a glimpse into how God views us and our role in His kingdom. It shows us something of our full potential in Christ.

"I find it hard to believe that Jesus came all the way from heaven, suffered as He did, and finally hung on a cross and died—all for the sake of creating the mediocre, anemic brand of Christianity that calls itself the church today. I believe the New Jerusalem is a parable of the dynamic and glorious kingdom Jesus died to establish."

I find it hard to believe that Jesus came all the way from heaven, suffered as He did, and finally hung on a cross and died—all for the sake of creating the mediocre, anemic brand of Christianity that calls itself the church today. I believe the New Jerusalem is a parable of the dynamic and glorious kingdom Jesus died to establish.

The word *mediocre* comes from two Latin words: *medi*, meaning halfway, and *ocris*, meaning a stony mountain. The Romans combined them to form an idiomatic expression which literally meant halfway up a mountain.

In my younger years, I was a mountain climber and scaled some of the best-known mountains in the world: the Matterhorn, Kilimanjaro, Mount Kenya, Mount Ranier, and others. I can tell you from those experiences that nothing is more demanding or exhausting than to keep climbing when everything within you cries out for relief and rest. I can also tell you that nothing is more devastating to the human spirit than getting all primed to go to the top of a magnificent and lofty peak, only to get stranded halfway up the mountain.

Friend, God is calling us to the very peak of His holy mountain. What's more, He is calling us to become kings and priests[73] of His holy mountain and the city perched on its pinnacle.

For too long now, we've been buying into the deception of the conspiracy that all the things we are promised and called to in the Revelation are out in the sky somewhere and out in the future sometime. The Apocalypse of Jesus Christ has unveiled Him in His Alpha and Omega form. He stands atop the holy mountain and says, "Come unto me!" His comings are at hand. His commands are heedable and obeyable—now! His blessings are available—now!

It's time to quit gazing off into the heavens looking for a physical city and to enter into His spiritual/physical reality to reign and rule with Him forever and forever.

Will you join me? Let's go—right now!

AFTERWORD

H arvard University provides a pitiful, painful example of what happens when the wisdom and revelation of God give way to the philosophies of men in our institutions.

When Harvard College was founded in 1636, just sixteen years after the pilgrims landed at Plymouth, Massachusetts, its mission was to train young men to preach the gospel and to do missionary work among the Indians. If John Harvard (the Puritan minister who gave so much of himself and his resources to its founding) were to return today, he would probably be shocked at how far removed his namesake is from his original vision for it.

Likewise, I believe that Jesus must weep today over the number of Christians who are refusing to reign and rule as kings and priests in the New Jerusalem, much as He wept over old Jerusalem a few days before His crucifixion.

> O Jerusalem, Jerusalem, you who kill the prophets and stone those sent to you, how often I have longed to gather your children together, as a hen gathers her chicks under her wings, but you were not willing.
>
> Look, your house is left to you desolate. For I tell you, you will not see me again until you say, "Blessed is he who comes in the name of the Lord."[1]

Notice that He did not say, "I *will not come* again until . . . " Rather, He said, " . . . *you will not see me* again until you say, 'blessed is he who comes in the name of the Lord'" (emphasis added). He comes! The question is do we see Him? He speaks! Do we hear Him?

He knocks! Do we open the door so He can come in and eat with us? He commands! Do we obey Him?

The two men dressed in white who appeared after Jesus ascended asked Jesus' disciples a very appropriate question: "Why do you stand here looking into the sky?"[2] The disciples had been given orders to follow, but they were just standing around waiting for something else to happen. Yet the Holy Spirit could not descend upon them until they obeyed.

It's still an appropriate question: "Why do you stand here looking up into the sky?" Hopefully, this book has made it clear that we have our marching orders. Jesus said, "It is done. I am the Alpha and the Omega, the Beginning and the End. . . . He who overcomes will inherit all this. . . ."[3]

Are you waiting around for something else to happen?

The Revelation was not given to us as literature or philosophy from the past, nor as a timetable for the future. It is an action book for the present. Its spirit-realm/physical-realm truths and realities were at hand in the first century; they have been at hand ever since; they are at hand, right here, right now; and they will continue to be at hand for future generations! Its fulfillments are countless.

What If I'm Wrong?

What if the end-timers are right? What if all the symbols in the Revelation are literal, physical, material, and chronological? What if there is only going to be a single, future coming of Jesus and a one-time, physical, corporate rapture, and a cosmic explosion that blows this present world out of existence to end human history?

Believe me, those are questions I have not taken lightly. No rational person would take them lightly when the Revelation ends with this somber warning: "I warn everyone who hears the words of the prophecy of this book: If anyone adds anything to them, God will add to him the plagues described in this book. And if anyone takes words away from this book of prophecy, God will take away from him his share in the tree of life and in the holy city, which are described in this book."[4]

No, I've weighed that warning very carefully. I've also weighed very carefully Jesus' warning about causing one of His little ones to sin.[5] I don't relish the idea of a fate worse than having a millstone tied around my neck and being drowned in the sea.

Therefore, I've sought diligently to rely on the Scriptures to explain themselves in interpreting every symbol. I've tried to keep my opinions to a minimum and, in the few instances where I've injected my opinions, I've identified them as such and not claimed that they were the Word of God.

Ultimately, you must ask God to give you His Spirit of wisdom and revelation and search out these mysteries for yourself.

If I am wrong, I believe I've erred on the safe side. First, if I have over-symbolized, I've followed the example set by none other than Jesus Christ, who repeatedly said, "The Kingdom of heaven is like . . ."

What's more, if sincere believers take the at-hand message seriously and go on to obey everything I've explained, future apocalyptic events hold no threat for them. If you go on to maturity in Christ, as I've encouraged you to do, you don't need to be worried about a final coming or a physical rapture. You're going! If you overcome and reign and rule with Christ in the kingdom of God, as I've repeatedly urged you to do, you don't need to worry about what's going to happen to this present world.

In short, if I'm wrong, so what?

But What If I'm Right?

What if the Revelation is to be applied individually and internally? What if it reveals the inner workings of the spirit realm, not a scenario of future events? What if the Revelation explains how and why the world works, why and how the church works? What if the primary purpose of the Apocalypse is to open the beauty of Jesus and His present-day ministry through His body?

If I'm right about the claims I've made in this book, then much in Christendom is under the judgment of God. The warnings I cited above apply not only to the evil spirit-realm conspirators who willfully distort God's Word, but to those who unwittingly or carelessly aid and abet them as tacit conspirators.

It's time for all of us to ask some hard questions. For example, are things like predicting timetables, interpreting spiritual/physical realities purely physically and pushing them out into the future, and telling people to watch for certain material-realm signs adding to the message of the prophecy? Do we subtract from the Apocalypse when we ignore the supernatural, or when we say these messages don't apply to us today, or when we refuse to grasp, heed, and obey the instructions to overcome and reign and rule with Christ?

If what I've said in this book is not my own, but the truth of God's Word,[6] it's time for us to quit playing church and get on with becoming kings and priests in the kingdom of God. It's time for us to face up to the judgments of God and to overcome—first in the spirit realm then in the physical/material realm. It's time for us to take back all of God's territory that Satan has seized—in our own lives, within our families, in our churches, and in the world.

It's time for us to take the Apocalypse seriously and dig into it with the eyes and ears of the Spirit—not just our physical eyes and ears. More than that, it's time for us to believe it!

"Oh," many will say, "I believe it." But to believe means much more than mental assent. In its biblical definition, to believe is to do. It has to be written believe/obey, and believe/act, and believe/be.

From the beginning of the human race, God planned for man to reign and rule over His earth. The Bible opens with God telling Adam and Eve to subdue the world and rule over it.[7] At its center, Jesus gives His disciples "the keys of the Kingdom" and instructs them to bind and loose in accordance with His instructions.[8] And it ends with a clear picture of the bride of Christ ruling and reigning over the world as His Holy City.[9]

If what has been said throughout this book is true, it's time for us to get off our religious and doctrinal hobby horses, get on our white horses with Christ, and fight with Him with the sword of His Word and by the power of His Spirit.

What Have I Not Said?

What a book doesn't say is often as important as what it does say. There have been several significant omissions from this book; some by necessity, some by design.

I'm sure this work will be accused of saying and implying many things that are not meant at all. I have no illusions that the conspirators will admit that I'm right, then roll over and play dead. And, I fear that many sincere Christians will reject the message of this book be-

---

"If what I've said in this book is not my own, but the truth of God's Word, it's time for us to quit playing church and get on with becoming kings and priests in the kingdom of God."

---

cause of what they think it may imply or what someone tells them it infers. But, if only a few receive it and take it to heart, the effort has not been wasted.

Obviously, I have not been able to cover many of the specific symbols and messages of the Revelation. There simply has not been enough room. Nor was explaining every detail my purpose. Perhaps more will come later. My objective was to give you a framework, a way of thinking about and seeking God, that will clarify the truths and realities of this vital prophecy. I trust that other men and women of God—even other laypeople—will take up the challenge, fill in some of the details of this admittedly sketchy outline, and bring out new treasures.[10] Hopefully, I've made their work easier and more productive.

Perhaps the most obvious omission has been in the area of applications to specific concerns and basic how-to's for one's daily life. That, too, has been intentional. Had I tried to address all the concerns and practices, name all the organizations, ministries, and churches that are participating as tacit conspirators and tried to tell people how to live, I would have obscured the central message. Besides, I might have alienated many people who otherwise might hear that message.

More important, it is not my prerogative (nor that of any man) to "teach you all things."[11] That's the work of the Holy Spirit. If you sincerely seek His wisdom and revelation and study God's Word, He will show you what all this means for you in your daily life. Jesus said, "There is nothing concealed that will not be disclosed, or hidden that will not be made known."[12] It's just a matter of how much you want to know and how willing you are to receive.

One of the joys during the process of writing this book has been the new songs of praise and worship the Lord has given me in my position as music director for my local church. They are drawing and prophetic songs centered around many of the truths and realities you have just read about. Below is the refrain from one of them:

> Prepare the way for the Lord
> Prepare the way for the Lord
> In the might
> And the power of the Spirit
> Prepare the way for the Lord

My goal has been to encourage people to take a new look at what they believe about prophecy, see how it squares with the Scriptures, and to prepare the way for the Lord in their own lives. If I've caused you to do that, I'm grateful for the privilege God has given me to share this journey with you.

Keep searching the Word and keep listening for the knock of our Lord. He comes! Open the door and let Him come in and reveal Himself fully to you! Please, do it now!

NOTES

Introduction

1. See Acts 4:13
2. See Ephesians 1:3–10
3. Ephesians 1:17
4. John 14:26
5. See Revelation 1:1–3, 3:22, 22:7, 18, 19
6. See Revelation 13:3, 17:6–7
7. See Exodus 15:22–26
8. See John 3:3–21

Chapter 1: Clearly, Something Is Wrong

1. Ann Hagedorn, "To Mark Year 2000, Some Events Will Be Out of This World," New York, *The Wall Street Journal,* June 27, 1988, p. 1.
2. Ibid.
3. Matthew 12:33
4. Revelation 7:14 (KJV)
5. See Revelation 1:5, 17:14
6. See Revelation 1:6
7. See Revelation 12:10–12
8. See Revelation 14:12–13
9. See Matthew 13:34–43; John 3:3
10. See Revelation 2:7, 2:11, 2:17, 2:29, 3:6, 3:13, 3:22
11. See John 4:4–26
12. Revelation 22:10 (KJV)
13. See Daniel 12:4
14. Revelation 1:1–3 (KJV)

15. Revelation 1:3 (KJV)
16. Revelation 22:7 (KJV)
17. Luke 17:21 (KJV)

Chapter 2: There Is a Conspiracy Against the Apocalypse

1. See Revelation 12:7–9, 16:14
2. John 8:44; Ephesians 6:12
3. See Revelation 1:17–18
4. See John 15:1, 7–8, 18–24
5. See 1 Corinthians 1:18–25, 3:19; Revelation 2:7, 2:11, 2:17, 2:29, 3:6, 3:13, 3:22
6. Matthew 13:13
7. Matthew 23:13–14
8. See Revelation 22:18–19
9. Matthew 16:6
10. See Matthew 16:12
11. Matthew 9:17

Chapter 3: How to Avoid Being Taken In by the Conspiracy

1. See Acts 1:6–8
2. Revelation 1:3 (KJV)
3. See Revelation 1:6
4. See Revelation 12:11, 17:14
5. See John 16:33
6. Revelation 1:3 (KJV)
7. Revelation 22:18–19
8. See Revelation 1:1
9. See Luke 3:7–19
10. See Matthew 5:17–20
11. See John 8:23, 17:16–18
12. Revelation 6:11
13. See John 15:18–27
14. John 16:33 (KJV)
15. See John 17:13
16. See James 1:22; Revelation 22:14
17. See John 14:12
18. See Revelation 2:26–27
19. See Revelation 1:6

20. See Matthew 10:7
21. See Revelation 1:5–6
22. See Ephesians 6:10–18
23. Revelation 1:1
24. See Revelation 22:12–15
25. John 3:7
26. Revelation 22:14
27. Ibid
28. Revelation 21:6
29. See John 17:20–23
30. John 5:19
31. See Revelation 5
32. Revelation 21:3
33. See Revelation 18:4–5
34. See Revelation 21:5–7
35. See Matthew 16:6
36. See John 8:44 (It is significant to note that Jesus was speaking here to the religious leaders of His day.)
37. John 14:30
38. Acts 19:15–16
39. Matthew 11:12
40. Ephesians 6:12
41. Revelation 1:18
42. Revelation 19:16
43. See John 13–17
44. John 17:15
45. John 17:20
46. John 17:18
47. John 17:21
48. Matthew 28:19–20
49. Revelation 12:11
50. See Acts 4:1–12, 5:17–18, 6:8–15, 7:54–60
51. John 16:33
52. See Ephesians 1:17–19

Chapter 4: How You Can Unravel the Mysteries of the Revelation

1. See John 3:1–13
2. John 4:24

3. See John 6:47–65
4. See John 16:5–16
5. See Luke 17:20–21
6. See Matthew 23
7. Revelation 1:3
8. Revelation 16:15
9. Revelation 22:14
10. Matthew 5:3, emphasis added
11. See Matthew 23:17
12. John 5:39–40, emphasis added
13. John 3:3, emphasis added (NASB)
14. John 3:5, emphasis added (NASB)
15. Revelation 1:19
16. Colossians 2:2–3, emphasis added
17. See Revelation 2–3
18. See Revelation 5–6
19. See Revelation 19
20. See Revelation 19:6–9
21. See Revelation 7
22. Revelation 19:16
23. See Philippians 2:10
24. Revelation 5:5
25. See Revelation 5:6
26. See Revelation 22:1
27. See Matthew 13:11–17
28. Revelation 19:10, emphasis added
29. Revelation 22:7, emphasis added
30. Revelation 22:10 (KJV), emphasis added
31. Revelation 22:13
32. Revelation 22:17
33. See Revelation 6:9
34. See Revelation 11:7–8
35. See Revelation 12:17
36. Luke 21:33
37. See Revelation 1:8
38. Revelation 1:1
39. Revelation 1:3 (KJV)
40. Revelation 1:4–5

41. Revelation 1:7
42. Revelation 1:20
43. Revelation 5:8
44. Revelation 12:9
45. Luke 1:17
46. Matthew 17:11–12
47. Matthew 11:13–14
48. See Matthew 10:5–42; Mark 16:20; Acts 3:1–10
49. See John 14:11–14; Revelation 12:11
50. Matthew 7:16
51. See Acts 9:1–6
52. See Revelation 1:12–16
53. Revelation 1:17
54. See Genesis 3:5
55. 1 John 3:2
56. See Acts 2:47–4:4

Chapter 5: Why You Don't Have to Wait Around for the Second Coming

1. See Revelation 22:19
2. See Acts 1:8 and note that the Greek word for "power" is "dunamis," from which we get our word "dynamite."
3. See Revelation 1:13
4. See Revelation 1:8–11, 4:8–10
5. See John 20:24–21:14
6. See Matthew 5:29
7. See Matthew 5:30
8. See John 20:19–31
9. See Jude 12, 14; 1 Thessalonians 3:13; Revelation 14:14
10. See Matthew 11:16, 12:41–42, 23:36
11. See Acts 7:55–56
12. See Acts 9:1–8
13. John 21:22–23; Revelation 1
14. John 14:21 (emphasis added)
15. Hebrews 9:28
16. See Luke 17:21
17. See Revelation 2–3
18. Revelation 21:3

19. Revelation 22:10 (KJV)
20. See Revelation 1:1
21. See John 3:8
22. Proverbs 2:1–6
23. Isaiah 6:9
24. Revelation 3:20 (emphasis added)
25. For other references to individual comings of Jesus, see: Mark 8:38; Luke 7:22–23, 9:26; John 3:15–16; Revelation 14:10–11, 19:15, 22:17.
26. Revelation 22:20

Chapter 6: How You Can Be Raptured Right Now

1. 1 Thessalonians 4:17
2. Proverbs 13:12
3. See 1 Thessalonians 4:15a
4. See Matthew 24:30–35
5. 1 Thessalonians 4:17
6. See Matthew 12:1–14, 23:1–33
7. See Matthew 24:26–27; Acts 1:7
8. See John 3:16–17
9. See John 17:15–23
10. See Matthew 16:21–28
11. See Genesis 2:7
12. 1 Thessalonians 4:17
13. See Hebrews 12:1
14. See Hebrews 12:22–24
15. See Revelation 20:4–5
16. See Matthew 3:7, 15:1, 16:6, 19:3, 22:23, 23:2; Luke 7:30
17. See Matthew 6:26, 8:20, 13:32
18. See Revelation 16:17
19. Luke 17:37 (KJV)
20. See Hebrews 12:1, 22–24; Jude 12
21. Revelation 20:4–5; 1 Thessalonians 5:1a
22. Revelation 11:15
23. Revelation 5:10 (emphasis added)
24. Matthew 24:31
25. Philippians 3:10–11
26. Ephesians 5:14
27. 1 Corinthians 15:50

28. 1 Peter 1:23 (emphasis added)
29. See Romans 6:13
30. See 2 Corinthians 5:4, Proverbs 12:28
31. See 2 Timothy 1:10; Romans 8:2; Revelation 21:4, 6
32. See John 8:51
33. See Genesis 3:10
34. 1 Corinthians 15:22
35. Luke 11:44
36. See 1 John 2:6
37. John 14:1–4
38. See John 13–17
39. See John 15:1–8
40. Colossians 1:27 (emphasis added)
41. See 2 Thessalonians 1:12
42. John 14:23
43. John 14:26
44. Revelation 20:4–6
45. See Hebrews 12:26–29

Chapter 7: How You Can Conquer the Awesome Creatures of the Apocalypse

1. See Ephesians 1:17
2. See Matthew 12:22–28
3. See Revelation 10:9b. For other prophetic Scriptures about scrolls see Ezekiel 2:9, Zechariah 5:1, Isaiah 29:18, Daniel 12:4, 7:10.
4. Revelation 10:11
5. Revelation 22:10
6. See Revelation 5
7. See Revelation 6, 8:1–5
8. See Revelation 8:6–9:21, 11:15–19
9. See Revelation 16
10. Revelation 11:1
11. See Acts 17:24; 1 Corinthians 3:16, 6:19; 2 Corinthians 6:16
12. See Revelation 10:10
13. See Revelation 6:11, 7:3, 3:21
14. See Revelation 7:14, 11:2, 3, 9, 11
15. Proverbs 14:12
16. See Revelation 1:1

17. See Revelation 1:17
18. See Revelation 5:11–12
19. See Revelation 4:6–8
20. See Revelation 19:6
21. See Revelation 4:10–11
22. See Revelation 15:4
23. See Revelation 4:11
24. See Revelation 5:9
25. See Revelation 3:7
26. See Revelation 1:18
27. See Revelation 9:1, 20:1
28. See Revelation 21:27
29. See Revelation 4:6
30. See Revelation 19:11–12
31. See Revelation 7:2–4
32. See Revelation 19:11
33. See Revelation 17:14
34. See Revelation 19:9
35. See Revelation 21:23–24
36. See See Revelation 2–3
37. See Revelation 6, 7 and 8:1–6
38. See Revelation 1:7–11:19
39. See Revelation 17
40. Revelation 17:2
41. See Revelation 17:4
42. Revelation 17:6
43. See Revelation 17:7ff
44. Revelation 17:6b
45. See Revelation 17:5b and chapter 18
46. See Genesis 11:1–9
47. See Daniel 1:1–2, 5:1–4
48. Revelation 18:4
49. See Revelation 13
50. See Revelation 12:9
51. Revelation 13:3b (emphasis added)
52. See Ephesians 2:2
53. See Revelation 13:16–17
54. See John 18:28–19:16

55. See Revelation 13:11, 18
56. See 2 Corinthians 10:4; Ephesians 6:11–12
57. See 1 John 4:2–3; 2 John 7
58. See Matthew 24:24; Revelation 13:4
59. See Revelation 2–3
60. See Revelation 12:11
61. See Revelation 3:20
62. See Revelation 5
63. See Revelation 6–8:5
64. See Revelation 8:6–13, 9, 11:15–19
65. See Revelation 10:9–10
66. See Revelation 11–14
67. See Revelation 15–16

Chapter 8: Why You Won't Find the Battle of Armageddon in the Middle East

1. See Revelation 16:14
2. See Isaiah 14:13
3. See 2 Kings 9:27
4. See Revelation 9:13–14, 14:14–20, 16:12–16
5. See Joel 2:32, 3:16–17, 21
6. See Exodus 15:17
7. Hebrews 12:22–23: Note also: Romans 9:33, 11:26; Revelation 14:1
8. See Revelation 1:12–20
9. Revelation 2:16
10. See Revelation 1:1
11. See Revelation 1:6
12. Revelation 1:1
13. See Revelation 1:3
14. See Revelation 7:14–17
15. See Revelation 16:15
16. See Revelation 14:4–5
17. See John 14:12, Revelation 2:26 (KJV)
18. See John 10:31
19. See Acts 4:7
20. Revelation 16:1
21. See Luke 10:12
22. See Genesis 2:14

23. See Genesis 15:18; Deuteronomy 11:24; 1 Chronicles 5:9

24. Revelation 22:1–2

25. Matthew 16:18

26. See Matthew 11:12

27. See Matthew 8:30–31

28. See Acts 16:16–19; Ephesians 6:12

29. See Acts 16:19

30. See John 9:1–34

31. See Matthew 26:35–45

32. See Genesis 3:8–10

33. See Revelation 2–3

34. Revelation 2:5 (emphasis added)

35. See Revelation 3:1–6

36. Revelation 3:20

37. Revelation 2:7

38. Revelation 2:11

39. Revelation 2:17

40. Revelation 2:26, 28

41. Revelation 3:5

42. Revelation 3:21

43. See Revelation 3:14–22

44. See 2 Timothy 3:5; Jeremiah 6:20

45. Luke 9:62 (KJV)

46. See Acts 5:1–11

47. See John 2:13–17

48. See Revelation 11:1–2; 1 Peter 4:17; Hebrews 12:5–6

49. Matthew 16:16

50. Matthew 18:17

51. 1 Corinthians 12:27

52. Revelation 19:11

53. See John 1:1

54. See Revelation 19:11

55. See Revelation 19:12

56. See Revelation 19:13

57. See Revelation 19:14

58. See Revelation 19:15

59. See Revelation 14:14

60. See Revelation 19:6–10

61. See Genesis 2:24; John 17:20–21
62. See Genesis 2:23
63. Revelation 1:6
64. See John 17:16

Chapter 9: How You Can Eat "The Wedding Supper"—Now

1. See Hebrews 12:28
2. See John 6:35
3. See John 4:10
4. See Luke 22:19–20
5. See Matthew 22:1–14
6. Matthew 22:11–14
7. Luke 22:15–19
8. Luke 22:28–30
9. See Psalm 23:5, (plus many other Old Testament references to table)
10. See 2 Samuel 7:11
11. See Psalm 23:6
12. See Isaiah 56:7
13. See Matthew 7:24
14. See John 14:2
15. 1 Peter 2:4–5
16. Proverbs 9:10
17. See Ephesians 1:9–10, 3:2–12; also see 1 Corinthians 4:1
18. See Ephesians 3:4–5
19. See Matthew 8:11
20. Revelation 3:20
21. Matthew 22:1–10 (Note: We won't repeat verses 11–14 since we covered them earlier in this chapter.)
22. See John 2:1–11
23. Matthew 9:14–15
24. See John 21:12
25. See Matthew 6:26
26. See Matthew 6:31–33, Romans 14:17
27. 2 Corinthians 5:16
28. Luke 24:5
29. See Exodus 25–40
30. See Hebrews 9–10
31. Hebrews 9:11–12

32. Hebrews 9:26b
33. John 6:30–31
34. John 6:32–33
35. John 6:48
36. John 6:51
37. John 4:32
38. John 4:33
39. John 4:34
40. See Matthew 25:1–13
41. Matthew 5:8 (emphasis added)
42. Jude 23
43. Revelation 19:8
44. Matthew 25:37–40
45. 2 Corinthians 5:16
46. 2 Corinthians 5:17
47. See Hebrews 10:20
48. John 10:27
49. Revelation 3:20

Chapter 10: Why Seven Years Don't Make a Week nor a Thousand Years a Millennium

1. See 1 Samuel 26:24; Matthew 13:21, 24:21, 29; John 16:33; Acts 14:22; Romans 2:9, 12:12; Revelation 1:9, 2:9–10
2. See Daniel 9
3. See Revelation 11:2–3
4. See Matthew 24:32–33
5. Daniel 9:21–27
6. See Matthew 24:34
7. Colossians 1:9
8. Colossians 2:2–3
9. Hebrews 9:10–15
10. John 2:18–22A
11. See 1 Peter 2:5
12. See Matthew 5:14
13. Revelation 11:1–6
14. See John 7:38–39
15. Matthew 10:34
16. John 16:33 (KJV)

17. John 15:18
18. John 13:16, 15:20
19. John 15:19
20. Revelation 11:11–13
21. Revelation 20:1–8
22. James Strong, *Strong's Dictionary of the Words in the Greek Testament,* reprinted 1983 by Broadman Press, Nashville, Tennessee; reference # 5507, page 77.
23. For examples, see Revelation 7:4, 11:13, 14:1
24. See Psalm 50:10
25. Note: For other examples see: Deuteronomy 1:11; Psalm 68:17; 84:10, 90:4
26. Daniel 7:27
27. Revelation 11:15, 22:5
28. Deuteronomy 7:9
29. See Revelation 7:4
30. See Revelation 14:1–5
31. See Luke 17:20–21
32. See John 18:36A
33. See Romans 14:17
34. Matthew 16:19
35. See Revelation 11:1–13
36. 2 Corinthians 6:14–17
37. 2 Corinthians 6:17–18
38. Matthew 6:10 (KJV)
39. See Daniel 9:24–27
40. John 19:30
41. Daniel 4:34

Chapter 11: Why It Won't Take a Nuclear Holocaust to Make Way for "a New Heaven and a New Earth"

1. Revelation 20:11–21:8
2. See Acts 2:16–21; Joel 2:28–3:3
3. See Revelation 4:1–11
4. Matthew 17:2
5. Revelation 1:14
6. See Revelation 2:17
7. Revelation 3:4
8. Revelation 3:5 (KJV)
9. Revelation 3:18 (KJV)

10. See Revelation 6:11, 7:9, 13–14
11. See Revelation 15:6, 19:8, 14
12. See Revelation 19:14
13. See Revelation 17–18
14. See Revelation 5:1–10
15. Revelation 3:21; see also Revelation 12:11
16. See Revelation 5:10
17. See Matthew 19:28
18. See Proverbs 16:12, 25:5
19. See Matthew 19:28, 25:31, 34; Revelation 3:21, 20:4
20. See Isaiah 66:1–2
21. Revelation 21:5
22. See Hebrews 9:27
23. See Romans 8:1–17
24. Revelation 21:6b (emphasis added)
25. Revelation 21:7 (emphasis added)
26. See Ezekiel 36:26–27; 1 Corinthians 3:16
27. See Psalm 103:14; 2 Corinthians 4:7
28. See Romans 12:1–2; 2 Corinthians 5:17
29. Romans 12:2
30. Ephesians 1:9–10 (emphasis added)
31. Isaiah 65:17
32. See Isaiah 66:14–16, 22
33. Isaiah 1:2
34. Revelation 21:5
35. Revelation 21:6
36. Amos 6:1
37. Jeremiah 48:10
38. Ephesians 5:6–14
39. See Revelation 21:23
40. See Psalm 118:22–24; see also Luke 17:22–37; 1 Corinthians 3:13; Hebrews 10:25
41. 2 Peter 3:10–13
42. See Galatians 4:3, 9
43. 2 Timothy 3:5
44. 1 Corinthians 15:47–49
45. 1 Corinthians 15:50
46. 2 Corinthians 4:7 (KJV)
47. Revelation 20:12b

48. Revelation 20:15
49. See 2 Corinthians 3:2–6
50. See John 1:1–5
51. See Matthew 25:31–46
52. Revelation 20:13
53. See Revelation 17:1, 15
54. Revelation 21:1b
55. See Ephesians 2:1–6
56. Matthew 8:22
57. Luke 15:24
58. Matthew 23:27b
59. See Romans 6–8 (especially note 6:11–13)
60. See Revelation 19:20
61. See Revelation 20:10
62. See Revelation 18:8b, 19:1–3
63. See Hebrews 12:29; Luke 12:49; 1 Thessalonians 5:19
64. See Genesis 19:24, 22:6–7; Exodus 3:2, 9:23–24, 14:24, 19:8, 24:17; Isaiah 5:24; Matthew 3:10–11; John 15:6; Acts 2:3
65. See Hebrews 2:14; John 8:51
66. Revelation 20:15
67. John 5:25 (emphasis added)
68. Revelation 21:1a
69. Revelation 21:2
70. Revelation 21:3
71. Revelation 21:4
72. Hebrews 9:10–11
73. Revelation 21:5
74. 2 Corinthians 5:17
75. Revelation 21:6
76. Ephesians 1:17
77. Romans 12:1–2
78. See Revelation 21:10
79. See Isaiah 66:22
80. Matthew 6:10
81. Revelation 21:7a
82. Revelation 21:7b
83. Revelation 21:8

Chapter 12: Why You Won't Find the New Jerusalem in the Middle East

1. See Galatians 4–5, especially 4:25–26
2. Revelation 21:9–10 (emphasis added)
3. See Revelation 19:7–9
4. See Revelation 7:3–8
5. See Revelation 14:1–5
6. See Revelation 21:1–22:5
7. Revelation 22:15
8. Read Revelation 17–18
9. Revelation 22:14
10. John 14:20
11. See Exodus 25–31
12. Matthew 5:48
13. See Hebrews 11:13–16
14. See Hebrews 8:13
15. Matthew 7:14
16. See Revelation 21:17
17. See John 14:1–4; 2 Corinthians 5:1; Colossians 1:5; Hebrews 11:10; Revelation 7:9, 21:1
18. Matthew 16:18 (KJV) (emphasis added)
19. Matthew 23:13
20. See Proverbs 8:3–11
21. Revelation 22:17 (emphasis added)
22. Psalm 100:4
23. Revelation 12:11 (emphasis added)
24. See Genesis 28:17
25. Matthew 13:45
26. See John 10:7
27. John 8:12; Matthew 5:14
28. See Matthew 7:24; Luke 6:46–49
29. Ephesians 2:19–21
30. See also 1 Corinthians 3:9 and all of chapter 15
31. See 1 Peter 2:5, (KJV)
32. See Exodus 28
33. See John 17, especially verse 22
34. Proverbs 25:28

35. See Revelation 17:4
36. See John 17:3
37. John 7:38
38. See John 15:1–8
39. Matthew 3:10
40. See Matthew 28:18–20; Mark 16:15; Luke 24:47
41. Isaiah 9:6–7
42. John 8:12
43. Matthew 5:14 (emphasis added)
44. Acts 13:47 (emphasis added)
45. Matthew 28:19–20
46. Matthew 28:18
47. See Matthew 16:17–19, 18:18
48. Revelation 21:15, also see 11:1
49. See Ephesians 4:7
50. See Ephesians 4:13
51. See Romans 12:3
52. See Revelation 22:7
53. See 2 Corinthians 10:7–15
54. See Matthew 7:15–23
55. See Galatians 5:22–26
56. John 14:12
57. Revelation 19:10
58. See 1 Corinthians 13:8–13
59. John 14:12
60. See Isaiah 9:6–7
61. See Matthew 16:19
62. See Revelation 1:6
63. See Isaiah 9:6–7
64. See James 2:14–26
65. See Titus 2:11–14, 3:14
66. Revelation 22:2b
67. Ephesians 6:12
68. 2 Corinthians 10:4
69. See Hebrews 8:7–13, 9:10
70. Revelation 21:5
71. See Matthew 11:12
72. See Romans 12:1–2; Galatians 4:19, 6:15; Ephesians 4:15; Colossians 1:27–28

73. See Revelation 1:6

Afterword

1. Matthew 23:37–39
2. Acts 1:11
3. See Revelation 21:6–7
4. Revelation 22:18–19
5. See Matthew 18:6
6. See John 7:15–18
7. See Genesis 1:28
8. See Matthew 16:19
9. See Revelation 21–22
10. See Matthew 13:52
11. John 14:26
12. Matthew 10:26

SUBJECT INDEX

SCRIPTURE INDEX

ABOUT THE AUTHOR

John Noē (pronounced no-ee) is the author of *Peak Performance Principles for High Achievers* and *People Power*. He is the president of a management service and training corporation as well as a songwriter, musician, mountain climber, familyman, and Christian activist.

The typeface for the text of this book is *Caledonia* which was created by the talented type and book designer, William Addison Dwiggins. Dwiggins, who became acting director of the Harvard University Press in 1917, was also known for his work with the publisher Alfred Knopf and for his other type designs, notably *Electra*. The name *Caledonia* is the ancient name for what is now the country of Scotland and denotes that the type was originally designed to parallel *Scotch Roman* (sometimes described as a *Modernized Old Style*). In creating *Caledonia*, Dwiggins was also influenced by the type that William Martin cut in 1790 for William Bulmer. Thus *Caledonia* is a modification of *Bulmer* and *Scotch Roman,* yet it is more business-like and versatile than the two older types.

Substantive Editing:
Michael S. Hyatt

Copy Editing:
Peggy Moon

Cover Design:
Steve Diggs & Friends
Nashville, Tennessee

Page Composition:
Xerox Ventura Publisher
Linotronic L-100 Postscript® Imagesetter

Printing and Binding:
Maple-Vail Book Manufacturing Group
York, Pennsylvania

Dust Jacket Printing:
Strine Printing Company
York, Pennsylvania